A CASE FOR CHARACTER

A CASE FOR CHARACTER

TOWARDS A LUTHERAN VIRITUE ETHICS

JOEL D. BIERMANN

Fortress Press
Minneapolis

A CASE FOR CHARACTER

Towards a Lutheran Viritue Ethics

Cover design: Tory Herman

Cover image: Luther rose; Schlosskirche, Wittenberg © Nick Thompson, University of Auckland

Library of Congress Cataloging-in-Publication Data is available

Print ISBN: 978-1-4514-7791-7

eBook ISBN: 978-1-4514-8434-2

The paper used in this publication meets the minimum requirements of American National Standard for Information Sciences — Permanence of Paper for Printed Library Materials, ANSI Z329.48-1984.

Manufactured in the U.S.A.

This book was produced using PressBooks.com, and PDF rendering was done by PrinceXML.

For Jasmine, Justine, and Jess
You've always known where I stand on things that matter;
now you have it in writing.

CONTENTS

Introduction

Following familiar paths, the liturgy has led the congregation on its weekly journey from invocation, through confession and absolution, prayer, Scripture, and hymns to the sermon. The pastor enters the pulpit with a sense of eagerness, ready to deliver a stirring and strong homily rich with solid doctrine, in tune with the season of the church and the world, scripturally accurate, and overflowing with magnificent gospel proclamation. The final feat will be no small accomplishment, especially considering his text for the day. Adhering to a self-imposed commitment to preach through an entire book of the Bible, the pastor's experiment in serial preaching has saddled him with a particularly difficult challenge from the latter part of Paul's letter to the Colossians:

> Wives, be subject to your husbands, as is fitting in the Lord. Husbands, love your wives and do not be embittered against them. Children, be obedient to your parents in all things, for this is well-pleasing to the Lord. Fathers, do not exasperate your children, so that they will not lose heart. Slaves, in all things obey those who are your masters on earth, not with external service, as those who merely please men, but with sincerity of heart, fearing the Lord. Whatever you do, do your work heartily, as for the Lord rather than for men, knowing that from the Lord you will receive the reward of the inheritance. It is the Lord Christ whom you serve. For he who does wrong will receive the consequences of the wrong which he has done, and that without partiality. (Col. 3:18-25, NASB)

Bound to a text focused entirely on right behavior within human relationships, a text that is brimming with what any reader would immediately recognize as ethical or moral directives and admonitions, the pastor nevertheless manages to save the sermon. That is, he transforms the ethical directions and encouragements from Paul into withering convictions of human sinfulness resolved in the gospel of grace. Paul's moral instruction is overcome by the pastor's assurance of forgiveness for his listeners' failures to be what they should be in their relationships. Against the odds, against the text itself, the pastor manages to salvage an otherwise dangerously moralistic text.

The congregation reaches the end of the sermon with its pastor and breathes a silent sigh of relief, having been assured that Paul's words about submission, obedience, sacrifice, service, rewards, and consequences within their most personal relationships are meant only to expose human inability and sin and their own crying need for God's forgiveness, which the sermon amply supplies. The hearers, then, are freed by the gospel from actually having to follow Paul's direction. Of course, there is an implicit expectation that God's good news should make some difference in their lives, but that's all left rather vague and unspecified—by intention. So the people return home still wondering what to do about the concrete realities and problems that have been plaguing them all week. The weary wife whose newly hired attorney will file on Monday her petition for divorce has heard again how impossible it is to have an "idealistic" biblical marriage, but takes solace in the assurance that there is always forgiveness. At hearing the Scripture read, the father with the petulant daughter began to consider what it might mean to "exasperate" his child but was dissuaded from the exercise, convinced by the sermon that the Bible isn't supposed to provide practical direction for modern problems like rearing a fifteen-year-old. For her part, when she heard the text read, the daughter shot a glance across the nave toward her family's usual place in the pews and wondered with a pang of guilt what it would be like actually to obey her parents in everything. But, like her father, she was restored by the preaching to the status-quo position that once one has grace, the specifics about what is right and wrong are determined by pragmatics and individual human hearts. After all, a book that endorses slavery can't have anything relevant to say to the world of the twenty-first century.

The problem is not the gospel. This must be understood. The imaginary pastor deftly preaching through the moralistic minefield of Paul's admonitions to the Colossians was not wrong to deliver the good news of the forgiveness of sins—all sins—through God's gift of the gospel. Indeed, the pastor was successfully accomplishing exactly what his education had trained him to do. He preached the forgiveness of sins, even when the text itself did not preach it. The gospel is central and is the unique message of the Christian faith. It deserves a prominent and permanent place in the preaching of the church. The problem is not the gospel. The problem is when the preaching of the gospel leaves no room for anything else. The problem is when the gospel is made to trump the call for a certain way of life on the part of God's people. The problem is when those who hear Christian preaching conclude that morality is a matter of personal preference and individual interpretation. The problem is when the preaching of the church undermines and even eliminates any place for the teaching of morality.

For some, the word *morality* may conjure uncomfortable and unwelcome visions and feelings, but it is simply the description of the way that a life is normed or shaped. For a Christian, morality means being formed according to the way that Christians live. But, of course, to state things so simply is to beg the question about whether or not such a thing as Christian morality actually exists. And in recognizing that such a question exists, we move considerably closer to the basic problem and the reason for this book. An emphatic and unapologetic concentration on the declaration of free forgiveness for the sake of the life, death, and resurrection of Jesus Christ is a hallmark of Christian faith—but it can also lead to a denigration and dismissal of any concrete or specific articulation of the way of life for Christians. In the name of "gospel freedom," it is sometimes insisted that the only acceptable norm for the Christian is the gospel of love, and that any attempt to spell out more clearly the content of that love is a faithless capitulation to morality and works righteousness. One purpose of this book is to consider this problem as a theological problem. Indeed, in the pages that follow, I will argue that the flight from ethics evident among some Christians is the outworking of a mistake in understanding the place of the gospel. It is a theological mistake. Complicating the situation exponentially is that this theological mistake is perpetrated in the context of an increasingly amoral society that has been made incapable of doing any meaningful moral reflection.

The extent to which the thinking of academics actually shapes the attitudes and actions of a culture is an old debate. Some see those in the "ivory tower" as irrelevant and insignificant. Others assume a slow and incomplete, yet inexorable, impact as the thoughts and paradigms of great thinkers trickle down into the everyday lives of citizens who live far from the halls of academia. While making no claim to be a shaper of society, Alasdair MacIntyre has proven to be a keen observer of the trajectories of Western thinking and a reliable teacher about the impact of such thinking on ordinary life. In the brief first chapter of his book *After Virtue*, MacIntyre skillfully employs an extended illustration of an imaginary displacement from and then reintroduction of natural science to common life and the subsequent absurdities and tragedies imposed on the society. His argument, however, is not about science and imaginary worlds: ". . . in the actual world which we inhabit the language of morality is in the same state of grave disorder as the language of natural science in the imaginary world which I have described. . . . we have—very largely, if not entirely—lost our comprehension both theoretical and practical, of morality."[1]

Publishing his text in 1984, MacIntyre had to address the fact that what he was presenting as an epic catastrophe, the defeat of "the language and practice of morality," was an event unrecognizable to all but a few.[2] He makes his case by arguing that, since academic history did not begin until after the catastrophe had already occurred, it would be unaware of the event and would actually be subject to the very problem itself. Thirty years later, it seems that the number of those aware of the catastrophe, or at least its ramifications, has increased significantly, perhaps in no small part because of MacIntyre's work. In 2000, James Davison Hunter was already chronicling this new interest in the morality of the American people: "There is much talk these days about the character of America and its people. A great deal of it is laced with anxiety."[3] Thus a new phenomenon arose, the "values industry." "Its premise is simple enough: if a tide of moral decadence is overtaking American society, then we must stem that tide by cultivating virtue and character among its people, especially among young people."[4] But Hunter is more than pessimistic about the possibility that such an industry might find success. He supports the declaration of his book's title, *The Death of Character*, with a "Postmortem" that precedes the book's introduction. The Postmortem begins: "Character is dead. Attempts to revive it will yield little. Its time has passed."[5] Hunter's book nicely complements MacIntyre's work. *After Virtue* provides the academic and intellectual history of the fall of morality and character in Western society, and *The Death of Character* provides the account of the more recent attempts and inevitable failure to revive and teach morality and character. Hunter concludes his Postmortem with a series of observations that capture perfectly the situation in which we who live in twenty-first-century America now find ourselves:

> We say we want a renewal of character in our day but we don't really know what we ask for. To have a renewal of character is to have a renewal of a creedal order that constrains, limits, binds, obligates, and compels. This price is too high for us to pay. We want character but without unyielding conviction; we want strong morality but without the emotional burden of guilt or shame; we want virtue

---

1. Alasdair MacIntyre, *After Virtue: a Study in Moral Theory*, 2d ed. (Notre Dame, IN: University of Notre Dame Press, 1984), 2.

2. Ibid., 3.

3. James Davison Hunter, *The Death of Character: Moral Education in an Age without Good or Evil* (New York: Basic Books, 2000), 3.

4. Ibid., 4.

5. Ibid., xiii.

but without particular moral justifications that invariably offend; we want good without having to name evil; we want decency without the authority to insist upon it; we want moral community without any limitations to personal freedom. In short, we want what we cannot possibly have on the terms that we want it.[6]

So, what's the point? What does the degradation of American moral culture and individual character have to do with the problem of Christian preaching so zealous to shun any hint of moralism that it willfully ignores a scriptural text and leaves its hearers without ethical direction? How does the problem of morality's collapse relate to the problem of impractical preaching? Most obviously, the moral wilderness of the Western world provides the context within which preaching occurs. In other words, those who listen to the preaching and are shaped by the teaching of the contemporary Christian church in America inhabit a world in which morality has little meaning and even less content. At the risk of sounding alarmist, this situation continues to degenerate for all the reasons that MacIntyre and Hunter so convincingly present. Those who listen to Christian preaching do not live in a vacuum, and the world handicapped by an inability to speak authoritatively about issues of morality has a profound effect on the average listener—whether or not he or the preacher realizes it. Simply put, Christians in America are not being positively shaped into having lives of basic morality and noble character merely by being a participant in the wider culture. Quite the opposite is the case. This is the context within which preaching occurs, and preachers must take care not to ignore this context.

Considering the present dearth of character and absence of ethical moorings, it might seem self-evident that a clear solution lies ready at hand: simply provide preaching and teaching within the church that will shape character and teach morality. This obvious and innocent suggestion brings us back to the driving concern of this book, because such preaching and teaching is precisely the thing that cannot happen. It is simply ruled out, as illustrated by this chapter's imaginary preacher who carefully crafted a sermon that left his congregation without ethical direction. There is a theological barrier that prohibits such a possibility; at least in some corners of the church today, there is such a barrier. The imaginary pastor inhabits such a corner; so do many people in my own denomination, the Lutheran Church—Missouri Synod (LCMS). The objective of this book is to address this theological barrier, to expose it, and then, more importantly, to overcome it. The hope is that once freed from mistaken theological notions, the church—even those corners now afflicted

6. Ibid., xv.

by an apparent aversion to morality—could actually do what it is uniquely positioned to do: it could provide a setting for the inculcation of morality and the formation of character that can work. All those essential ingredients for morality that Hunter details, ingredients summarily rejected by the wider society yet ingredients without which character can neither be taught nor sustained, are present—indeed, are held precious—in the church. The church is perfectly poised to be a place of remarkable relevance in the world because the church is capable of producing the people of character and moral conviction that society desperately needs. But this cannot happen until the theological problem is addressed.

For those who empathize with my imaginary preacher and who share his concern about the threat of moralism, what I have been suggesting is likely to cause genuine concern and a compelling urge to toss this text aside with a dismissive declaration, "Legalist!" Or the reader may be tempted to pronounce a yet more damning condemnation and invoke the withering charge of pietism. The temptation or urge to dismiss my argument out of hand is, of course, exactly the problem that this book seeks to address. For too many, it is assumed that when morality enters, the gospel is displaced; this is the upshot of the muddled theological thinking that will be the focus of the investigation presented in the following pages. It will take some time for the case to unfold, which will require the reader's patience. I hope that such patience will be granted—and I hope that it will not be disappointed. Suggesting a place for morality and character formation within the church does not necessitate a corresponding loss of the gospel in the church's preaching and teaching. Assertions cannot stand alone, of course, and it is my purpose to substantiate this claim and dispel the fears of those who treasure the gospel of free grace above all. I include myself among that number. Nothing matters more than the clear proclamation of the forgiveness won by Christ and delivered in his church. Justification by grace through faith in Jesus Christ alone remains the church's central doctrine and *raison d'être*. It is not, however, the only thing that the church can do or is called to do.

While those who occupy our pews and listen to sermons may have grown to expect the concerns and challenges of their mundane existences to be all but ignored by preachers intent on doing one thing and assiduously avoiding anything that might compromise that one thing, they are nevertheless being ill served. Faced with the relentless barrage of life's trials and woes, people certainly need the undiluted balm of the gospel's comfort and assurance. Yet, faced with those same trials and woes, people certainly also need the challenging and directing standard of bona fide Christian ethics. People need practical answers to their utterly practical concerns. This is the province of Christian ethics. Rightly understood, Christian ethics is not so much concerned with end-of-life questions or societal justice as it is with simply teaching what it means to live the Christian life. As the argument develops in the chapters that follow, much consideration will be given to those who have made similar observations about the state of the contemporary Christian church, particularly its Lutheran manifestation and the role of ethics within that church. Two of the most important thinkers, however, provide interesting corroboration of the thesis that the church, even extending well beyond its instantiation in the LCMS, is marked today by a distinct distaste for questions of ethics. Stanley Hauerwas, who will be more fully introduced in the chapter that follows, observes that in the church today, "no matter how sincerely many believe what it is they believe about God, they in fact live lives of practical atheism."[7] Elaborating on his term, Hauerwas writes: "quite profound and sophisticated theological systems can be developed, but the theological discourse seems to 'float,' making no difference for how we live."[8]

Hauerwas's observation coincides with the scenario of the irrelevant imaginary preacher. The theological system is duly impressive, but it does not touch the daily lives of the people. What takes place in the sanctuary on a Sunday morning leaves no detectable impression on the remaining hours and days of the week. The mundane and ordinary struggles of living seem somehow unspiritual and untheological. Consequently, life is met without the practical resources available to the church; and Christians live, Monday through Saturday, in the routine of life, as if God makes no difference. Whether God exists or not is not the point. Nor would any of these church-going people deny God's existence. Regardless of the ontological reality, however, too many believers continue to live as if God does not exist. What Hauerwas calls practical atheism is, then, another way of describing the ethical difficulties of the church already noted.

Reinhard Hütter also provides a memorable phrase in his attempt to articulate the malady that he detects within the contemporary church and within Lutheranism in particular. The current aversion to ethical questions that is pandemic in significant portions of the church Hütter terms "Protestantism's Antinomian Captivity."[9] Hütter contends that in its unflagging quest for

---

7. Stanley Hauerwas, *A Better Hope: Resources for a Church Confronting Capitalism, Democracy, and Postmodernity* (Grand Rapids: Brazos, 2000), 140.

8. Ibid.

9. Reinhard Hütter, "(Re-)Forming Freedom: Reflections 'After *Veritas Splendor*' on Freedom's Fate in Modernity and Protestantism's Antinomian Captivity," *Modern Theology* 17, no. 2 (April 2001): 117–61.

"freedom," Protestantism has shunted away the law and with it any meaningful ethics. "When the ethics of autonomy construes freedom to be the very core of subjectivity," argues Hütter, "it—from the very outset—eliminates the law's otherness and therefore reception."[10] What is left is the inevitable harvest of such autonomy and rejection of the law: "individual sovereignty, will to power, and license."[11] Hütter's description is essentially that of Hauerwas but considered from a somewhat different perspective. Unable to affirm or appreciate the place of the law, those captive to their antinomianism demonstrate the same sort of ethical failure, or practical atheism, identified by Hauerwas.

The licentiousness that Hauerwas and Hütter describe is at bottom precisely the problem illustrated in the opening account of the irrelevant pastor. A distaste for the law, a Sunday-only Christianity, and a disregard for the practical concerns of daily living are all different facets of the common problem, a problem readily recognizable in many of today's churches. Personal encounters and routine engagements with this ethical malaise were the catalyst for the study that eventuated in the present volume. I hope that the research and conclusions presented herein will help to treat the malady, end the atheism, and point a way out of the captivity. The parish pastor, of course, is certainly in mind as the argument is developed; by virtue of Christ's call through the congregation, every pastor is compelled to contend with the realities of the current situation of ethical distrust. However, it is for the person in the pew, who listens to sermons, and who eagerly desires to face the realities of practical life in ways that reflect his faith, that the argument which follows is presented. While pastors are no more easily generalized and classified than any other segment of humanity, it seems safe to assume that virtually all of those serving in parish situations have some sense of the reality and urgency of their parishioners' practical concerns. Unfortunately, the awareness of this need is too often met with unhelpful or unfaithful responses ranging from cavalier dismissal to the uncritical adoption of the latest theologically errant, but often practically useful, teaching fads.

The intent, then, is first simply to offer a way that parish pastors can rethink the place and the legitimacy of providing ethical direction and character training in a parish setting. Of course, I hold out hope that the reader will also put these new ways of thinking into actual practice so that a renewed emphasis on character and morality may find its way into parish life. In other words, rather than simply making another appeal for such an emphasis that is grounded in the acute need, the argument that is developed in the pages of this

10. Ibid., 120.
11. Ibid., 121.

book will offer a theological foundation for the work of forming character and giving direction for ethical living at the parish level that is at once orthodox and pragmatically useful. It is my intention at the very least to encourage further discussion of the appropriate place of training in ethics—that is, teaching the practical matters of living the Christian life. Understood scripturally, the goal is quite simply to provide a way for congregations faithfully to practice the Lord's parting instruction to make disciples—baptizing them, yes—*but also* "teaching them to observe all that I commanded you" (Matt. 28:20, NASB). A critical, but too often overlooked, aspect of such teaching is the work of character formation, which will be particularly emphasized. This emphasis is meant to further the understanding of Christian ethics less as the adoption of a set of basic rules of behavior or the provision of answers to perplexing moral dilemmas and more as the shaping of individual character.[12] Ethical training is neither the anticipation and resolution of every conceivable quandary that a Christian may eventually encounter nor the development of an exhaustive list of right activity. Rather, ethical training is about equipping and shaping individuals to be people of character so that, in whatever circumstances they may find themselves, they act virtuously—that is, in conformity with God's will for God's people.

The Shape of This Book

A call for training in virtue and shaping of character is a defining characteristic of a rediscovered school of thought known as virtue ethics. Virtue ethicists do not strike out into new territory but, rather, seek to retrieve what has in recent centuries been neglected or forgotten. A proponent of providing training in virtue, Josef Pieper insists on this characteristic: "In this realm, originality of thought and diction is of small importance—should, in fact, be distrusted. It can hardly be expected that there will be entirely new insights on such a subject. We may well turn to the 'wisdom of the ancients' in our human quest to understand reality, for that wisdom contains a truly inexhaustible contemporaneity."[13] The rise and essential tenets of virtue ethics will be considered in chapter 1. Special attention will be given to one of the most prominent proponents and outspoken voices in the contemporary reclamation of virtue ethics, Stanley Hauerwas. Hauerwas's significance for this study will be made clear as that chapter unfolds.

---

12. The shaping of character should not be perceived, however, as antithetical to directions for living or commandments meant to guide behavior. Indeed, they cannot be divorced. Nevertheless, the recent climate in which character and the virtues have been neglected argues for a special emphasis on character development and its place within the Christian life.

13. Josef Pieper, *The Four Cardinal Virtues: Prudence, Justice, Fortitude, Temperance* (Notre Dame, IN: University of Notre Dame Press, 1967), xii.

Of special interest for this book's focus is the challenge that virtue ethics presents to contemporary manifestations of Lutheranism. Chapter 2 will then listen to four important Lutheran theologians who have committed themselves to a careful analysis of Lutheranism's struggles with the ethical task in the context of contemporary America. Their observations will highlight and support the importance, as well as the relevance, of the present study. Not only will their observations be considered, but their proposed solutions will be examined and the various arguments' strengths as well as shortcomings, whether actual or potential, will be assessed.

Chapter 3 will turn to the first generation of sixteenth-century Lutherans in an effort to discern their attitude toward the concept of shaping character and training in virtue. This chapter's investigation will center on Lutheranism's formative and norming documents: the Lutheran Confessions, particularly the Apology of the Augsburg Confession and the catechisms. The intent of this chapter is to discern whether Lutheranism is, as some have charged, *inherently* incapable of providing a meaningful account of Christian ethics. That is, do the theological presuppositions and emphases of Lutheran doctrine require a de facto disqualification of any attempts to articulate a Lutheran understanding of ethics? This chapter will seek an answer in the work of the reformers.

Having considered the contemporary situation within the Lutheran church and the relative faithfulness of the current manifestation of Lutheranism vis-à-vis the teaching of the reformers themselves, chapter 4 will consider possible avenues out of Lutheranism's ethical predicament. Potential solutions to the problem of locating ethics within Lutheran theology will be examined and evaluated, particularly in the light of the findings of the previous chapter. These will include readily recognized 'standard' solutions, as well as some less familiar.

Chapter 5 will continue the task initiated in the prior chapter but will begin the constructive work of proposing and defending a framework that is able to overcome the shortcomings of those previously considered. Ultimately, the chapter will suggest a paradigm or framework within which one may ably conduct the tasks of theology and ethics in a way that is wholly faithful to Lutheran doctrine. This is my driving concern, and will mark the heart of the book's argument.

Finally, chapter 6 will articulate conclusions that can be drawn from the material presented in the preceding chapters. Additionally, concrete practical applications of the study as well as avenues for further investigation suggested by the study will be considered. In particular, the ability of Lutheran doctrine, when faithfully articulated and practiced, to provide a compelling answer to the problem of contemporary society's moral crisis will be explored. Far from perfunctory addenda, these suggested applications should be recognized as the compelling purpose that has fueled this study from the outset. It is the theological and practical needs of parish pastors and their parishioners that have always motivated and directed the research and writing of this book, even from its earliest days when it first took shape as a dissertation. It is for the sake of the church and her people that this book was written.

DEFINITIONS

Providing a careful account of key terms and definitions at the beginning of a book is an enterprise fraught with peril. Such material seems to take on a life of its own and quickly results in overwrought and tedious text that demands too much of the reader. Aware of the dangers, it is nevertheless necessary to make some effort to provide a common vocabulary and starting point for the work that follows. In particular, the terms *ethics, virtue, formation,* and *character* require some definition and clarification in order to forestall any confusion or misunderstanding.

As the term will be used in the following pages, *ethics* refers to the overarching responsibility of the Christian to live all of life in conformity to Christ. Hauerwas rightly notes that "ethics is never finally a matter of theory; rather it is a reflective activity not easily learned."[14] Broadly considered, ethics can rightly be understood as reflection on the subject of sanctification, or discipleship, as those terms are popularly understood to name the challenge of living in a way that is shaped by the scriptural account of Christ heard within the church. Ethics is concerned with all that it means practically to be a Christian in this world. Robert Benne provides a succinct definition: "the disciplined reflection on Christian moral life," or "critical and constructive reflection on Christian moral practice."[15] While this definition certainly leaves space for questions about what should or should not be done in difficult "borderline situations," in concert with the focus of this book, it reflects an interest in questions of Christian identity and the shape of the unexceptional routine of Christian living.

Less easily defined, *virtue* names the skills, habits, and ways of being that enable one to conform more nearly to an accepted standard or goal.

14. Stanley Hauerwas, *The Peaceable Kingdom: A Primer in Christian Ethics* (Notre Dame, IN: University of Notre Dame Press, 1983), xv.

15. Robert Benne, "Lutheran Ethics: Perennial Themes and Contemporary Challenges," in Karen L. Bloomquist and John R. Stumme, eds., *The Promise of Lutheran Ethics* (Minneapolis: Fortress Press, 1998), 11.

Significantly, such a goal or telos should not be assumed or understood to be inherent or universal among human beings. Hauerwas's recurrent assertion that all ethics must be qualified by an adjective[16] articulates the truth that different communities adopt different understandings of the telos of human existence. The particular telos which is adopted or enforced in turn determines the virtues necessary to achieve or arrive at that telos. Hauerwas poignantly explains the particularity of a community's telos and subsequent virtues: "Christian ethics is not written for everyone, but for those people who have been formed by the God of Abraham, Isaac, Jacob, and Jesus. Therefore Christian ethics can never be a minimalistic ethic for everyone, but must presuppose a sanctified people wanting to live more faithful to God's story."[17] The fact that even Christians often seem incapable of complete agreement on the telos of Christian life corroborates the claim that virtues are far from universal. It is impossible, then, to define virtue simply by producing a list of noble skills or behaviors. Another proponent of virtue ethics, Brad Kallenberg, observes, "the first step in ethics, therefore, is to identify the *telos* of human life."[18] Having done that, virtues can be considered. After his own meticulous discussion, Lutheran theologian and ethicist Gilbert Meilaender comes close to a precise definition of virtue: "The moral virtues—those excellences which help us attain the furthest potentialities of our nature—are, then, not simply dispositions to act in certain ways. They are more like skills which suit us for life generally—and still more like traits of character which not only suit us for life but shape our vision of life, helping to determine not only who we are but what world we see."[19] Virtues are the specific traits, skills, and behaviors that serve both to define and guide those on the journey toward the agreed-upon telos.[20]

Formation describes the process by which an individual is shaped or nurtured into the adoption and espousal of a particular community's telos and attendant virtues. Formation is a complex process that takes place throughout

---

16. Hauerwas, *Peaceable Kingdom*, 1.

17. Ibid., 97.

18. Brad J. Kallenberg, "Positioning MacIntyre in Christian Ethics," in Nancey Murphy, Brad J. Kallenberg, and Mark Thiessen Nation, eds., *Virtues & Practices in the Christian Tradition: Christian Ethics after MacIntyre* (Harrisburg, PA: Trinity Press International, 1997), 52.

19. Gilbert Meilaender, *The Theory and Practice of Virtue* (Notre Dame, IN: University of Notre Dame Press, 1984), 11.

20. The illustration of an athlete in training is helpful. The telos is an Olympic gold medal. En route to that goal, however, the athlete must adopt and achieve a score of auxiliary goals requisite for the fulfillment of the desired end. Thus goals, or virtues, are established relevant to strength, skill, speed, endurance, resilience, etc. While certain commonalities would no doubt arise, each sport would advance its own peculiar "virtues."

life in virtually every area of life as the community strives, intentionally or not, to conform a person to that community's way of life. Obviously, formation entails vastly more than a high school or college course on "values clarification"; and it will not be accomplished via a school signboard broadcasting the virtue of the month or through fifteen minutes of basic morality instruction at the outset of each school day. Formation is best understood in the broadest possible sense as it includes a community's unique teaching, conversations, observation of rituals, and practices extending from infancy to death.

While it hardly qualifies as the definitive source for theological purposes, it is interesting that even Webster's etymology for the word *character* captures the intimate connection between formation and character: "*fr. charassein* to scratch, engrave."[21] Put too simplistically, character is the resultant impact of formation on a person's being. More specifically, Webster helpfully provides this definition of character: "the complex of mental and ethical traits marking and often individualizing a person, group, or nation."[22] Individual traits or habits of thinking and behaving make up the composite of factors that combine to be described as a person's character. Seeking to clarify the distinction between our doing and our being, Hauerwas writes, "Character is a designation that marks the continuity present throughout the changes that constitute a complete human life."[23] Understood in a thoroughly practical way, character "is not a theoretical notion, but merely the name we give to the cumulative source of human actions."[24] In other words, character is the essential identity and impetus manifest in a person's thinking, speaking, and doing.

Character describes the matrix of personal traits that define, direct, and name an individual. Hauerwas clarifies that character is roughly synonymous with what is understood by identity. A person does not exhibit character as an external reflection of one's more central identity or agency. The person and the person's character are indistinguishable. They are one. He writes, "Our character is not merely the result of our choices, but rather the form our agency takes through our beliefs and intentions. . . . character is not a surface manifestation of some deeper reality called the 'self.' We are our character."[25]

21. *Webster's New Collegiate Dictionary* (Springfield, MA: G. & C. Merriam Co., 1979), 185.

22. Ibid.

23. Stanley Hauerwas and Charles Pinches, *Christians among the Virtues: Theological Conversations with Ancient and Modern Ethics* (Notre Dame, IN: University of Notre Dame Press, 1997), 126.

24. Stanley Hauerwas, with Richard Bondi and David B. Burrell, *Truthfulness and Tragedy: Further Investigations in Christian Ethics* (Notre Dame, IN: University of Notre Dame Press, 1977), 29.

25. Hauerwas, *Peaceable Kingdom*, 39.

Hauerwas makes this point even more emphatically and, given the importance of this definition, it is worth hearing him at length:

> Nothing about my being is more "me" than my character. Character is the basic aspect of our existence. It is the mode of the formation of our "I," for it is character that provides the content of that "I." If we are to be changed in any fundamental sense, then it must be a change of character. Nothing is more nearly at the "heart" of who we are than our character. It is our character that determines the primary orientation and direction which we embody through our beliefs and actions.[26]

Quite rightly, this definition of character offers no grounds for differentiating between an individual's identity and that individual's character. Such psychological or anthropological distinctions appear arbitrary at best. To shape character, then, is to shape the person.

Conclusion

The definitions suggested here raise important questions for the theologian, whether pastor or parishioner, especially for the Lutheran theologian striving to maintain an unencumbered proclamation of divinely accomplished salvation by grace alone through faith alone. If God is the creator of our persons and the author of our renewal, in what sense can it be said that character is shaped and formed by human effort? If virtue is shaped by the particular telos embraced by the individual and the community, do Christians have anything to gain ethically from pagan philosophers, regardless of the possible civil nobility of those philosophers? And, what exactly is the telos for a Lutheran believer? Finally, does the church that focuses on the delivery of the gospel have anything significant, much less definitive, to say to a culture, or even its own Christian people, about morality and character? The consideration of these and related questions will direct the investigation in the chapters that follow.

---

26. Stanley Hauerwas, *Character and the Christian Life: A Study in Theological Ethics* (San Antonio: Trinity University Press, 1975), 203.

1

Virtue Ethics and the Challenge of Hauerwas

William Bennett touched a national nerve in 1993 when he published his bestseller, *The Book of Virtues*.[1] Many Americans seemed to be longing for the sort of ethical foundation that Bennett endorsed. The idea that there are enduring virtues that deserve to be taught appealed to many who had grown weary of living in a climate of moral uncertainty rife with ethical ambiguities. In Bennett's thick book, everything was reassuringly black and white. Here were stories with heroes to be emulated and villains to be despised. Here was right and wrong that could be grasped and taught. Of course, not all agreed with Bennett's implied understanding of what constitutes the virtuous life, and some offered alternate anthologies of stories and suggestions for their use.[2] That such debate exists is one of the problems besetting the wider culture, which possesses no means of judging between competing claims.[3] Even if agreement on what actually constitutes a universal list of the virtues may well be altogether impossible, the desire for such a list, or even lists, illustrates that there is a chord in contemporary American society responsive to the idea of virtue. It should be noted, though, that the efforts of Bennett and others to champion the restoration of the moral fiber of contemporary culture is but the populist tip of a significant body of work that has come to be called virtue ethics, or an ethics of virtue.

---

1. William J. Bennett, ed., *The Book of Virtues: A Treasury of Great Moral Stories* (New York: Simon & Schuster, 1993).

2. Colin Greer and Herbert Kohl, eds., *A Call to Character* (New York: HarperCollins,1995).

3. The reasons for this are complicated and have more to do with politics and sociology, rather than with what is immediately theological. James Davison Hunter ably explores this reality in *The Death of Character: Moral Education in an Age without Good or Evil* (New York: Basic Books, 2000); see esp. 205–20.

THE RISE OF VIRTUE ETHICS

The academic antecedents to Bennett's popular efforts began several years earlier. Indeed, it is easily and safely argued that an ethics of virtue is as old as Aristotle or even Plato. It was Plato who identified and Aristotle who thoroughly expounded what by the Middle Ages had become the first four of the "seven cardinal virtues" (prudence, justice, fortitude, and temperance). Aristotle's carefully considered ethics supplied the enduring framework for thinking about the virtues and their human manifestations.[4] It was he who set the standard for virtually all subsequent virtue thinkers, including Christian teachers of ethics such as Thomas Aquinas and Philip Melanchthon. Contemporary virtue ethics certainly is interested in the classic virtues as presented by Aristotle and made complete with the addition of the three "theological virtues": faith, hope, and love.[5] Still, today's interest in an ethics of virtue is about much more than the promulgation of anthologies describing virtuous individuals or a school district's decision to assign a virtue for each month in the academic calendar in the hope of encouraging the cultivation of correspondingly virtuous behavior in students and perhaps even faculty.[6]

Having been overshadowed and displaced by the Kantian and later utilitarian directions of Enlightenment ethics, an ethics of virtue began a renaissance in the last part of the twentieth century. "The past fifteen years," wrote Gregory Trianosky in 1990, "have witnessed a dramatic resurgence of philosophical interest in the virtues."[7] He continues, "The charge that modern philosophical thought neglects the virtues . . . once apposite, is by now outmoded; and the calls for a renewed investigation of virtue and virtue ethics are being answered from many quarters."[8] Of the many quarters providing answers to the call for a retrieval of virtue ethics, or at least the study of virtue, one of the most important is Alasdair MacIntyre. MacIntyre is generally credited with fueling the resurgence of interest in an ethics of virtue by attracting the attention not only of the philosophical community but of the

---

4. Aristotle, *Nicomachean Ethics*, esp. Books II-VII.

5. The work of Josef Pieper not only serves as an excellent example of contemporary interest in the ancient virtues, but also provides an outstanding discussion of these virtues and their relevance to life in the church today. See Pieper, *The Four Cardinal Virtues: Prudence, Justice, Fortitude, Temperance* (Notre Dame, IN: University of Notre Dame Press, 1967).

6. This practice has been in evidence on the roadside signboards of St. Louis-area schools for the past fourteen years and counting.

7. Gregory Trianosky, "What Is Virtue Ethics All About?," *American Philosophical Quarterly* 27 (October 1990): 335.

8. Ibid.

wider academic community and even, to some extent, the general public. With his sharp insight and compelling prose, MacIntyre fully deserves his continuing position of influence and prominence.

ALASDAIR MACINTYRE AND AFTER VIRTUE

MacIntyre's *After Virtue* was published in 1981 and still inspires interest and discussion, as well as no shortage of detractors.[9] In this landmark volume, MacIntyre argues that without the moorings provided by a unified community that prizes and nurtures virtue, isolated moral imperatives make no sense. How can there be agreement on questions of morality when there is no agreement on what is good or virtuous? The result is social moral conflict that is "interminable." "I do not mean by this," writes MacIntyre, "that such debates go on and on and on—although they do—but also that they apparently can find no terminus."[10] He cites the ongoing cultural angst over abortion as a prime example. With essentially antithetical conceptions of what is good, it should be small wonder that opposing forces in the current debate find little room for agreement. Because unity cannot be achieved solely through reason, the tone of this and other moral debates inevitably becomes increasingly shrill. MacIntyre's harsh analysis of modernity's moral paralysis still rings with authenticity. Yet, the very truth of his critique provides not even a remote possibility for societal curatives. Indeed, MacIntyre holds out meager hope for the intentionally pluralistic society at large. Essentially abandoning the wider society, he seems instead to advocate or desire the founding and flourishing of intimate communities modeled on an Aristotelian standard. Recognizing the significant monastic contribution to medieval society, MacIntyre hopes that the modern refuges he envisions might replicate the monastic success and be bastions in which virtue can be taught, morality encouraged, and the future of civilization itself guarded.

While MacIntyre's cultural assessment may well be accurate and important, what is most of interest for theological ethics and for the present study is his

9. MacIntyre recognizes that his critique of contemporary culture is an attack on the "Enlightenment Project," his label for the Enlightenment agenda largely responsible for the present ethical collapse in the West. Naturally, his work provokes the anticipated negative reactions from those yet committed to the tenets of modern liberalism. See, for example, Richard J. Bernstein, "Nietzsche or Aristotle? Reflections on Alasdair MacIntyre's *After Virtue*," *Soundings* 67 (Spring 1984): 6–29. See also John Horton and Susan Mendus, eds., *After MacIntyre: Critical Perspectives on the Work of Alasdair MacIntyre* (Notre Dame, IN: University of Notre Dame Press, 1994).

10. Alasdair MacIntyre, *After Virtue: A Study in Moral Theory* (Notre Dame, IN: University of Notre Dame Press, 1981), 6.

success in returning virtue to the forefront of ethical discussion and thought. En route to that end, he has also served the development of virtue ethics by providing many of the concepts and terms that now make up the vocabulary of thinkers in virtue ethics. Two of the most significant of these terms are *narrative* and *practice*. The ideas signified by these terms have become foundational for the movement that has come to be known as "virtue ethics." The tremendous influence of these concepts and their importance as underpinnings for this book warrant a closer examination.[11]

By *narrative*, MacIntyre refers to the relationships, responsibilities, and experiences that combine into the particular shape taken by an individual's life. The narrative in which a person lives will in turn direct and explain much of what that person does. A simple example is that "getting dressed for work" and "warming up" will mean quite different things for a concert pianist and a football player. Each lives in a different narrative, each of which in turn relates to a wider community of others in similar narratives. MacIntyre writes, "For the story of my life is always embedded in the story of those communities from which I derive my identity."[12] MacIntyre's concept of narrative is closely related to the idea of practice.

Though often referenced by subsequent thinkers in virtue ethics, MacIntyre's definition of a *practice* is less succinct or simple than one might hope.[13] A practice is:

> . . . any coherent and complex form of socially established cooperative human activity through which goods internal to that form of activity are realized in the course of trying to achieve those standards of excellence which are appropriate to, and partially definitive of, that form of activity, with the result that human powers to achieve excellence, and human conceptions of the ends and goods involved, are systematically extended.[14]

11. Indeed, some Christian ethicists have seen "a *theory* of Christian ethics lurking in his [MacIntyre's] writings," and elaborated a Christian ethics accordingly. "Preface and Acknowledgments," in Nancey Murphy, Brad J. Kallenberg, and Mark Thiessen Nation, eds., *Virtues & Practices in the Christian Tradition: Christian Ethics after MacIntyre* (Harrisburg, PA: Trinity Press International, 1997), xi (emphasis in original). Kallenberg's essay "The Master Argument of MacIntyre's *After Virtue*" is quite helpful, but also acknowledges the difficulty of succinctly explaining MacIntyre. "The tricky part of his analysis is that each of the central concepts—*virtue, practice, narrative,* and *tradition*—can be defined only, finally, in terms of the other concepts." Ibid., 20.

12. MacIntyre, *After Virtue*, 221.

13. Kallenberg accurately observes: "MacIntyre defines a *practice* somewhat tortuously" ("Master Argument," 21).

Brad Kallenberg derives a Christian ethic from the work of MacIntyre and provides some guidance in unpacking MacIntyre's rather unwieldy phraseology. He helpfully identifies four central concepts in MacIntyre's definition. First, he observes that practices are human activities that are more than social, but are also "complex enough to be challenging, and coherent enough to aim at some goal in a unified fashion."[15] "Second," continues Kallenberg, "practices have goods that are internal to the activity."[16] Thus, while external goods, such as economic benefits, fame, or societal prestige, certainly attend some practices, "true practices are marked by *internal* goods—those rewards that can be recognized and appreciated only by participants."[17] So it is that baseball players have been known to testify that it is "the love of the game" that motivates their play regardless the financial compensation.

Making his third point, Kallenberg asserts, "practices have standards of excellence without which internal goods cannot be fully achieved," that is to say, those involved in the practice know what counts as great success because they have been taught by the "historical community of practitioners" or, more plainly, by those who have gone before them. "The joy of chess is in having played *well*."[18] Finally, Kallenberg's fourth point is that in MacIntyre's definition, "practices are systematically extended." Practices are not static but demonstrate advances that are an essential aspect of the practice itself. The practice of medicine has progressed dramatically since the time of Hippocrates, and even since the accomplishments of Christiaan Barnard, yet the practice is still that of medicine and there is a continuity with and appreciation for what preceded. Having a better grasp of MacIntyre's understanding of practice, it is now possible more fully to appreciate another important contribution of *After Virtue*: MacIntyre's definition of virtue as ". . . an acquired human quality the possession and exercise of which tends to enable us to achieve those goods which are internal to practices and the lack of which effectively prevents us from achieving any such goods."[19]

14. MacIntyre, *After Virtue*, 187.

15. Ibid. Kallenberg gives several examples: "Building a house is a practice, while taking long showers is not. The game of tennis is a practice, but hitting a backhand is not" (ibid.).

16. Ibid.

17. Ibid.

18. Ibid. (emphasis in original).

19. MacIntyre, *After Virtue*, 191.

IMPORTANT ASPECTS OF VIRTUE ETHICS

The influence of MacIntyre's thought will become apparent as our investigation of virtue ethics proceeds. One of the immediate and readily detectable results of MacIntyre's work has been a shift within the entire field of ethics. MacIntyre's emphasis on the classical virtues was eagerly embraced by many who were dissatisfied with the traditional choice between doing ethics either as a deontologist or as a consequentialist. An ethics of duty, or deontology, achieved its clearest articulation in the monumental and enduringly influential work of Immanuel Kant.[20] Affirming the reality and authority of absolutes, deontologists teach that there is a universal duty that one must follow in order to be moral. Utilitarian, or consequentialist, ethicists advocate a decidedly different approach. Represented well by John Stuart Mill, utilitarians discount the existence of absolutes and argue that moral actions are determined not by duty but by what brings the greatest good to the greatest number.[21]

Christian ethics in the recent past typically busied itself with the task of discerning the appropriate interface and emphases within the space marked out by these modern ethical approaches.[22] In Christian circles, the debate hinged on whether theological ethics was better described as doing a duty anchored in the divine nature or as focusing on the extrinsic goal of meeting the needs of others.[23] While questions of duty and utility deservedly retain a place within the dynamic of ethical discussion, the revival of interest in the virtues provides a way around the limits imposed by ethical systems that consider only these two possibilities. Virtue ethics is best seen not as an alternative or third way but, rather, as a wider view of the ethical task, one that encompasses the concerns and contributions of both deontological and utilitarian ethics.

Advocates of virtue ethics regard both deontological ethics and ethics of utility in their usual narrow manifestations as insufficient for the most critical task of ethics. Describing the recent rise of virtue ethics, William

---

20. See Immanuel Kant, *Grounding for the Metaphysics of Morals*, trans. James W. Ellington (Indianapolis: Hackett, 1981).

21. The best-known account is Mill's essay "Utilitarianism," first published in *Fraser's Magazine* in 1861. One of many reprints can be found in Steven M. Cahn, ed., *Classics of Western Philosophy*, 5th ed. (Indianapolis: Hackett, 1999).

22. For a representative contemporary example of this constrained understanding of the purview of ethics, see Norman L. Geisler, *Christian Ethics: Options and Issues* (Grand Rapids: Baker, 1989).

23. While innumerable examples are available, two roughly contemporary representatives could be found in Joseph Fletcher, with his infamous dictum that love for neighbor overrides all else, and Dietrich Bonhoeffer, who taught that man's task is to live in concert with the will of God as revealed within the structure of creation itself.

Spohn observes that "almost all proponents of virtue ethics consider it more adequate than utilitarianism or neo-Kantianism because it provides a more comprehensive picture of moral experience and stands closer to the issues of ordinary life."[24] Indeed, this is the great strength and attraction of virtue ethics. Trianosky concurs: "Perhaps the most persuasive argument in favor of studying the virtues is simply that they are the stuff of which much of the moralities of everyday life are made."[25] Rather than obsessing over moral quandaries arising out of difficult, though exceptional and rarely encountered, ethical dilemmas, an ethics of virtue concentrates on the development of people who display virtuous character in the mundane routines of ordinary life. Proponents of virtue ethics find little value in plaguing those venturing into the work of ethics with artificial situations that demand a decision, such as the ubiquitous "Should a person lie to save a life?" Those who embrace virtue ethics believe, rather, that it is far more important that students be nurtured by their communities, according to the norms and standards of those communities, into people of virtuous character who will make ethically virtuous decisions in all the ordinary as well as the extraordinary circumstances of life.

Certainly, extraordinary moments of ethical perplexity do arise. Nonetheless, "an ethic of virtue," Gilbert Meilaender observes, "seeks to focus not only on such moments of great anxiety and uncertainty in life but also on the continuities, the habits of behavior which make us the persons we are."[26] Put another way, an ethics of virtue focuses on "being" while traditional ethics of duty or utility tend to focus on "doing." Stanley Hauerwas concurs: "Christian ethics is concerned more with who we are than what we do."[27] He adds, however, a clarification which eliminates any notion that virtue ethics is perhaps unconcerned about questions of behavior: "This is not to suggest that our actions, decisions and choices are unimportant, but rather that the church has a stake in holding together our being and behaving in such a manner that

24. William C. Spohn, "The Return of Virtue Ethics," *Theological Studies* 53 (March 1992): 60.

25. Trianosky, "What Is Virtue Ethics All About?," 342. Hauerwas offers a more basic, if less flattering, explanation for the rise of virtue ethics: "For in effect the paradigm of ethics inherited from Kant has been burdened by so many anomalies, has died the death of so many qualifications, that a new alternative simply needed to be suggested. Thus some may well have been attracted to the emphasis on virtue and character because if offered a relief from boredom." Stanley Hauerwas, "A Retrospective Assessment of an 'Ethics of Character': The Development of Hauerwas's Theological Project (1985, 2001)," in *The Hauerwas Reader*, ed. John Berkman and Michael Cartwright (Durham: Duke University Press, 2001), 77.

26. Gilbert Meilaender, *The Theory and Practice of Virtue* (Notre Dame, IN: University of Notre Dame Press, 1984), 5.

27. Stanley Hauerwas, *The Peaceable Kingdom: A Primer in Christian Ethics* (Notre Dame, IN: University of Notre Dame Press, 1983), 33.

our doing only can be a reflection of our character."[28] Virtue ethics, then, strives to join the expected ethical questions concerning behavior and choices of right versus wrong with the broader issues of the formation of enduring character and the cultivation of virtue.

Another contribution of ethics centered on virtue is the recognition that an individual's character has much to do with that individual's perception of ethical situations. Put differently, the sort of virtues that shape a person's life will determine how that person thinks about moral questions. One man's paralyzing moral dilemma is another's black-and-white conclusion. One woman's compelling sense of moral obligation is for another a casually dismissed sense of preference. Meilaender notes, "What we ought to do may depend on the sort of person we are. What duties we perceive may depend upon what virtues shape our vision of the world."[29] Those who advocate virtue ethics recognize that it is quite impossible to practice a deontological or a utilitarian ethic without that ethic's being shaped by one's virtues or lack thereof. In fact, whether acknowledged or not, the essential truths of virtue ethics have always been in operation even when the ethical task was assumed to be limited to questions of duty or utility. Contemporary virtue ethics seeks to articulate these broader truths and so enrich the field of ethics and its wider contributions and applications to individuals and society.

Virtue ethics, then, certainly is concerned with, among other things, the promotion and cultivation of virtue. Obviously, however, this is not virtue according to the traditional populist understanding: that peculiar asset of women who have lived chastely and maintained their sexual purity. Neither is the understanding of virtue to be diminished into what Meilaender terms the "cardinal virtues of our time, sincerity and authenticity—in short, being true to oneself."[30] In contrast to a subjective morality of individual autonomy, an ethics of virtue contends that there do exist objective standards for human being, the pursuit of which is encouraged and enhanced by the adoption of virtues. Virtues, then, are significantly more than guidelines for polite human interaction. Virtues "call attention not only to certain basic obligations which we owe each other; they call us out on an endless quest toward the perfection of our being."[31] Virtues direct individuals toward some goal or standard. Meilaender captures the significance of virtues when he calls them "those excellences which help us attain the furthest potentialities of our nature."[32] More

28. Ibid., 33–34.

29. Ibid.

30. Meilaender, *Theory and Practice*, 4.

31. Ibid., 7.

than "simply dispositions to act in certain ways," virtues are "like skills which suit us for life generally—and still more like traits of character which not only suit us for life but shape our vision of life."[33] Hence, virtue ethics actually encompasses the particular interests and emphases of both deontological and teleological or utilitarian ethics. There are standards grounded in the authority of absolutes, and there is an end or a telos that serves as a goal for human beings.

At first blush, it would seem that those within the church would enthusiastically applaud the rise of virtue ethics. Certainly, virtue ethics appears particularly attractive when considered in the light of the great ethical fad that swept church and society in the latter part of thetwentieth century. Traditional Christian believers found little to admire in the situation ethics of Joseph Fletcher. In Fletcher's hybrid ethics, where one's duty is to do the most loving thing, norms and mores that had been in place for millennia seemed to be carelessly jettisoned and the moral relativity of the culture justified.[34] By comparison, virtue ethics allows church and society to return to an unapologetic affirmation of traditional morality and ethical education. How can the church argue with a movement that produces people of virtuous character, that is, people who live morally decent, upright lives, and who support standards of thinking and acting that can conform even to biblical norms? But, of course, things in the church are not always simple, and the obvious is not always recognized as such. In fact, the church has found a way to argue even with an ethics of virtue.

THE PLACE OF VIRTUE IN CHRISTIAN HISTORY

It is worth digressing here for a brief consideration of the history, or what might be seen as the rise and fall, of virtue within the church. The current effort to establish a place for virtue within Christian theology is actually better understood as retrieval rather than innovation. There was a significant period when virtue was encouraged as the superior explication of Christian ethics. In a helpful study, Robert Bast traces virtue's ascendancy to the second century, when Ireneaus contended that Christian ethics excelled Jewish law, even as Jesus exceeded the limits of the Decalogue with his amplifications.[35] In the late sixth century, Pope Gregory the Great advanced the argument by drafting

32. Ibid., 11. It is not difficult to detect the influence of MacIntyre in Meilaender's definition of virtue.

33. Ibid.

34. Joseph Fletcher, *Situation Ethics: The New Morality* (Philadelphia: Westminster, 1966).

35. Robert James Bast, *Honor Your Fathers: Catechisms and the Emergence of a Patriarchal Ideology in Germany 1400–1600*, Studies in Medieval and Reformation Thought 63, ed. Heiko A. Oberman (Leiden: Brill, 1997), 33.

an entire moral system based not on the Ten Commandments but on New Testament imperatives. "Culling ethical imperatives and prohibitions almost exclusively from the Gospels, the Epistles, and patristic theology," writes Bast, "Gregory created a patchwork of moral teaching organized into seven virtues and seven vices (or 'deadly sins')."[36] Christian ethics based on the virtues and their corresponding vices held sway in the church for better than half a millennium. Thomas Aquinas contributed to the secure position of the virtues with his own explication of the virtues in the *Summa Theologica* and his affirmation of Aristotelian ethics.[37] Gradually, however, through a combination of factors, the Decalogue regained its place within Christendom. Bast credits Hugh of St. Victor and then Peter Lombard with the beginning of the reemergence of Christian interest in the Commandments.[38] This interest gained momentum in subsequent generations: "Though it [the Decalogue] never entirely replaced the Gregorian system of the virtues and vices, by the fifteenth century it had become the single most popular guide for moral instruction in much of Europe—a position confirmed in the catechetical programs of Protestants and Catholics in the sixteenth century."[39] Bast attributes the mounting interest in the Decalogue at the time of the Reformation to the unrest and chaos in society. The Commandments were "the intended tonic for a critically ill Christendom . . . a tool to fashion an ordered, godly society."[40]

It is interesting to note that at least through the Reformation period, the Commandments were not perceived as a replacement for the system of virtue. Rather, they could be reckoned as complementary, the Decalogue providing guides for specific behavior, whereas the virtues "generally dealt with feelings rather than actions."[41] The Lutheran reformers, as later chapters will

36. Ibid., 34. Gregory's vices were: vainglory, envy, anger, melancholy, avarice, gluttony, and lust. Corresponding in number to these vices were the "highest virtues": prudence, temperance, fortitude, justice, faith, hope, and love. (Other "intermediary virtues," such as patience, chastity, humility, etc., were added as necessary specifically to combat the vices.) Peter of Waltham, *Source Book of Self-Discipline: A Synthesis of* Moralia in Job *by Gregory the Great: A Translation of Peter of Waltham's* Remediarium Conversorum, trans. Joseph Gildea, American University Studies Series 7, Theology and Religion 117 (New York: Peter Lang, 1991), 86–87, 241–42. The remarkable influence of Gregory's system in subsequent centuries, indeed, even down to the present, provides sufficient argument of its importance. Nevertheless, a more thoroughgoing analysis of his detailed proposal lies beyond the scope of the present investigation.

37. MacIntyre observes that "Aquinas' commentary on the *Nicomachean Ethics* has never been bettered" (*After Virtue*, 178).

38. Ibid., 35.

39. Ibid., 36.

40. Ibid., 43.

demonstrate, embraced the Commandments yet continued to use the language of virtue. Eventually, however, interest in the system of virtues faded as the Commandments "became the normative guideline for teaching and enforcing morality."[42] The virtues continued their decline, especially within Protestantism, until today's present interest in the virtues is typically perceived as an innovation. While there are relevant historical factors involved in the rise of the Ten Commandments and erosion of the place of the virtues, Josef Pieper supplies perhaps the most convincing explanation for the present displacement of virtue within Christian theology. He candidly observes: "It is true that the classic origins of the doctrine of virtue later made Christian critics suspicious of it. They warily regarded it as too philosophical and not Scriptural enough. Thus, they preferred to talk about commandments and duties rather than about virtues."[43] Writing in the middle of the twentieth century, Pieper sought to overcome that suspicion and offered a compelling case for renewed study and application of the virtues. He was convinced that the pursuit of virtue should be taught and encouraged for the sake of the actual lives and witness of Christian people: "The doctrine of virtue . . . has things to say about this human person; it speaks both of the kind of being which is his when he enters the world, as a consequence of his createdness, and the kind of being he ought to strive toward and attain to—by being prudent, just, brave, and temperate."[44] That others agree with Pieper accounts for what has come today to be known as virtue ethics. It was a time of cultural and civil crisis that brought a resurgence of interest in the Commandments before and during the Reformation. Perhaps the same motivations are driving the call for a return of virtue. There yet remain, though, a few crucial theological factors that may very well militate against a Lutheran endorsement of virtue. And in arriving at those factors, we have, of course, arrived at a central focus of this book's argument.

THE LUTHERAN DILEMMA

While churchly supporters of virtue ethics such as Josef Pieper are increasingly common, a more considered evaluation quickly raises some fundamental concerns. In the minds of some Christians, Lutherans in particular, the idea of cultivating virtues is tied too closely to popular notions of self-fulfillment.[45]

41. Ibid., 44.

42. Ibid., 45.

43. Pieper, *Four Cardinal Virtues*, xi.

44. Ibid., xii.

45. See, for example, Ivar Asheim, "Lutherische Tugendethik?," *Neue Zeitschrift für Systematische Theologie und Religionsphilosophie* 40 (1998): 239–60.

People who achieve a state of virtue, it is thought, are people who have arrived at self-realization, and efforts at self-realization hardly seem compatible with the New Testament's teaching of self-sacrifice. Virtue ethics could be charged with complicity in the creation of the very egocentric, self-serving individuals so prevalent in contemporary culture over which the Christian church typically and loudly laments. Meilaender clearly articulates a perhaps even greater concern: "Furthermore, the very notion of character seems to suggest—has suggested at least since Aristotle—habitual behavior, abilities within our power, an acquired possession. And this in turn may be difficult to reconcile with the Christian emphasis on grace, the sense of the sinner's constant need of forgiveness, and the belief that we can have no claims upon the freedom of God."[46] Could it be that virtue ethics actually promotes the most damnable and dangerous of all enemies of Christian truth: self-righteous legalism? Indeed, doesn't any emphasis on behavior and virtuous character run the risk of advancing the works righteousness that seems always to lurk just outside the door of orthodoxy?

These are weighty questions for any heir of the Reformation. For Lutherans in particular, the tenets of virtue ethics can arouse substantial theological concerns. An ethics of virtue elevates the pursuit of character and extols the practice of habituation as an integral aid in the cultivation of character. Of course, these were central concepts in the Scholastic theology against which the reformers fought with such vehemence. In fact, a favorite teacher of many virtue ethicists is none other than Thomas Aquinas, the oft-quoted and misquoted patron of many of the Scholastics whose works righteousness the reformers found reprehensible. Luther, and the reformers who bore his name after him, placed the doctrine of justification by grace through faith in Jesus Christ alone at the heart and center of their theology. Anything that threatened this doctrine was to be resisted and rejected. Of course, the actual practice of applying this central article of the faith while still encouraging a life of Christian obedience led to significant debates within Lutheranism even during Luther's life and certainly after his death. Nevertheless, the legacy of that article by which the church stands or falls continues to provide the essential shape of Lutheran doctrine and practice today. And some would conclude that this legacy does not allow for the kind of emphases found in virtue ethics.

At the risk of stating the obvious, it is certainly a very good thing that the free gospel of forgiveness is held dear as the definitive message and work of the church. It is to their credit that Lutherans teach the doctrine of justification

46. Meilaender, *Theory and Practice*, 6.

with great zeal and devotion. But does this legitimate priority of promoting and defending the central teaching of the church render impossible any meaningful appropriation of the benefits of virtue ethics? It is not without cause that jokes about the Lutheran reluctance or perhaps inability to handle theological ethics continue to abound.[47] There is enough truth behind the in-house and classroom comedy, however, that it can be rightly classed as gallows humor. Lutheranism's arguably infamous detachment from ethics has prompted a number of contemporary critics to voice their concern over the apparent failure of Lutheranism to articulate a significant place for the ethical task within the work of the church.[48] *Ethical task* here refers not to questions of social action, moral management of new technologies, or guidance in making difficult decisions in borderline situations. The ethical task that seems too often beyond the grasp of Lutheran theologians and thinkers is the fundamental, altogether practical, work of providing concrete guidance and intentional shape to the routine Christian life. Bill Bennett, a politically savvy Roman Catholic, can do it, but can Lutheran pastors and people do it?

There are some who would conclude that they cannot. Surprisingly, or maybe not so surprisingly, there are some even from within the Lutheran community who question the ability of Lutherans to provide a compelling account of the Christian life and the ethics that describe that life. One of the clearest articulations of the Lutheran failure to handle the concerns of ethics, however, comes from the pen of a Methodist named Stanley Hauerwas.

An Introduction to Stanley Hauerwas and His Work

A brief consideration of the work of Stanley Hauerwas actually serves a twofold purpose within the scope of this discussion. Not only does an examination of Hauerwas yield an increased understanding of the challenge that virtue ethics poses to some contemporary interpretations of Lutheran doctrine, but as a recognized representative of virtue-centered ethics, Hauerwas provides a fuller grasp of the concerns and contributions of virtue ethics. Hauerwas is the Gilbert T. Rowe Professor Emeritus of Divinity and Law at Duke Divinity School.

---

47. A case in point is the introduction of a speech Gilbert Meilaender delivered to fellow Lutherans: "The letter of invitation . . . asked that I 'point with pride to some past Lutheran accomplishments' in the field of ethics and that I speak for about an hour. Taken together, of course, these requests might be thought to constitute a rather difficult assignment, but the letter bore no traces of irony, nor did it even hint that to combine 'Lutheran ethics' and 'accomplishments' might be what the logicians call a *contradictio in adjecto*." Gilbert Meilaender, "The Task of Lutheran Ethics," *Lutheran Forum* 34, no. 4 (Winter 2000): 17.

48. Representative voices will be considered in the chapter that follows.

Through his teaching and writing career, he has gained the deserved reputation as one of the prominent spokespersons of contemporary virtue ethics. John Berkman identifies him as "a seminal figure in the 'recovery of virtue' in theological ethics."[49] Nancey Murphy recognizes that "there has been a sea change in *Christian* ethics, due largely but not exclusively to the prolific Stanley Hauerwas."[50] Hauerwas is of further specific interest in relation to the scope of this book, however, in that he directly addresses the apparent inability of Lutheran doctrine to handle the necessary questions of growth in virtue and character development.

Not a clergyman, Hauerwas nevertheless regularly contends, with some justification it seems, that he is more theologian than ethicist. "I am a Christian theologian who teaches ethics," he writes, adding, "Being a theologian has become a habit for me that I cannot nor do I wish to break. I am also an ethicist, but I do not make much of that claim."[51] Early in his academic career, Hauerwas characterized his own "central concern" as the "task of finding the most appropriate means to articulate how Christians have understood, and do and should understand, the relationship between Christ and the moral life."[52] In words that have proven to be normative for his subsequent career, Hauerwas described his work and its emphasis: "I have tried to reclaim and to develop the significance of character and virtue for the moral life. Character is the category that marks the fact that our lives are not constituted by decisions, but rather the moral quality of our lives is shaped by the ongoing orientation formed in and through our beliefs, stories and intentions."[53] This is indeed a precise description of Hauerwas's work and, it should be noted, of virtue ethics itself. Raised a Methodist, Hauerwas earned his doctoral degree at Yale and taught at Notre Dame before making the move to Duke. Confirming in his own life his insistence on the crucial significance of one's community in the shaping of character, Hauerwas's work amply evidences the influence of each

49. Quoted in John Berkman, "An Introduction to *The Hauerwas Reader*," in Berkman and Cartwright, eds., *The Hauerwas Reader*, 3.

50. Nancey Murphy, "Introduction," in Murphy, Kallenberg, and Nation, eds., *Virtues & Practices*, 1. "Prolific" accurately describes the work of Hauerwas: "He has authored or edited over thirty books and well over three hundred and fifty scholarly articles." Berkman, "An Introduction," 3.

51. Stanley Hauerwas, *Sanctify Them in the Truth: Holiness Exemplified* (Nashville: Abingdon, 1998), 201.

52. Stanley Hauerwas, "The Ethicist as Theologian," *The Christian Century* 92 (April 1975): 409. Decades later, Hauerwas confirmed his contention: "Given the nature of my subsequent work, I think it is apparent my primary agenda was and always has been theological." Hauerwas, "A Retrospective Assessment," 79.

53. Hauerwas, "Ethicist as Theologian," 411.

of these communities.[54] Throughout the scores of published essays and books that bear his name, several themes consistently appear and reappear. Naturally, as an ethicist, Hauerwas is compelled to address some of the pressing ethical quandaries of the day including abortion, homosexuality, and the breakdown of the family. His impassioned advocacy of many traditionally conservative causes has led some to label him accordingly. Though Hauerwas does regularly occupy positions in sympathy with those of more conservative Christians, he defies easy categorization.

Always near the forefront of Hauerwas's practical concerns is an appeal for Christian pacifism, or as he usually refers to it, nonviolence. Hauerwas consistently advocates the standard of thoroughgoing nonviolence for God's people and church.[55] Hauerwas also regularly returns to the question of people with handicaps and the tremendous importance and significance of their being welcomed into Christian families and communities.[56] Finally, another representative issue occurring with some regularity in Hauerwas's corpus is a deep suspicion of the modern capitalistic, democratic nation-state. While Hauerwas is no Marxist, he has concerns about the Enlightenment-formed foundation that underlies the American experiment.[57] Throughout all of his occasional writing, however, the recurrent and foundational themes are the ones staked out in 1975: the importance of virtue and character. Nancey Murphy concurs that these are the central aspects of Hauerwas's efforts: "Hauerwas tends to talk about Christian morality in terms of *narratives* and *community, virtue* and *character*."[58] The twofold emphasis on virtue and character is joined with the pair, narrative and community, which receive particular emphasis in his discussions on church and theology.

Making good on his own self-categorization, Hauerwas demonstrates an able competence in facing the challenges that the discipline of theology poses. Trained at Yale by, among others, Hans Frei and George Lindbeck, Hauerwas reflects common postliberal ideals such as the importance of the community

---

54. Not surprisingly, Hauerwas is quite candid about the various influences that shaped him theologically and ethically. See, for example, his "On What I Owe to Whom" in Hauerwas, *Peaceable Kingdom*, xix–xxv.

55. For example, see his discussion connecting the resurrection of Christ to "the establishment of a kingdom of forgiveness and peace," in Hauerwas, *Peaceable Kingdom*, 87–91.

56. Stanley Hauerwas, with Richard Bondi and David B. Burrell, *Truthfulness and Tragedy: Further Investigations in Christian Ethics* (Notre Dame, IN: University of Notre Dame Press, 1977), 147–56.

57. Stanley Hauerwas, *A Community of Character* (Notre Dame, IN: University of Notre Dame Press, 1981), 72–86.

58. Murphy, "Introduction," 1 (emphasis in original).

in shaping individuals and the centrality of narrative in theology. These are themes that have been present in his work from the beginning. As he began his career, he wrote of his hope that the church would "stand as an alternative society that manifests in its own social and political life the way in which a people form themselves when truth and charity rather than survival are their first order of business."[59] In *Resident Aliens*, his only book aimed specifically at a popular audience, Hauerwas and co-author William Willimon write: "The challenge of Jesus is the political dilemma of how to be faithful to a strange community, which is shaped by a story of how God is with us."[60] Here both themes coalesce. The church is political in a broad sense in that it is about people gathered together in community or *polis*. For Hauerwas, the community in which a person should be shaped and formed in character is none other than the church, and that community should be shaped in turn by its faithful commitment to the story of Jesus as recorded in the Gospels.

Hauerwas closely binds these twin concerns of narrative and community in other places as well. In *A Community of Character*, "the primary task of the church," he tells us, "is to be itself—that is, a people who have been formed by a story that provides them with the skills for negotiating the danger of this existence trusting God's promise of redemption.[61] This is such a prominent aspect of Hauerwas's work that it would be difficult to overemphasize it. In yet another place, he states his position this way: "The nature of Christian ethics is determined by the fact that Christian convictions take the form of a story, or perhaps better, a set of stories that constitutes a tradition, which in turn creates and forms a community."[62] It is this emphasis on the creating and norming narrative of the church that guides Hauerwas to his critique of the way that Lutheran doctrine too frequently approaches questions of virtue and character formation. Hauerwas is convinced that ethics must be intimately bound to the doctrinal task of the church. He is also convinced that Lutheranism has too often shown itself ill-suited for achieving and maintaining such a union.

HAUERWAS'S CRITIQUE OF LUTHERANISM

It is important to recognize that the essence of Hauerwas's critique of Lutheran doctrinal practice springs from his commitment to the narrative nature of

59. Hauerwas, "Ethicist as Theologian," 411.

60. Stanley Hauerwas and William H. Willimon, *Resident Aliens: A Provocative Christian Assessment of Culture and Ministry for People Who Know That Something Is Wrong* (Nashville: Abingdon, 1989), 30.

61. Hauerwas, *Community of Character*, 10.

62. Hauerwas, *Peaceable Kingdom*, 24.

the Christian faith. In other words, Hauerwas contends that one must look at the Christian life not as two parts, namely what a Christian believes and what a Christian does. Instead, as Hauerwas sees it, what a Christian believes and what a Christian does are so thoroughly interrelated and interdependent as to be indistinguishable. This is what he means when he says, as he often does, that ethics and doctrine must be bound together: "Theological claims are fundamentally practical and Christian ethics is but that form of theological reflection which attempts to explicate this inherently practical nature."[63] Christian doctrine and Christian ethics should not, then, be divided into two separate disciplines. They are equally significant and interdependent aspects of one unified story. Hauerwas insists that the division between ethics and doctrine, so commonplace in contemporary Christianity, was not always so: "Once there was no Christian ethics simply because Christians could not distinguish between their beliefs and their behavior. They assumed that their lives exemplified (or at least should exemplify) their doctrines in a manner that made division between life and doctrine impossible."[64] This is not to say that it is impossible or imprudent to distinguish at times between theology and ethics. "The task of the theologian," Hauerwas explains, "is not to deny that for certain limited purposes ethics can be distinguished from theology, but to reject their supposed ontological and practical independence."[65] Hauerwas takes sharp issue, therefore, with seminary curricula that require the completion of systematic theology as prerequisites for courses on ethics. "In such a context theology begins to look like a 'metaphysics' on which one must get straight before you can turn to questions of ethics."[66] This alienation between theology and ethics, Hauerwas believes, leads to the diminution of both. Theology becomes increasingly theoretical and removed from the practicalities of Christian living. Ethics, in turn, struggles to find a ground that lends it legitimacy and significance in the life of the church.

As Hauerwas sees it, a combination of factors contributed to this unfortunate divorce between theology and ethics. A chief culprit was the Enlightenment, which eroded confidence in Christian truth-claims and left theologians trying "to secure the ongoing meaningfulness of Christian convictions by anchoring them in anthropological generalizations and/or turning them into ethics."[67] Put another way, "enlightened" theologians felt

---

63. Ibid., 54.
64. Hauerwas, *Sanctify Them*, 20.
65. Ibid.
66. Ibid., 32.
67. Ibid., 30.

compelled to abandon the embarrassingly exclusive propositional claims of Christianity and embraced instead the more palatable and sophisticated pursuit of humanity's assumed common ethical foundation. But it is not just the Enlightenment that is to blame for the disastrous bifurcation between doctrine and ethics that typically leaves ethics shrouded in a cloud of suspicion. Hauerwas also finds fault with the Reformation itself:

> Yet the polemical terms of the Reformation could not help but reshape how ethics was conceived in relation to theology. Faith, not works, determines the Christian's relationship to God. Moreover works became associated with 'ethics,' particularly as ethics was alleged to be the way sinners attempt to secure their standing before God as a means of avoiding complete dependence on God's grace. So for Protestants the Christian life is now characterized in such a way that there always exists a tension between law and grace.[68]

It should be noted, though, that Hauerwas does not credit this division with Luther. He insists, "Neither Luther or [sic] Calvin distinguished between theology and ethics," and offers Luther's treatise "The Freedom of a Christian" as his evidence.[69] The rift between theology and its practical form demonstrated in the Christian life, what we commonly call ethics, came about, ironically enough, when a zeal to guard the Reformation's central doctrine led subsequent reformers into positions eschewed by the very forebears credited with the doctrine's rediscovery.[70]

Hauerwas indulges in historical consideration not for its own sake. He does it only to reinforce his case that things are not now as they once were—or should be. Always, his concern is with the contemporary situation. He decries the ongoing failure of Christians to rectify the unwarranted division between theological truth and the ethical task. He levels his complaint against Protestantism in general and sharpens his thrust with a specific rebuke of contemporary Lutheranism. Lutheranism, he alleges, is particularly culpable for perpetuating the estrangement between ethics and theology. Presumably, Hauerwas is acquainted with a number of theologians who might be considered Lutheran. However, it is Gilbert Meilaender and his work that receive particular consideration in Hauerwas's essays. Since Meilaender is one of the few Lutheran

---

68. Ibid., 27.

69. Ibid.

70. The teaching of the reformers, particularly Philip Melanchthon, will receive greater attention in chs. 3 and 4.

ethicists writing in support of virtue ethics, it is reasonable that Hauerwas would choose to interact with him. Further, Meilaender specifically addresses the relation of ethics to theology, providing Hauerwas ready material for evaluation. In at least two separate essays, Hauerwas takes up Meilaender's argument and considers its merit. It is prudent, therefore, to offer a brief overview of Meilaender's position as critiqued by Hauerwas.[71]

The Christian life, as Meilaender describes it in one of his early essays, may be pictured as both dialogue and journey. According to the dialogue paradigm, the Christian life is a movement back and forth between the two words of God: law and gospel. The law condemns and convicts, driving the despairing believer into the gospel. Comforted and confident in the wake of the gospel encounter, the believer is freed to return to the law—only to be crushed again and so driven back once more to the gospel. And so it goes: back and forth, back and forth. "On this model," observes Meilaender, "there can be no notion of progress in righteousness; for righteousness is purely relational in character."[72] Before God, *coram Deo*, this is precisely the way that Christians experience life. Yet, this is but half the picture.

The Christian life, Meilaender argues, can also be understood as a journey, that is, "the process by which God graciously transforms a sinner into a saint, as a pilgrimage (always empowered by grace) toward fellowship with God."[73] In this image, the Christian life is aiming at a particular goal. It is going *some*where, not just back and forth. Both portrayals have their strengths and weaknesses. Both testify to critical aspects of the Christian's life. Both find support in Scripture. Both, Meilaender insists, must be kept in tension in the Christian life: "The tension between these two pictures of the Christian life cannot be overcome, nor should we try to overcome it."[74] Hauerwas, however, is unconvinced and takes exception to Meilaender's Lutheran argument: "This strikes me as what a good Lutheran should say—namely, that it is crucial to keep the two metaphors in dialectical tension so that the full range of Christian existence coram deo is before us. But I am not a good Lutheran, and I want to argue that the metaphor of the journey is and surely should be the primary one for articulating the shape of Christian existence and living."[75] Concerned that "Meilaender's faithful Lutheranism" extends, and indeed exacerbates, the

---

71. Meilaender and his work will be examined more thoroughly in ch. 2.

72. Gilbert Meilaender, "The Place of Ethics in the Theological Task," *Currents in Theology and Mission* 6 (1979): 200.

73. Ibid.

74. Ibid., 210.

75. Hauerwas, "A Retrospective Assessment," 87.

unfortunate divide between doctrine and ethics, Hauerwas presents a vision of the Christian life that joins Meilaender's two separate paradigms into one unified portrayal. From Hauerwas's perspective, Meilaender's Lutheranism is no small part of his problem. "Meilaender's account of dialogue is too Lutheran for me," Hauerwas avers. "After all, a dialogue can be an ongoing conversation in which one can certainly make progress."[76] Hauerwas is dissatisfied with the seemingly endless circularity of Meilaender's account of dialogue and sees an emphasis on the journey metaphor as the way to escape what he sees as a stultifying cul-de-sac. "The metaphor of dialogue only makes sense as a necessary and continuing part of the journey."[77] For Hauerwas, the truth of the Christian's forgiveness through Christ's life and resurrection belongs to the overall narrative of the Christian's life. What Lutherans name as justification, in distinction from sanctification, Hauerwas makes a part of (and a normative part of) the journey that is the Christian's story as it is lived in relation to Christ's story.

Hauerwas frankly admits that his concentration on the metaphor of journey, including his move to subsume the dialogue metaphor—and with it the doctrine of justification—within that journey image, may well be misconstrued. Writing with Charles Pinches, he concedes, "We no doubt appear to leave justification behind in emphasizing sanctification and the virtues it makes available."[78] Determined to dispel this appearance, however, Hauerwas strives to demonstrate that the Christian's forgiveness is at once the beginning as well as the context for the journey that describes the Christian's life: "Suppose we fix on what is perhaps the most rudimentary notion of justification imaginable: by justification we are made just before God. As Paul makes plain, something decisive has occurred in Jesus that has changed our status as God sees us. Put this way, we can see that 'justification' begs for narrative display: what we were before, what are we now, and where is this change taking us?"[79] Far from negating the importance of justification, Hauerwas seeks to impart particular prominence to justification by considering it within an eschatological context. "Paul's emphasis upon justification, and virtually all else he says," according to Hauerwas, "is incomprehensible apart from his eschatology."[80] It is the Christian's life, his eschatologically oriented journey, which becomes the

---

76. Hauerwas, *Sanctify Them*, 127.

77. Ibid.

78. Stanley Hauerwas and Charles Pinches, *Christians among the Virtues: Theological Conversations with Ancient and Modern Ethics* (Notre Dame, IN: University of Notre Dame Press, 1997), 116.

79. Ibid., 117.

80. Ibid., 118.

"narrative display" or the concrete shape of his justification, even when this is understood in a strictly forensic sense.

This emphasis on eschatology, pointing to the telos of the Christian narrative, bolsters Hauerwas's case for the sufficiency of the journey motif, without recourse to Meilaender's separate dialogue paradigm. "The metaphor of dialogue," Hauerwas argues, "only makes sense as a necessary and continuing part of the journey."[81] For Hauerwas, the truth of the sinner's justification before God is contained within and illuminated by the idea of growth or journey: "We can grow in Christian virtue, yet it is best to describe this as growth in grace, whose hallmark is forgiveness."[82] For Hauerwas, this growth, naturally, is bound up in eschatological reality: "If we refuse to be forgiven, we grow neither in virtue nor in grace. . . . Our acceptance of forgiveness is the means by which our souls are expanded so that we can hope. Through hope we learn to endure suffering, confident that God has given us the character faithfully to inhabit the story of the redemption of all creation, of which we are part."[83] Dialogue or justification, and journey or sanctification, thus blend into a single narrated account. Seen from Hauerwas's viewpoint, then, Meilaender's portrayal of two distinct paradigms is not a helpful way of considering the Christian life, but an unnecessary and unhappy division that perpetuates the disastrous divorce between theology and ethics.

Hauerwas is insistent on the necessity of overcoming Meilaender's tension between dialogue and journey because of his conviction that ethics and doctrine, or practice and belief, must not be driven into separate corners. He charges that Meilaender's (and Lutheranism's?) approach needlessly supports precisely this separation. "The problem," Hauerwas explains, "is that when either justification or sanctification becomes an independent theological notion something has gone wrong."[84] The correction of this wrong turn is a consistent concern of Hauerwas and motivates his criticism of Meilaender's Lutheranism. In *The Peaceable Kingdom*, Hauerwas explicitly expresses the importance of adopting a structuring horizon for the Christian life wider than the maintenance of perpetual tension. This is perhaps his clearest articulation of the relationship between justification and sanctification, and so demands careful attention:

---

81. Hauerwas, *Sanctify Them*, 127.

82. Hauerwas and Pinches, *Christians among the Virtues*, 128.

83. Ibid.

84. Hauerwas, *Sanctify Them*, 127. As subsequent chapters will indicate, this is a statement that many Lutherans would willingly affirm.

For the language of "sanctification" and "justification" is not meant to be descriptive of a status. Indeed, part of the problem with those terms is that they are abstractions. When they are separated from Jesus' life and death, they distort Christian life. "Sanctification" is but a way of reminding us of the kind of journey we must undertake if we are to make the story of Jesus our story. "Justification" is but a reminder of the character of that story—namely, what God has done for us by providing us with a path to follow.[85]

The essential ideas of justification (what God does for us) and sanctification (our response of holy living) are retained, but Hauerwas places both in the wider context of a narrated theology. The Christian life is not understood as a tension between theology and ethics, or between dialogue and journey. Christianity, as Hauerwas sees it, is as wonderful and as simple as the Christian learning to make his story part of Jesus' story. Justification and sanctification are merely components of that wider frame.[86] Accepting as the norming horizon an irresolvable tension between dialogue and journey or between doctrine and ethics, Hauerwas would charge, leads inevitably to an ethics set adrift and consequently a lackluster interest in the cultivation of virtue and character formation.

Recognizing the significance of this point of doctrine, Hauerwas has considered it more than once. A thorough summary of his distinctive theological position appears in *The Hauerwas Reader* and provides a fitting last word on this discussion:

> I am aware that my claim for the priority of the journey metaphor for the display of the Christian life can only reinforce the suspicion of some that I have abandoned the central Christian contention of the priority of God's grace. I know of no way in principle to calm such fears. Moreover I am aware it is not sufficient to claim, as I have here and elsewhere, that I have no intention of qualifying the necessity of God's grace for the beginning, living, and end of the Christian

---

85. Hauerwas, *Peaceable Kingdom*, 94.

86. Obviously, many Lutheran as well as other theologians would take exception to Hauerwas's definition of justification and the inclusion of justification within the journey imagery. The Lutheran concerns with Hauerwas's teaching on justification are considered more fully in the next chapter. For now, it is sufficient to suggest that from a Lutheran perspective justification might better be understood as the fact that the reality of Jesus' story before, and outside of, the believer is wholly sufficient for that believer's eschatological acquittal, entirely independent of the believer's own subsequent efforts to live the story.

life. What I hope is now clear, however, is that I refuse to think the only or best way to depict the priority of God's grace is in terms of the dialogue metaphor. This has certainly been the dominant mode among Protestants, but exactly because it has been so, we have had difficulty articulating our sense of the reality of and growth in the Christian life.[87]

CONCLUSION

Virtue ethics, it seems, poses a significant challenge to Lutheran theology. Lutheranism's proclivity for tension and duality is well known and readily documented. Equally recognized is Lutheranism's typical ambivalence toward issues of ethics, as it seems to prefer instead an emphasis on the church's central article of justification. Appearances notwithstanding, however, the intent of this book is to demonstrate that virtue ethics and Lutheranism are in fact altogether compatible. Contemporary virtue ethics has much to contribute to the Lutheran church of today, and reciprocally, the field known as virtue ethics can learn important lessons from Lutheranism. Of course, a Lutheranism ready both to receive from and to contribute to an ethics of virtue will likely look substantially different from the one Hauerwas recognizes. Interestingly, the portrayal of Lutheranism I will offer may also be altogether unfamiliar to some of those who today bear the reformer's name. It is hoped, however, that while the account of Lutheran theology presented here may appear foreign to certain contemporary manifestations and understandings of Lutheranism, it will nevertheless prove to be one that the reformers themselves would have readily recognized. As the reformers knew and taught, there is a place within Lutheran theology for ethics. Today, that place can be filled remarkably well by ethics that focus on the cultivation of character and the promotion of the virtues. Before that case is made, though, some time should be spent listening to a few notable representative voices within contemporary Lutheranism.

---

87. Hauerwas, "A Retrospective Assessment," 88.

2

Contemporary Lutheran Voices

Since the days of Luther, Lutheranism has widely enjoyed a reputation for meticulous, insightful, and often influential theology. Roughly corresponding to this enviable reputation for astute and perhaps even profound theology is the antithetical assumption that the cultivation of great ethical thinkers is not to be expected from Lutheran soil. Of course, there have been notable exceptions. The tribulation of Nazi Germany proved an effective fertilizer for ethical reflection, and both Dietrich Bonhoeffer and Helmut Thielicke demonstrated Lutheranism's capacity for the production of capable ethical thinkers when demanded. The next chapter will present the case for similarly considering Philipp Melanchthon and some of his contemporaries as Lutherans who took seriously the questions and challenges of ethics. But first, the present chapter will consider some current Lutheran theologians whose continuing work may yet successfully overcome the common caricature of Lutheran ethical inadequacy or inability.[1]

Lutheran Critiques of Contemporary Lutheranism

Through the spokesman of Stanley Hauerwas, contemporary virtue ethics confronts Lutheran doctrine with a significant challenge, accusing it of a failure to address adequately important ethical questions with regard to the cultivation of Christian character and development of virtues within the individual Christian's life. For Hauerwas, the specific problem is Lutheran theology's complicity in the persistent rift between doctrine and ethics, which in turn fosters widespread ethical ignorance and indifference among Christians. Undue

---

1. Typical of this caricature is the summarizing comment of Max Stackhouse and Dennis McCann in their rebuttal of Robert Benne's critique of their own work: "But we do not want to rub this in. It is difficult enough being a Lutheran ethicist—if one always has a bad conscience for speaking of good works." Stackhouse and McCann, "Responses to a Postcommunist Manifesto: Ethics, Economics and the Corporate Life," *The Christian Century* 16 (January 23, 1991): 83.

obsession with the doctrine of justification that overshadows all else is a regularly cited cause of Lutheranism's ethical difficulties. In varying degrees, the writers considered in this chapter will take up the challenge posed by virtue ethics. Their willingness to address concerns similar or even identical to those raised by Hauerwas is the reason for their inclusion here. Certainly, it comes as no great surprise that a non-Lutheran theologian like Hauerwas would detect problems in Lutheran doctrine. It is noteworthy, however, that the thinkers considered below are also willing to recognize substantial shortcomings with the account of Lutheran theology sadly typical among both laity and clergy today. This chapter will examine the observations and diagnoses offered by four contemporary theologians. Their insights will demonstrate many affinities with the concerns of virtue ethics. A consideration of their proposed solutions will create space for the subsequent work of this investigation.

DAVID YEAGO

For many years, David Yeago taught systematic theology at Lutheran Theological Seminary of the South, a seminary of the Evangelical Lutheran Church in America (ELCA). In 1993, he wrote a brief essay that proved to be a potent catalyst for the work of others who recognized the validity of his argument and shared his concern for the church. His essay remains perhaps the clearest succinct articulation of the unintended but arguably inevitable consequences of using a law-and-gospel polarity as a basic structure for thinking theologically. In "Gnosticism, Antinomianism, and Reformation Theology," Yeago argues that today's Protestant church is perilously infected with insidious forms of the "isms" identified in his title. Their pervasive yet often unrecognized presence within Protestantism he traces to what he terms a "misconstrual" of the polarity between law and gospel.

> What I am contesting is the view that the distinction and opposition of law and gospel constitutes the last horizon of Christian belief, that the opposition of law and gospel to one another is the prime structuring principle which bounds and orders the conceptual space within which the coherence of Christian belief must be thought out. I am suggesting that the law/gospel distinction, however indispensable it may be, is not the principle in terms of which Christian belief hangs together, and that to assume that it is such a principle has disastrous consequences which we can see all around us.[2]

Yeago argues that when law and gospel are set against one another, the gospel inevitably gains its definition in antithesis to the law itself. The gospel becomes our liberator not from our failure to keep the law and the consequent just wrath of God; rather, it becomes our liberator from the law per se. Hence, any word that comes to a Christian as command, direction, or guidance is ruled out by the liberating gospel. "If the law/gospel distinction is a final antithesis," Yeago concludes, "then *any* call for one ordering of life rather than another, will by definition be the law from which the gospel frees us."[3]

In this theological climate, of course, antinomianism thrives. "Indeed," Yeago charges, "much twentieth century Protestant theology has been antinomian all along; the practical antinomianism now regnant in many churches is simply a long-standing theoretical antinomianism achieving the courage of its convictions."[4] But there are further consequences of the law/gospel paradigm's overextension. Yeago's marquee accusation of Gnosticism derives from the same thesis of a misconstrual of the law/gospel dichotomy: "The logic is simple: if form is enslavement, then a God who took form in history would be an enslaving God. The liberating God must therefore be a formless God, a God at most dialectically related to any particular form, a God who is everywhere and nowhere, whose faceless elusiveness frees us from the tyranny of the particular and ordered and definitive."[5] Thus, various forms of "soft Gnosticism" so frequently encountered in today's church also find a source in the common problem of the misuse, or overuse, of the law/gospel distinction.

In separate essays, Yeago maintains that this state of affairs is not inherent within Lutheranism. This point should not be missed. "Even in the sixteenth century," Yeago observes, "the Reformers were well aware that there is more to the gospel promise than assurance that we will not be damned."[6] Along with comfort for guilt-ridden souls, Yeago argues, the gospel entails positive content: "the promise of the gospel is not simply that we will not be condemned; it is the promise that we will *live* in, with, and through Jesus Christ."[7] In other words, the gospel carries not only negative content (freed *from* something),

2. David S. Yeago, "Gnosticism, Antinomianism, and Reformation Theology: Reflections on the Costs of a Construal," *Pro Ecclesia* 2, no. 1 (Winter 1993): 38–39 (emphasis in original).

3. Ibid., 42 (emphasis in original). Once freed from the law, it should be noted, people are at liberty to choose whatever pleases them and to take their cues about acceptable behavior from the culture or from whatever other source is convenient or comfortable.

4. Ibid.

5. Ibid., 44.

6. David S. Yeago, "The Promise of God and the Desires of our Hearts: Prolegomena to a Lutheran Retrieval of Classical Spiritual Theology," *Lutheran Forum* 30, no. 2 (May 1996): 25.

7. Ibid., 26.

but also positive content (freed *for* something). "The free gift of God in Christ Jesus, we need to say is that we *get to do* all sorts of splendid things as his priestly people."[8] This Reformation view of the gospel, Yeago asserts, stands in stark contrast to contemporary understandings: "After some years of listening to Lutherans argue about justification, sanctification, faith, and the sacraments, I have become convinced that the tendency to think of the gospel in negative terms, as 'the word which lets us off,' is quite widespread among us, often the tacit premise even of those who would be very embarrassed to say so explicitly."[9]

Yeago has no patience for thinking and behavior in ordinary church life that derive from the antinomian and Gnostic theology present among Lutherans. He laments the "contemporary tender-minded rhetoric about all those 'hurting people' who need more than anything else to be liberated from all order and absolved of all expectations by the redemptive 'inclusivity' of the antinomian church."[10] Yeago also denounces the effects on worship, education, and ethics as congregations increasingly jettison extensive catechesis and ritual/liturgical observances in favor of formats deemed less demanding, more contemporary, and presumably more meaningful. Interesting in this regard is Yeago's own affirmation of a primary concern of Hauerwas.

> The simplest way to adapt Lutheranism to modern culture is to identify the substance of Lutheranism with a doctrine, a theological teaching, and to separate doctrine from practice so that the doctrine can live a disembodied existence in the mind. The notion of adiaphoron can then be summoned to establish the required distance between the inward essence of religion and its secondary outward expression.[11]

Two of Hauerwas's chief concerns with contemporary Lutheranism, then, are acknowledged and reinforced by Yeago's observations. Not only does Yeago express concern over what he considers the routine misunderstanding that allows only negative content to the gospel, but he also regrets the split between doctrine and practice. Yeago, then, offers an analysis of contemporary Lutheranism that agrees substantially with Hauerwas's observations.

---

8. David S. Yeago, "Sacramental Lutheranism at the End of the Modern Age," *Lutheran Forum* 34, no. 4 (Christmas/Winter 2000): 14.

9. Yeago, "Promise of God," 25.

10. Yeago, "Gnosticism," 42.

11. Yeago, "Sacramental Lutheranism," 9 (emphasis in original).

ROBERT BENNE

Professor Emeritus at Roanoke College in Virginia, Robert Benne is another ELCA Lutheran willing to concede certain "weaknesses and lacunae" within today's manifestations of Lutheranism as it contends with the questions of Christian ethics.[12] Like Yeago and Hauerwas, Benne believes that much of the problem stems from a misappropriation of the definitive Lutheran emphasis on justification. "Dazzled as they are by the wonder and profundity of God's justifying grace in Christ," writes Benne, "Lutherans are tempted to think that the only really interesting ethical question is the motivational one."[13] He cites this Lutheran predilection for "soteriological reductionism," as he dubs it, as the reason for the commonly recognized "lack of ethical substance" in Lutheran doctrine.[14] The ethical life of Christians that results from this attitude lacks content and clarity. The believer is provided with little more than a vague notion of love that "becomes both a permissive affirmation of any behavior and a rather amorphous serving of the neighbor."[15]

It would be mistaken, however, to conclude that Benne is willing to concede the existence of an ethical Achilles's heel within Lutheranism or even ready to admit that Lutheranism is ill-equipped for handling the serious business of ethics. To the contrary, Benne is fully prepared not only to defend the ethical sensibilities of Lutheran theology, but to argue with conviction that "perennial themes" in Lutheranism provide it "with a coherent and persuasive account of Christian ethics in both its personal and social dimensions."[16] Any alumni of the most rudimentary instruction in Lutheran doctrine would readily recognize the themes that Benne goes on to identify as perennial. While Benne acknowledges that a misconstrual of the doctrine of justification fosters serious problems, he does not hesitate to propound the doctrine's legitimate location at · the core of theology and ethics. "The central principle of Lutheran ethics," he declares, "is identical with its central theological principle: justification by grace through faith on account of Christ."[17] In thoroughly Lutheran language, Benne expounds the gospel's determinative role in ethics: "Our faith becomes active in love. This love expresses itself in deeds that follow spontaneously from faith and

12. Robert Benne, "Lutheran Ethics: Perennial Themes and Contemporary Challenges," in Karen L. Bloomquist and John R. Stumme, eds., *The Promise of Lutheran Ethics* (Minneapolis: Fortress Press, 1998), 11.

13. Ibid., 27.

14. Ibid.

15. Ibid., 28. Again, the result of such a move is the triumph of culture or perhaps individual ego to supply any norms or specific direction for behavior.

16. Ibid., 27.

17. Ibid., 12.

no longer from the compulsion of the law. Such love is creative and dynamic. It goes beyond the limits and structures of the law but does not violate them."[18]

Benne's unflinching Lutheranism makes his observations about ethical shortcomings within his doctrinal community the more poignant. Lutheranism's soteriological reductionism is a serious concern, particularly when coupled with the collapse of the old general morality, which, until recently, had been cultivated by the surrounding culture. Benne offers an excellent analysis of this significant factor in Lutheranism's ethical difficulties:

> Like other mainstream Protestants, Lutherans have relied on the general culture to do their work for them. The general Protestant Ethic had established notions of marriage and sexual ethics, the calling, and humane values of justice and civility. But that established culture has been fractured by the new world that surrounds us. Lutherans need a more specific notion of the Christian life if they are to respond to this chaotic world. They cannot do that by relying solely on justification.[19]

Like Yeago, Benne recognizes the need for Lutheranism to attend to questions regarding the shape and structure of the Christian life. Yet, such an emphasis is fraught with serious obstacles for a Lutheran. Such an intentional effort at ethical instruction could appear to flout "the ecstatic notion of motivation with which they [Lutherans] have operated for so long."[20] The reach and strength of this difficulty is reflected in the fact that, earlier in the same essay, Benne himself seems to endorse the very notion he later questions, asserting, "love expresses itself in deeds that flow spontaneously from faith."[21] Benne represents well the peculiar ethical challenge confronting Lutheran theologians.

---

18. Ibid., 14. Taken by itself, Benne's comment could yet lead one to a diminished understanding of the law, assuming, as it seems to, that the law always and only compels or limits. This faulty idea will be addressed in what follows, most immediately in the discussion of Hütter's work.

19. Ibid., 28. It should be noted that the disintegration of what Benne calls the "general Protestant Ethic" lends urgency to the thesis of this study. When the surrounding culture is providing a sufficient standard of morality, it could be argued that the church need not so carefully or intentionally tend to the cultivation of ethical behavior among its members; in a time of societal licentiousness, however, it could be argued that such a casual stance toward character formation is no longer acceptable.

20. Ibid., 29.

21. Ibid., 14.

REINHARD HÜTTER

Now writing and teaching at Duke as a Roman Catholic theologian, until 2004, Reinhard Hütter wrote and worked as a Lutheran and was numbered among those who had something to say about Lutheran ethics. In the same volume on Lutheran ethics with Benne's essay is a contribution from Hütter. In large part, Hütter concurs with Benne's assessment of the ethical failings of the Lutheranism of his day; but, of course, Hütter elaborates his own particular concerns. In line with both Yeago and Benne, Hütter traces Lutheranism's ethical difficulties to a misuse of the doctrine of justification. Hütter sharpens the critique to a provocative point by declaring an ethics built solely from and by justification fallacious: "The decisive core fallacy of modern Protestant ethics is a broadly shared assumption about justification: What makes Christian ethics 'Protestant' is the conviction that everything must ultimately be framed by and derived from the one and only central article of Protestantism, namely, justification by grace through faith alone."[22] It would be a mistake, though, to read here a foreshadowing of his later move to Rome, or a budding distaste for central Lutheran theological formulations. Hütter clarifies his critique of the mishandling of the doctrine, of justification saying, "I am not challenging the centrality of the doctrine of justification by faith alone; instead I am seeking to safeguard it from the misuse of applying it beyond and against the Reformation's intention."[23] Certainly, this was the goal for Hütter at the time he wrote; he sought to do ethics in the same spirit as that of the reformers.

Hütter substantiates his concerns with contemporary Lutheranism's mishandling of ethical issues through a thorough consideration of the theology in question. Offering a brief historical analysis of the developments that led to the current misuse of justification, Hütter concludes that the contemporary culmination and manifestation of this mishandling of justification is a thoroughly negative understanding and appropriation of the law:

> The focus on an exclusively forensic understanding of justification fostered the assumption that the gospel had only a negative relationship to God's law. This primarily negative relationship, of course, had to have inherently antinomian consequences. If the gospel is interpreted as radically opposed to the law, the freedom that results in the gospel's acceptance can only be construed as a "negative

22. Reinhard Hütter, "The Twofold Center of Lutheran Ethics: Christian Freed om and God's Commandments," in Bloomquist and Stumme, eds., *Promise of Lutheran Ethics*, 33.

23. Ibid. The accuracy of Hütter's assessment of the reformer's view of justification will be considered in the chapter that follows.

freedom," as the freedom from all alienating, authenticity-inhibiting restrictions. The "law"—and not humanity under the condition of sin faced by God's law!—becomes the central problem.[24]

This observation reinforces Hütter's specific thesis that the issue that most needs to be addressed and corrected before today's Lutherans will be able to deal with their widely recognized ethical challenges is "the deeply problematic opposition that many allege exists between 'freedom' and 'law.'"[25]

Hütter makes the point that an erroneous understanding of freedom as autonomy leads not only to the antinomianism already noted, but also to a denigration of form and structure. This line of argument meshes with the threat Yeago identifies as Gnosticism, the first half of the pair of evil infiltrators he discerns within today's Lutheranism. Yeago and Hütter share much common ground in their assessment of contemporary Lutheranism and its attempt to handle the challenge of providing a meaningful ethics.

Hütter provides an insightful depiction of the sort of populist attitudes commonly cited among Lutherans who oppose a developed Christian ethic on principle. He understands this way of thinking quite well, observing that, "If there is one thing modern Protestant ethics is dogmatic about—with a very good conscience—it is the protection of human freedom from the dangers of legalism and works-righteousness."[26] These twin threats to personal autonomy, as much of contemporary Lutheranism would understand it, Hütter dubs the "one unforgivable double sin in Protestantism."[27] Protestantism's abhorrence of this "sin" stems directly from its strict adherence to the "Protestant fallacy" of making the doctrine of justification the "ceiling that has to cover everything instead of the very floor on which we stand."[28] The failure properly to understand and locate justification, Hütter observes, fosters the disregard and even aversion for serious consideration of ethics and morality so typical in modern Protestantism. Any talk of commandment, direction, or even responsibility is perceived as a threat to the flawed understanding of justification as a declaration of individual autonomy.

Ironically, though, even the most ardent proponents of justification as freedom from all forms of autonomy-limiting law inevitably advance their own norms and rules for right behavior. It will become clear as the book's

---

24. Ibid., 34.
25. Ibid., 32.
26. Ibid., 36.
27. Ibid.
28. Ibid., 33.

investigation unfolds that this is an outcome that portends dire consequences for the gospel itself. Hütter notes that "modern Protestant ethics has become antinomian and at the same time very legalistic about particular 'correctnesses' that are reflective of distinct social and political agendas."[29] So, for example, the use of inclusive language, the ordination of women, or the freedom of sexual expression become issues deemed worthy of impassioned defense and even church discipline, while concerns about chastity or doctrinal fidelity are considered passé and peripheral to "genuine" Christianity. Hütter unequivocally rejects antinomian versions of Lutheranism as antithetical to the position of the reformers themselves and argues for a retrieval of the law as commandment. Believing himself in hearty agreement with the reformers, he advocates the zealous study and appropriation of God's commandments as a great good. "Christian ethics in the tradition of the Reformation should, of course," Hütter declares, "always end with praise of God's commandments."[30] Happy to oblige, Hütter does so—literally, concluding his essay with a portion of Psalm 119[31]—but not before joining Yeago and Benne in harshly criticizing popular notions of what it means for Lutherans to do ethics.

GILBERT MEILAENDER

Meilaender joined this conversation in the previous chapter as the foil for Hauerwas's critique of Lutheranism. Unlike the previous three theologians, Meilaender is a clergyman of the Lutheran Church—Missouri Synod. Like the previous three theologians, he is quite concerned about the dismissive or even suspicious attitude toward ethics that exists in the church today. Although he doesn't specifically follow Yeago, Benne, and Hütter in expressly identifying a misconstrual of justification as the prime culprit, he views their work sympathetically.[32] Meilaender makes clear that ethics from a Lutheran standpoint must always be vigorously anti-Pelagian, but adds an unmistakable word of caution in the spirit of the Lutheran critics already considered:

29. Ibid., 37.

30. Ibid., 53.

31. Ibid., 54. Hütter ends his essay by quoting verses 129–136 (KJV): "Thy testimonies are wonderful; therefore my soul keeps them. The unfolding of thy words gives light; it imparts understanding to the simple. With open mouth I pant, because I long for thy commandments. Turn to me and be gracious to me, as is thy wont towards those who love thy name. Keep steady my steps according to thy promise; and let no iniquity get dominion over me. Redeem me from human oppression, that I may keep thy precepts. Make thy face shine upon thy servant, and teach me thy statutes. My eyes shed streams of tears, because they do not keep thy law."

32. Gilbert Meilaender, "Reclaiming the Quest for Holiness," *Lutheran Quarterly* 13 (Winter 1999): 488. Meilaender considers Yeago's "deconstructive analysis," considered above, to be "unanswerable."

Quite probably we Lutherans suppose that this is our strong point. We are certainly anti-Pelagian. Eager to make the preaching of Jesus necessary, we will not want to deny our need for him. And there's something to that. From another angle, however, seeing only this may sometimes have been the bane of Lutheran ethics. Emphasizing so strongly that every form of order is finally disorder, we can only negate any and every piece of moral guidance as inevitably disordered.[33]

In such an atmosphere of suspicion toward moral guidance—one readily recognized by Meilaender, and likely by others who share his church culture—every moral directive and every good deed is ultimately deemed corrupt. Hence, there is a ring of truth in the well-circulated quip that the trouble Lutherans have with ethics is that they see no difference between helping a little old lady across the street and pushing her in front of an oncoming bus. The taint of sin clings hopelessly to both acts. Such is the perspective when considered through a lens focused on justification and fearful of works righteousness.

Such a pessimistic view of ethics results in the conviction that for a Christian the only safe and legitimate use of ethics is to reveal and condemn human sin and weakness. Ethics serves purely as "propaedeutic to preaching," as Meilaender puts it.[34] According to this understanding, ethics condemns sinners and their actions but has nothing positive to say about the "form and structure" of the Christian's life. The "hard work" of speaking to the mundane and routine issues and questions of daily life is left to others.[35] The inadequacy and disingenuousness of the position that all moral guidance is inevitably disordered is starkly exposed by the free use made of the efforts of these "others" when it comes to the pressing practical concerns of moral conduct and behavior. Even greater is the irony that this parasitic appropriation of the ethical efforts of others is frequently complemented with disdainful criticisms of the theological deficiencies of the very ones whose ethical contributions are being employed.

With the accuracy of an insider, Meilaender illustrates the typical Lutheran attitude toward ethics. "We cannot talk about progress in grace or growth in holiness," he charges, "without immediately emphasizing that even the best of our righteousnesses are as filthy rags—and that, therefore, our need is less for

---

33. Gilbert Meilaender, "The Task of Lutheran Ethics," *Lutheran Forum* 34, no. 4 (Winter 2000): 20.

34. Ibid.

35. Ibid. Meilaender names "Roman Catholic, Orthodox Catholic, Anglican, Presbyterian, Methodist, and (yes, even) Baptist brothers and sisters" among the "others."

continued moral analysis and reflection than for hearing the gospel."[36] This attitude he labels the "peril of much Lutheran ethics in the twentieth century."[37] Attuned to the species of temptation peculiar to Lutherans, Meilaender cautions against a now familiar malady stemming from Lutheranism's difficulties with ethical concerns: "We must be wary of the antinomianism that always lies near at hand, of an emphasis on motive that leaves no room for reflection upon the body and the created order, of a lingering complacency that is too ready to suppose that worldly wisdom is one thing and the mind of Christ another."[38] Clearly, Meilaender is not unsympathetic to the concerns of the other theologians considered in this chapter who desire to make room for an effective understanding of ethics within Lutheranism.

Meilaender strongly affirms the centrality of the gospel and saving faith that vindicates before God without any conditions being added, "as if something more were needed to enter the kingdom that Jesus establishes."[39] "Nevertheless, it would be a mistake," he continues, "to suppose that the Scriptures exist only to bear witness to Christ, as if they were the norm for the church's faith but not also for her life."[40] This, of course, is a critical point; to be able to hold two distinct truths at once while challenging, is, as will become increasingly clear, an essential attribute of a faithful theologian. Like Yeago, Benne, and Hütter, Meilaender believes that the church can proclaim the gospel clearly without being compelled to succumb to ethical vacuity.

> The church's moral discipline does not set up conditions for entering the kingdom; rather, it offers a description of what the life of discipleship should be like—a description of what it means to follow Christ. In setting forth such a description of her way of life, in understanding that description as a discipline to be undertaken, the church does not raise any other standard than the Christ who is confessed. . . . We seek, that is, to give content and structure to the meaning of love.[41]

36. Meilaender, "Reclaiming the Quest," 484.

37. Ibid.

38. Meilaender, "Task of Lutheran Ethics," 22. The neglect of the created order as identified by Meilaender is a significant concern and will be addressed at length in ch. 4.

39. Gilbert Meilaender, *Things That Count: Essays Moral and Theological* (Wilmington, DE: ISI Books, 2000), 60.

40. Ibid.

41. Ibid., 61.

The conviction that the church can provide meaningful ethical guidance without compromising the centrality of the gospel is common to all four of this chapter's thinkers who approach the question from a Lutheran point of view. Nevertheless, while it may appear that they and Hauerwas occupy substantial common ground, significant differences certainly do remain, particularly for Meilaender.

LUTHERAN CONCERNS WITH HAUERWAS'S VIEW OF JUSTIFICATION

Despite the extensive agreement between Meilaender and Hauerwas on a number of significant fronts, including Lutheranism's ethical shortcomings, Meilaender is not prepared fully to endorse Hauerwas's theological move and subsume justification within the journey idea of Christianity. Meilaender's description of justification, his "dialogue" image of Christianity, does not permit an understanding of justification as simply one element in the process of becoming part of the story of Jesus. Of course, this is precisely the way that Hauerwas suggests it be understood. To follow Hauerwas's understanding of justification, Meilaender believes, is ultimately to sacrifice the gospel's capacity to extend unadulterated comfort and unconditional assurance to sinful people. Meilaender insists that any attempt to resolve the tension between journey and dialogue, which he maintains is inherent within the Christian's life, will lead to a gift of grace that is "radically ambiguous."[42] The "gift" will be tied inextricably to the tasks of the moral life. When Christians fail for whatever reason to do what the gift generates, can they be confident that the gift is indeed theirs? There are times, perhaps many times, when Christians need precisely what the gospel has to give. "They need to hear," urges Meilaender, "the word of God's acceptance untrammeled by talk about progress in righteousness."[43]

It seems that Meilaender would find it necessary to disagree not only with Hauerwas but with Yeago as well. In his effort to heal the breach between justification and ethics, Yeago suggests a notion often voiced by those who would like to make the pursuit of upright living relevant in the context of justification: "the free gift of God in Christ Jesus, we need to say, is that we *get to do* all sorts of splendid things as his priestly people."[44] Yeago puts it well, but the idea is essentially a populist one: good works are not a "have-to" but

---

42. Gilbert Meilaender, *Faith and Faithfulness: Basic Themes in Christian Ethics* (Notre Dame, IN: University of Notre Dame Press, 1991), 83.

43. Gilbert Meilaender, "The Place of Ethics in the Theological Task," *Currents in Theology and Mission* 6 (1979): 202.

44. Yeago, "Sacramental Lutheranism," 14 (emphasis in original).

a "get-to." Appealing as the idea may be, this description of the Christian life sounds strikingly similar to the sort of thing that by Meilaender's estimation actually may undermine the essential characteristic of justification as word of pure grace. While Meilaender is eager to establish in Lutheran theology a vital place for the ethical task and character formation, he nevertheless wisely proceeds with caution lest the gospel's power to speak comfort to afflicted consciences be diminished in any way. Such an outcome would be tragic, indeed. As Meilaender writes, "The danger, after all, is that the effort—traced here—to make place for serious attention within Lutheran theology to ethics and to the commanded shape of the Christian life could undercut our ability to offer a word of forgiveness to those who—seeing few evidences of holiness in their life—may be moved to doubt God's favor toward them."[45] Exactly. This must always be the concern of the faithful theologian. Making room for the work of ethics must never diminish the theologian's ability to speak a word of unvarnished and unconditional gospel to a sinner defeated by personal moral failures. Such a crushed sinner does not need a pep talk or the cheery assurance that as God's child one "gets to do" all sorts of wonderful things. These are, of course, the very things he has failed to do. The desperate and repentant sinner needs only one thing: the word of forgiveness. The gospel must be available to be delivered as necessary.

This issue is of some significance for Meilaender, one that he has considered at length in more than one essay. An extended treatment of the question appears in a volume responding to John Paul II's *Veritatis Splendor*. Meilaender's contribution reflects the depth and degree of his wrestling with the topic and provides further insight into Lutheran concerns with Hauerwas's desire to bring justification under the umbrella of the Christian life.[46] In the essay, Meilaender considers the believer who still struggles with sin and even falls prey to the temptation of deliberate wrongdoing. The case of King David in his sin with Bathsheba stands as a supreme example. Meilaender insists on the necessity of distinguishing between the "judgment of the person and judgment of the work."[47] What a person wills and what a person works may not be consistent, argues Meilaender. "To one whose will we judge to be so deeply

---

45. Meilaender, "Reclaiming the Quest," 491.

46. Gilbert Meilaender, "Grace, Justification through Faith, and Sin," in Reinhard Hütter and Theodor Dieter, eds., *Ecumenical Ventures in Ethics: Protestants Engage Pope John Paul II's Moral Encyclicals* (Grand Rapids: Eerdmans, 1998), 60–83. For other examples of Meilaender's interest in this question, see Meilaender, "Place of Ethics"; idem, "Reclaiming the Quest"; idem, *Faith and Faithfulness*, ch. 4; and idem, *The Theory and Practice of Virtue* (Notre Dame, IN: University of Notre Dame Press, 1984), ch. 5

47. Meilaender, "Grace, Justification through Faith, and Sin," 79.

divided that he clings to Christ even in his sin, another kind of response [as opposed to the kind of response for one "smugly persisting in sin"] is necessary."[48] In other words, the minister must be able to speak the law as well as the gospel as the situation warrants.

The possibility of abuse is not lost on Meilaender, who readily admits as much. Nevertheless, such risks are necessary, he believes, if the work of the gospel is to enjoy its full range of application. Meilaender considers this position to be peculiarly Lutheran: "a Lutheran, at least, should be willing to run some risks in order to be certain that we are theologically positioned to speak the gospel to anyone whose self is deeply divided and who seeks God's promise of grace."[49] Meilaender's ardent defense of the gospel as sheer declaration of pardon stems from his potent interpretation of *simul iustus et peccator* (at once saint and sinner). "When we turn away," he maintains, "we need the warning of the law, but we also need—when our wills are sorely divided—a gospel that is not transforming power but sheer declaration of pardon, a declaration that we are pardoned precisely in our ungodliness."[50] Linking justification with the Christian's life of discipleship, Meilaender fears, could well compromise a vital aspect of the gospel.

Still, it bears reiterating that Meilaender's concern about the compromise of the gospel is not intended to quell efforts at resuscitating ethics within Lutheranism. Meilaender is consistently adamant about the need to overcome Lutheranism's ethical maladies. And he is a strong advocate of the usefulness of training in virtue as a means toward this necessary end. Meilaender's reluctance to proclaim justification simply a part of "learning to live the story of Jesus" stems not from a misdirected though sincere Lutheran piety, but from a genuine and carefully considered concern for the gospel's unique work of speaking grace and comfort to those who know well the tenacious grip of sin.[51] As he sees it, the twofold solution is the only solution. The Christian life is dialogue, a word of undeserved grace—period. The Christian life is journey, a word of unmitigated challenge—for all. It is, and must be, both.

Meilaender concedes that the simple distinction between law and gospel, as he prefers to label his insistence on the purely declaratory potential of the gospel, is no sort of foundation for an ethical system. "We should not, I repeat, attempt to spin an ethic out of the distinction between law and gospel."[52]

---

48. Ibid., 78.

49. Ibid., 79.

50. Ibid., 81.

51. One might supplement this concern with the equally compelling concern fittingly to laud Christ and his work of atonement accomplished in first-century Palestine and recorded in the Gospel accounts.

Neither is the *simul* to be construed as an ethical foundation. "To suggest, as I have," writes Meilaender, "that deliberate intention to commit grave sin may sometimes coexist with saving faith is not a claim upon which to build an ethic."[53] The veracity of the theological truth of the gospel spoken to a person desperate for a word of grace does not legitimate its being pressed into the service of Christian ethics. This truth serves a different purpose altogether. Thus Meilaender reasserts the need for an ethical system capable of speaking meaningfully to present-day Christians:

> No Christian ethic can say everything that needs saying solely through the Reformation language of "faith active in love." If we dare never say for certain that a particular deed makes the simul of faith impossible, we ought not deny that our deeds do shape our character—and that they have the power to make of us people who no longer trust God for our security in life and death.[54]

Ethics, then, retains a prominent place for Meilaender, as does the ability to speak words of pardon and forgiveness unencumbered by attachments to the responsibilities of living Christianly. Meilaender insists on the maintenance of the twofold reality. He resists Hauerwas's unifying proposal in order to assure that the uncomplicated purity of the gospel's declaration of grace is in no way diminished.[55] To what extent the other theologians considered here would subscribe to Meilaender's position is not entirely clear. It is certainly possible that some would actually be more amenable to Hauerwas's account and take issue with Meilaender. Regardless, Meilaender maintains his position and founds it upon solid Lutheran ground. It is difficult to find fault with such a compelling concern for the gospel's pure proclamation. And yet the difficulty remains for the Christian and for the Christian church: how to practice a

52. Ibid., 79.

53. Ibid., 77.

54. Ibid., 82.

55. Obviously, the concern to maintain the unique declaratory power of the gospel is not the only potential trouble spot between Lutherans and proponents of virtue ethics. One of the other more notable areas of contention is the charge that an ethics of virtue encourages egocentric self-development, in stark contrast to the gospel's preaching of self-sacrifice and a focus on the other rather than self. For a representative example of this critique, see Ivar Asheim, "Lutherische Tugendethik?" *Neue Zeitschrift für Systematische Theologie und Religionsphilosophie* 40 (1998): 239–60. Meilaender is cognizant of this and other criticisms of virtue ethics and ably addresses them in his *The Theory and Practice of Virtue*, esp. pp. 13–17. While these issues will be considered more fully in a later chapter, it is worth noting that the charge of egocentrism does appear to be somewhat preoccupied with the question of motive.

singular proclamation of the gospel with clarion clarity while also encouraging a zealous pursuit of ethics and formation. On this count, all four men agree that a serious problem remains with the way that today's Lutherans, with unfortunate consistency, typically approach the ethical task. The usual frame is too limited. It is inadequate to the demand of proclaiming both the gospel of absolute unconditional forgiveness as well as a Christian ethic of lifelong formation that invariably necessitates ongoing transformation. What solutions, then, do these men offer?

PROPOSED SOLUTIONS TO THE LUTHERAN PROBLEM

A faithful theologian seeking to serve well should not merely offer a critique without suggesting some direction toward a solution. The thinkers considered in this chapter are not negligent in their responsibility, and their solutions deserve attention.

DAVID YEAGO

After his broadside against the antinomianism and Gnosticism that spring from the misuse of the law/gospel dynamic, David Yeago makes a foray into providing a solution to the ailments of Protestantism. His suggestions range from solutions altogether simple and mundane to rather ethereal and speculative theological considerations. Yeago is well aware of the insufficiency of an ethic established only on the narrow foundation of divine commandment. "If salvation is by free grace through faith alone," queries Yeago, "is it *necessary* for believers to live a renewed life?"[56] Granting the apparent truth of the statement, Yeago next considers four possible ways to understand this necessity. Two possibilities, conditional and coercive, he dismisses as outside the pale of Lutheranism. The third, the "necessity of commandment," Yeago deems inadequate:

> "When the light turns red, it is necessary for all drivers to come to a halt." The new life is, of course, necessary in this sense, simply because God commands it, but this is not an adequate answer. A renewed life is necessary for *all* humans by necessity of commandment; our present concern is for the distinctive necessity of a renewed life for believers in particular.[57]

56. Yeago, "Promise of God," 27 (emphasis in original).
57. Ibid. (emphasis in original).

Perhaps Yeago is somewhat hasty in dismissing this third sense of necessity, but he moves past it because he is convinced that a better option is found in the fourth sense: a necessity of consistency.

As Yeago sees it, a renewed life is the only reasonable response to the reception of the gift of salvation. There is a logical or, perhaps better, ontological connection that binds salvation to living the Christian life, Yeago contends, much as there is a connection between two people being in love and their choice to spend generous amounts of time with one another. The two *necessarily* belong together. The profession of love and the desire to be together are inseparable. So it is, Yeago asserts, with a believer and a life of steady moral renewal. There is an obvious attraction to this understanding of the Christian's life of willing obedience and its necessary connection to the gift of justification. Nevertheless, this solution may be a bit superficial, and even Yeago realizes that this life of renewal will not flourish without encouragement and direction. The sort of direction and encouragement Yeago deems effective happens in things as common as reading Bible storybooks and singing hymns in church.

> If we do not teach the catechism, if our people do not learn to participate in the liturgy, if our children do not know the Bible stories and cannot sing along in worship, if we do not begin to recover practices of formation, ways of prayer and meditation and fasting and celebration, that bind daily life with the worshipping assembly in a priestly mode of common life, then our churches will simply fade into spiritual inconsequence over the coming decades, however many new members we have and whatever the outcome of our ecclesiastical politics.[58]

Yeago is quite right, of course. It is the unheralded, indeed often disparaged, routine of church life that provides training in and strengthening of the necessary connection between salvific grace and Christian living. Yeago's high praise for the mundane yet powerful elements of parish life is certainly in order and welcome. However, his contention that salvation and Christian holiness are necessarily bound in some ontological sense is made less convincing by his admission of the need for consistent training in the Christian life. If holiness follows necessarily of its own accord, then why such an ardent plea for training in Christian habituation? Meilaender's account of the *simul*, which cleaves even the holiest of saints, seems to ring closer to reality than Yeago's perhaps overly optimistic rendering.

---

58. Yeago, "Sacramental Lutheranism," 16.

Leaning in a more "spiritual" or even mystical direction, Yeago supplements his proposal for the recovery of a viable theological ethic within Lutheranism by emphasizing the incarnation and ultimately deification. "The notion of holiness expounds the conviction that by the union of our lives with the incarnate God we may be 'formed' to his image in specific and describable ways and, precisely in the concrete particularity of our finite lives, become the bearers of his Spirit."[59] This statement reinforces Meilaender's move in the direction of virtue ethics, emphasizing the way that God conforms our story to God's story. Yeago, however, binds the connection considerably more tightly than Meilaender or even Hauerwas. In fact, Yeago finally suggests a meaningful solution in the world of deification or theosis. Commending the work of Tuomo Mannermaa, who advocates reading Luther through the Eastern Orthodox lens of theosis, Yeago tries to establish a critical connection between Christ's incarnation and the Christian life of holiness: "The reality of the incarnation grounds the reality of holiness: God has truly given his own life to humankind in the concrete flesh and blood of his Son Jesus, and so we may be truly 'deified by grace' (as the Fathers teach us) through our conformation to that flesh and blood."[60] While Yeago's effort to ground Christian holiness in concrete realities is a move in the right direction, his advocacy of the Christian's deification unnecessarily obscures the picture he would illuminate. The doctrinal world of theosis or deification may enjoy a prominent place within much Eastern Orthodox theology, but it is alien to Lutheran thought and creates far more questions and problems than insight and answers. An exploration into the complexities of theosis would lead us far afield, and can be safely left to others.[61] Moreover, it is hoped that a resolution of the Lutheran ethical dilemma that is both meaningful and doctrinally accurate can be accomplished without recourse to an explanation grounded in the intricacies, potential vagaries, and numerous difficulties of a doctrine of theosis.

ROBERT BENNE

In his essay included in *The Promise of Lutheran Ethics*, Robert Benne does not attempt to offer a thoroughgoing solution to the ethical malaise he correctly identifies within Lutheranism. This is not necessarily a shortcoming, however, as he makes clear in this essay that his task is simply review and analysis.[62] When

---

59. Yeago, "Gnosticism," 42.

60. Ibid., 48.

61. For a thorough critique of the "Finnish interpretation" of Luther that would bind him to the ideas of theosis as Yeago suggests, see William Schumacher, *Who Do I Say That You Are? Anthropology and the Theology of Theosis in the Finnish School of Tuomo Mannermaa* (Eugene, OR: Wipf & Stock, 2010).

he does provide a more exhaustive treatment of Lutheranism's handling of ethical questions, Benne is content to emphasize typically Lutheran nuances.[63] It is evident that he places a great deal of confidence in the maintenance of classic Lutheran paradoxes as fruitful avenues toward a correct handling of ethics. Benne's paradoxical vision includes the *simul iustus et peccator*, God's right-hand and left-hand rule, and the now-but-not-yet reality of God's kingdom. It is in living out of these tensions, Benne believes, that Christians rightly meet and fulfills their ethical responsibilities. He offers a forthright account of the Christian pursuing a sober life of service within the world:

> Yet life in this world means inescapable responsibility for Christians. God has not abandoned the world, and the Christian calling is certainly not to reject responsibility within a world that God intends to preserve. While the world is not the final home for the Christian, it is an abode that God wants us to care for. This will mean that all people, Christians included, will be involved in some worldly responsibilities that will not appear directly as works of love. Christians may have to be soldiers. Luther thought they could be hangmen. Worldly responsibility will mean coming to terms with the finitude and fallenness of the world.[64]

Christians are to be involved in pursuing a course of ethical integrity, Benne tells us, simply because God desires citizens of the earthly kingdom so to act. Benne seems to be satisfied that this connection or relation between the believer's justification and their ethical responsibilities is sufficient. In truth, however, following Benne's suggestion amounts to an admission that there is no connection. The believer's justification has no apparent impact on the way that one then lives in the world. Putting this another way allows the introduction of two terms that will be helpful. In effect, Benne's depiction of the Christian life leaves the believer's relationship *coram Deo* altogether disconnected from personal relationships and responsibilities *coram mundo*. This pair of Latin terms *coram Deo* (before God) and *coram mundo* (before the world) captures the distinction that exists between a creature's standing before God, and that same individual's standing in the eyes of the world within which she lives. The former is sometimes referred to as the vertical relationship while

62. Benne, "Lutheran Ethics," 11.

63. Robert Benne, *The Paradoxical Vision: A Public Theology for the Twenty-first Century* (Minneapolis: Fortress Press, 1995).

64. Ibid., 85.

the latter is termed the horizontal relationship. In Benne's description of the Christian moral life, there is no meaningful connection between the vertical, *coram Deo*, and the horizontal, *coram mundo*, dimensions of Christian existence.

Benne's mundane version of the Christian life that is all but disconnected from justification is not, however, his last word on the subject. In his 1998 essay, he suggests, somewhat cryptically, another avenue of inquiry: "Lutherans need a more specific notion of the Christian life if they are to respond to this chaotic world. They cannot do that by relying solely on justification. Lutheran ethics will have to be more trinitarian."[65] Without further elaboration from Benne, it is difficult to determine exactly what he might have intended by referencing the Trinity. What is clear, though, is that Benne identifies the frame of justification (or perhaps law/gospel) as it is commonly employed by contemporary Lutheranism to be insufficient for addressing the realities of Christian living. For that task, a wider frame is needed, and Benne prods those who would seek such a frame to look in a trinitarian direction. Benne is content to drop the hint and does not venture beyond his promising nudge toward trinitarian theology. With thanks to Benne, the objective of this book is to follow his suggestion and to pursue a trinitarian approach to thinking about the Christian life. But that constructive work lies ahead in chapter 5.

REINHARD HÜTTER

As noted earlier in this chapter, even before his move to the Roman Church, Hütter was sharply critical of Lutheranism's inability to grapple with the place of ethics, contending in several essays written while yet within the Lutheran fold that an inordinate aversion to the law accounts for much of the problem. In these essays, Hütter argues that this vilification of the law is neither scriptural nor genuinely Lutheran. But Hütter does not only offer criticism; he also contributes helpfully to the present effort to discover a remedy to Lutheranism's ethical ills. Hütter provides a strong defense of God's law (or, as he prefers to distinguish it, commandment[66]) as more than merely accuser. Hütter urges

---

65. Ibid., 28.

66. In his contribution to *Promise of Lutheran Ethics*, Hütter follows the lead of most "Luther Renaissance" scholars and rejects a "third use" of the law. The term *law* he reserves for its application to humans in the condition of sin. *Commandment*, on the other hand, he uses to describe "the goods constitutive of the way of life in communion with God." As Hütter further elaborates, "Yet by grasping Christ in faith, Christian freedom receives its distinct *gestalt* through a way of life according to the commandments: the Decalogue, the Sermon on the Mount, and the double-love commandment." Hütter, "Twofold Center," 182–83n.16. Interestingly, in a subsequent essay, Hütter is less certain of the need tenaciously to preserve the distinction between law and commandment. "While I am basically

his readers to recapture the understanding of the commandments as being a great and good gift, indeed, something not to be hated, but loved. Ethics that is genuinely Lutheran, Hütter contends, will actually prompt praise of the commandments and embrace them "as creaturely ways of embodying our love of God and neighbor."[67] For Hütter, the key to the Christian's ethical life is learning to see the commandments of God not as a burden from which to be freed, but as a great blessing. Turning to Luther for support, Hütter endorses a potent and dynamic understanding of justification's impact on the believer. He finds much to support his case in Luther's "The Freedom of a Christian." In particular, Hütter finds much significance in his observation that for Luther being "in faith" or "in union with Christ" actually means that "the Christian is restored to the original state of prelapsarian life with God."[68] This is an important point that will figure centrally in the ideas developed in later chapters. It is worth hearing Hütter at some length:

> Now we are in a much better position to understand the radical perspective behind Luther's rather innocent-sounding claim that "in faith" human beings are "back in paradise": they are back in communion with God, back—*sola gratia* and *sola fide*—in that righteousness that God's commandment presupposes and to which God's commandment gives creaturely form and shape! And this is precisely why for Luther the "freedom of a Christian" never contradicts God's commandments and never comes without them, but rather rejoices in them and welcomes them as ways of creaturely embodying our love of God and of neighbor.[69]

The commandments of God (and within this term Hütter is careful to include the Decalogue) serve as the "shape and form of believers' lives with God."[70] For Hütter, the doing of the commandments is part of the Christian's relationship with God. "God's commandments," writes Hütter, "allow us to embody our

sympathetic to it [Althaus's sharp distinction between *Gesetz* and *Gebot*] and have used it myself, I increasingly wonder about the merits of using the term "law" in an analogical sense which obviously brings me into the vicinity not only of Aquinas but also of the much and wrongly disparaged Melanchthon." Idem, "(Re-)Forming Freedom: Reflections 'After *Veritatis Splendor*' on Freedom's Fate in Modernity and Protestantism's Antinomian Captivity," *Modern Theology* 17, no. 2 (April 2001): 160.

67. Hütter, "Twofold Center," 43.

68. Ibid., 42.

69. Reinhold Hütter, "'God's Law' in *Veritatis Splendor*: Sic et Non," in Hütter and Dieter, eds., *Ecumenical Ventures*, 109.

70. Hütter, "Twofold Center," 44.

obedience to God and our service to humanity in concrete historical practices and activities."[71] God's commandments, then, serve a positive function in the Christian's life. They form and shape the believer according to the will and purposes of God.

The significance of Hütter's insight should not be underestimated. Not only has he salvaged a viable and prominent role for the commandments (or, less restrictively defined, the law) in the life of the believer, but he has also provided a significant correlation between the believer's justification *coram Deo* and the believer's life *coram mundo*—and in a move that should delight and calm Lutheran readers, he has used Luther to do it. As Hütter sees it, it is fully in accord with the spirit and explicit teaching of Luther to hold that justification returns the newly forgiven sinner to God's original intent for humanity. Justification not only makes a person right with God, it also makes the person the kind of human that God had created in the beginning. This restored creature serves God and fellow creatures according to God's plan for creation. "God's commandments," Hütter observes, "are nothing else than the concrete guidance, the concrete social practices which allow us as believers to embody—in concrete creaturely ways—our communion with God, which always includes God's other creatures."[72] Hütter's careful reading of Luther and theological insight certainly serve the effort to claim a meaningful and relevant place for ethics within Lutheranism. In particular, his concentration on God's intent for creation is both helpful and hopeful for the purposes of this book.

GILBERT MEILAENDER

Remarkably enough, Meilaender—who was the direct target of Hauerwas's critique for, as Hauerwas alleges, allowing his Lutheranism to disconnect ethics and doctrine and so render ethics ineffective, and who in spite of Hauerwas's criticism insists on the importance of the gospel's sheer declaratory power—actually suggests a view of the ethical life that bears a striking resemblance to Hauerwas's argument. Meilaender steadfastly argues for the legitimacy and necessity of a twofold tension within the Christian life—and also honestly admits its shortcoming:

> On the one hand, our substantive virtues may be few, yet we may be accepted and righteous before God. On the other hand, our substantive virtues may be many, yet if we rely on them we may

71. Ibid.
72. Hütter, "'God's Law,'" 108.

lack the faith which *is* virtue before God. There need be, it would seem, little correlation between our virtue understood substantively and our virtue understood relationally.[73]

Still, Meilaender is not satisfied simply to leave the issue in such an untidy state. Seeking some way to overcome this detrimental separation that provides "little correlation" between the gift of virtue and the pursuit of virtue, he writes of the certainty of a coming day when the author of our Christian life himself will resolve the tension: "The tension between these several views of virtue cannot, I think, be removed from the Christian perspective. Its theoretical resolution lies in the narrative Christians tell and retell—a story, not yet finished, in which God is graciously at work transforming sinners into saints. But that story, because it is not yet finished, must be lived."[74] Meilaender's "story that is lived" sounds very much like Hauerwas's recurrent theme when he describes the Christian life as a narrative, a living out of the Christian story, or learning to make the believer's story part of Jesus' story. To help solve Lutheranism's ethical dilemma, Meilaender looks where Hauerwas looks and turns to the insights of a narrated theology. This is not a bad place to look for answers.

Thinking about the Christian life in terms of story leads in many helpful directions. Meilaender emphasizes especially the thick and latently powerful eschatological element that is an essential aspect of narrative and story. "The narrative of the Christian story which provides the contours for Christian living," writes Meilaender, "envisions a day when these several evaluations of our character meet, are reconciled, and no longer stand in tension."[75] For Meilaender, the eschatological element provides the resolution between the two different ways of understanding virtue. "God," concludes Meilaender, "is committed to transforming people who are partly saint and partly sinner into people who are saints *simpliciter*—who are substantively what they are already in relation to him."[76] The eschaton will resolve the tension. This side of the eschaton, though, no resolution should be expected. The use of narrative theology provides an ultimate answer for the ethical questions that nag Lutherans—once the narrative is concluded; in the meantime, however, while the Christian story is being lived, the answers provided are perhaps a bit meager.

While they wait for the eschaton, Meilaender argues, Christians should be striving for ethical improvement: "Until that day, however, we live within the

73. Meilaender, *Theory and Practice*, 121 (emphasis in original).
74. Ibid., 125.
75. Ibid., 122.
76. Ibid.

constraints of a temporal narrative—adding virtues piecemeal, shaping being by doing, unable to see ourselves whole."[77] As Meilaender explains, Christians do this because it matters to God: "He [God] is intent upon renewing us after the image of his Son, and we must therefore be just as intent upon seeking that renewal—that holiness—in our being and our doing."[78] Meilaender seems to suggest that one should be busy about the task of formation into Christian character for the simple reason that it is important to God. Since this is God's intended goal for God's people, he might say, one may as well get a decent start on it now. No doubt, this is true as far as it goes; however, it is worth asking whether it goes far enough. Still, the eschatologically weighted narrative does supply a way of managing Lutheran concerns for guarding the gospel of faith while encouraging the practical need of providing ethical direction for life.

What is not altogether certain, however, is whether Meilaender's solution provides an account of the relationship between the gospel and a life of virtue that is at once comprehensible and compelling for the average Christian parishioner. Meilaender recognizes that finally what is most important in thinking about virtue and ethics is not theory, but actual practice, the doing. "Even if the approach I have taken is sound and is to be recommended," he admits, "we need finally to acknowledge for ourselves and fellows that the trick is not only to see or say this but to live it."[79] Meilaender provides hints, however, that perhaps his own efforts at a viable solution are not entirely satisfactory in exactly this regard of ready applicability. "Even if the discussion above helps locate the place of virtue in the Christian life," he concedes, "we need not deny that it may prove difficult to translate theory into practice and find a way to do justice to both senses of virtue [what God gives, as well as what Christians achieve] in our lives."[80] Difficulty translating theory to practice, it could be argued, is a shortcoming of Meilaender's proposed solution to Lutheranism's ethical ills. His assessment is accurate and his theory theologically precise. Yet in this case, the accuracy and precision are, perhaps, not coupled with an explanation of the ethical life of Christians that lends itself to effective explanation and implementation in a parish setting. While Meilaender succeeds in retrieving a Lutheran way of thinking about ethics, and even teaching virtue, his explanation is so intricately and densely woven that it could well prove impenetrable to some who occupy Lutheran pews. Moreover, it is not apparent that Meilaender's solution would have a ready response to the

---

77. Ibid.
78. Meilaender, "Reclaiming the Quest," 490.
79. Meilaender, "Task of Lutheran Ethics," 22.
80. Meilaender, *Theory and Practice*, 123.

inevitable and worn "insight" that if God is going to complete the Christian's story by perfecting growth in virtue, then wouldn't it be prudent to stay out of the way while God is busy doing the requisite divine work? The devout and humble believer piously—and conveniently—leaves the entire job to God. More needs to be done to defend the place of ethics accurately and meaningfully yet in a way that is both immediately accessible and broadly compelling to the majority of Christians, clergy and laity alike.

Conclusion

In varying degrees, the four theologians considered in this chapter have recognized and then in divergent ways addressed the critique of Lutheranism's ethical difficulties implicit in virtue ethics and made explicit by Hauerwas. Together, all agree that typical contemporary expressions of Lutheranism are unable to address effectively the ethical challenge presented by virtue ethics and the need for those responsible within the church to be able to speak authoritatively and meaningfully about the shape of the Christian life. These writers point in promising directions as they attempt to recover a viable place within Lutheranism for talk of ethics, cultivation of virtue, and formation of character. Yeago's recognition of habituation, Benne's nudge toward trinitarian thinking, Hütter's insights into the results of justification and the role of God's commandments, and Meilaender's emphasis on the narrative shape of the Christian life are all important components in the attempt at providing an answer to the place of ethics within Lutheranism. Each provides important ideas that will aid the project of this book, the formulation of a yet broader and more thoroughgoing way of thinking about the ethical task and its relationship to Lutheran doctrine.

In seeking answers to the ethical dilemma of Lutheranism, each of this chapter's four theologians have looked back to the sixteenth century and sought guidance from the reformers themselves. Their example is worthy of imitation—where better to learn about Lutheran theology than from Luther and the Lutheran Confessions? Accordingly, the next chapter will examine the Confessions, with a special emphasis on the Augsburg Confession and its Apology, from the standpoint of the reformers' understanding of the ethical task, particularly the place of virtue and the formation of character, within the church's teaching. The goal here is to provide a convincing case that, as the confessional writers carried out their work, they made use of a theological framework within which questions of ethical instruction and Christian character formation appropriately and readily fit.

3

The Lutheran Confessions

Lutheranism yet today continues to find itself struggling to locate Christian ethics meaningfully within its justification-centered theology. Already several centuries old, the struggle has evaded an entirely satisfactory resolution, as witnessed in the variety of efforts surveyed in the previous chapter. The reality and persistence of Lutheranism's notorious quandary over ethics is readily admitted by Lutherans themselves. Some theologians working from a Lutheran perspective such as Yeago and Hütter seek and suggest remedies for this ethical impairment. There are others, though, who actually discourage the pursuit of typical ethical concerns, in particular the encouragement of virtue, deeming this to be a threat to Lutheran doctrine.[1] Such attitudes only serve to bolster the accusations of those like Hauerwas who contend that Lutheran theology itself is the source of the problem.[2] To see problems with the current practice of Lutheran theology in line with the observations made in the previous chapter is one thing. To fault Lutheran theology itself is another thing altogether. But that is precisely the charge that is being made. Handicapped by what might be called justification-induced myopia, Lutheran doctrine, it is asserted, suffers from an inherent incapacity for ethical concerns, which leaves Lutheran believers poorly equipped to address practical issues of Christian living. Sadly, as witnessed by the previous chapter's criticisms, much of contemporary Lutheranism may very well substantiate the charge of proffering feeble or inadequate ethical tools. What must be understood, however, is that the fault for this failure lies not with the doctrine itself but with some of the current claimants to the legacy of Lutheranism. The object of this chapter is to support this assertion

1. Cf. Gerhard O. Forde, "The Exodus from Virtue to Grace: Justification by Faith Today," *Interpretation* 34 (1980): 32–44.

2. Stanley Hauerwas, *Sanctify Them in the Truth: Holiness Exemplified* (Nashville: Abingdon, 1998), 27–28.

by considering the best possible authority on the true position of Lutheran theology: the Lutheran Confessions themselves.

Why Consider the Confessions?

In their effort to address the problem of Lutheranism's allegedly inherent ethical inadequacy, some of the theologians considered in chapter 2 looked with success to the work of Luther himself. This is a move in the right direction: thinking about Lutheran theology, it is probably a good idea to hear what Luther thought, and there is much in the great reformer's writing that is of significant value in refuting the charge of Lutheranism's systemic ethical incapacity. Still, Lutheran pastors and teachers do not subscribe to Luther's extensive corpus, but to the Lutheran Confessions. The Confessions enjoy a unique authority and surpass Luther alone. So, in this chapter, we will specifically consider the Augsburg Confession (also known as the Augustana) and the Apology of the Augsburg Confession. There are several reasons for this choice. Penned by Philipp Melanchthon, these Confessions are important by virtue of their priority in the confessional corpus historically and formatively. Further, these documents are of special interest since their foil is the sixteenth-century Roman Catholic Church, a church that had carefully cultivated the idea of habits and disciplines of piety—key components of what today is called virtue ethics. It is helpful, then, to explore Melanchthon's attitude toward the possible continued usefulness of such practices in the churches of the Reformation. This is especially important in light of the Lutheran rejection of Rome's understanding of the Christian life and Rome's oft-repeated accusation that Lutheran theology was undermining morality.

Finally, there remains at least one last factor that favors the use of the Augsburg Confession and its Apology. Contemporary Lutheranism's near-universal recognition of the primacy and authority of the Augustana and, for most, also the Apology, confer a particular significance and sphere of influence on these confessions. If the charge that ethical incapacity is an intrinsic aspect of Lutheranism is accurate, one should legitimately expect to discover corroborating evidence within these foundational confessional documents. If, however, these documents exhibit a concern for questions of Christian ethics, and an interest in formation of Christian character, not only will the charge collapse, but those Lutherans content to dismiss ethical issues will perhaps be obliged to reevaluate the propriety of their position. To that end, this chapter will consider representative passages from the Confessions, especially the Augustana and the Apology, which provide significant bridges to the concerns of contemporary virtue ethics. Chapter 4 will then suggest a framework within which to organize and understand these data gleaned from the Confessions.

THE PROMINENCE OF GOOD WORKS IN THE CONFESSIONS

The Confessions' keen interest in encouraging good works is the most obvious "ethical" element in the Lutheran symbols and provides a reasonable place to begin a search for potential connections between Lutheran theology and modern virtue ethics. Little more than a cursory reading of the Lutheran Confessions is required to recognize that the believer's life after justification was a significant concern for the reformers.

THE AUGSBURG CONFESSION

Of course, the primary Lutheran confession is the Augsburg Confession, and one needs to proceed no further than article 6 of that symbol to discover explicit evidence of the reformer's desire to cultivate and multiply good works in the lives of Christian people: "Likewise, they teach that this faith is bound to yield good fruits and that it ought to do good works commanded by God on account of God's will and not so that we may trust in these works to merit justification before God."[3] This article, provided with the title "The New Obedience" in early editions of the Confession, is later supported by article 20 of the Augustana, "Concerning Faith and Good Works." Here, a similar importance is attached to good works: "Further, it is taught that good works should and must be done, not that a person relies on them to earn grace, but for God's sake and to God's praise."[4] Even beyond these articles specifically committed to an exposition of the significance of good works, *The Book of Concord* contains a wealth of additional material that highlights the reformers' keen interest in good works and the Christian's life after justification.

The author of the Augustana emphasizes the importance, indeed the *necessity*, of good works in several articles primarily dedicated to other issues. Article 12 of the Augustana, "Concerning Repentance," confirms that good works are the fruit of repentance: "Faith believes that sins are forgiven on account of Christ, consoles the conscience, and liberates it from terrors. Thereupon good works, which are the fruit of repentance, should follow."[5]

---

3. "The Augsburg Confession (1530)" (hereafter CA) 6, 1, in Robert Kolb and Timothy Wengert, eds., *The Book of Concord: The Confessions of the Evangelical Lutheran Church* (Minneapolis: Fortress Press, 2000), 41.

4. Ibid., 56 (CA 20, 27).

5. Ibid., 45 (CA 12, 5-6).

Article 16, on civil affairs, establishes that "lawful civil ordinances are good works of God," and reflects the central elements of the reformers' teaching of two realms and their corresponding kinds of righteousness.[6] Article 18 treats the topic of free will and further develops the doctrine of two different kinds of righteousness: "Concerning free will they teach that the human will has some freedom for producing civil righteousness and for choosing things subject to reason."[7]

THE APOLOGY

Besides multiple passing references to the place and importance of good works in the Christian life, the Apology also contains several extended discussions about the good works of Christians as well as the two kinds of righteousness. Given the repeated accusations being leveled against the Lutherans that their doctrine was undermining civil righteousness, such an emphasis is hardly unexpected.[8] Friedrich Mildenberger lucidly outlines the logic of the charge against the Lutheran reformers' doctrine:

> If salvation is the free gift of God's grace, then we have no need to trouble ourselves with trying to lead a God-pleasing life. Rather, we are free to do or not to do whatever pleases us. This reproach was close to the surface and was easily confirmed by experience—for people's religious and moral activities are always open to criticism. The statement that Lutheran preaching resulted in immorality was an effective argument and the Lutherans had to defend themselves against this accusation.[9]

6. Ibid., 49 (CA 16, 1). This confessional affirmation of two distinct kinds of righteousness, the righteousness of faith *coram Deo* and civil righteousness *coram mundo*, will prove to be a critical aspect of the present effort to locate the ethical task within Lutheran theology. The righteousness of faith indicates believers before God where they are the totally passive recipients of God's gift of salvation. Civil righteousness, on the other hand, refers to individuals in their interactions with other creatures and names the humanly recognized achievements of rightly ordered living.

7. Ibid., 51 (CA 18, 1).

8. This was no small factor for Melanchthon, who was already defending the Lutheran position from such attacks by Erasmus. For an excellent account of Melanchthon's scholarly interactions with Erasmus, see Timothy J. Wengert, *Human Freedom, Christian Righteousness: Philip Melanchthon's Exegetical Dispute with Erasmus of Rotterdam* (New York: Oxford University Press, 1998), esp. ch. 5.

9. Friedrich Mildenberger, *Theology of the Lutheran Confessions*, trans. Erwin L. Lueker, ed. Robert C. Schulz (Philadelphia: Fortress Press, 1986), 91.

Melanchthon took the charge seriously and addressed it at length. His argument begins with paragraph 122 in article 4 of the Apology and runs for the remainder of the article—almost thirty-three pages in the Kolb-Wengert edition. Exhibiting his skill as a dialectician, Melanchthon contends that good works and faith are not at odds, but intimately related. "Thus good works ought to follow faith as thanksgiving toward God. Likewise, good works ought to follow faith so that faith is exercised in them, grows, and is shown to others, in order that others may be invited to godliness by our confession."[10] For Melanchthon and the argument of the Apology, good works are not optional but an integral part of the Christian life.

THE SMALCALD ARTICLES AND THE CATECHISMS

In a somewhat ironic twist, the vast majority of the Lutheran Confessions did not come from the pen of Luther. Luther's Smalcald Articles and catechisms, then, occupy a unique place in the confessional corpus as we hear from the great reformer himself. And here we continue to find a marked concern for the importance of good works in the life of the believer. Article 13 of the Smalcald Articles addresses both justification by faith and the good works that are to follow. Here, Luther lays heavy stress on the absolute necessity of faith before any work can be considered good.

> Good works follow such faith, renewal, and forgiveness of sin, and whatever in these works is still sinful or imperfect should not even be counted as sin or imperfection, precisely for the sake of this same Christ. Instead, the human creature should be called and should be completely righteous and holy—according to both the person and his or her works—by the pure grace and mercy that have been poured and spread over us in Christ.[11]

In other words, Christ justifies not only the person, but also that person's works. A good work is good not by virtue of the motive driving it, nor in light of the result it produces. It is good only because the forgiveness of Christ covers and redeems it. For Luther, it is simple: Christ makes both the person and that person's works holy and righteous. The transformation is complete.

Nevertheless, Luther's most enthusiastic endorsement of good works in the life of the Christian is yet to come. Within the confessional corpus, the

---

10. "Apology of the Augsburg Confession (September 1531)" (hereafter Ap) 4, 188, in *Book of Concord*, 150.

11. "The Smalcald Articles (1537)" (hereafter SA) 13, 2, in ibid., 325.

Small Catechism and the Large Catechism together provide perhaps the most impressive evidence of the emphasis placed on good works or Christian living in the teaching of the first Lutherans. Scandalized by his bitter firsthand experience during the 1528 church visitation of electoral Saxony and Meissen, Luther hoped that the catechisms and their place in the daily routines of believers would help to lead the people out of their shameful state of licentiousness.[12] The problem is best explained by Luther himself. In his preface to the Small Catechism, the reformer complains that the "ordinary person, especially in the villages," is woefully ignorant about the most basic tenets of the Christian faith. "As a result," Luther laments, "they live like simple cattle or irrational pigs and, despite the fact that the gospel has returned, have mastered the fine art of misusing all their freedom."[13]

Similarly, in the Large Catechism's longer preface addressed to "preachers and pastors," Luther identifies a moral crisis in the churches of Saxony as a precipitating force behind the catechism's production and urges the regular reading and teaching of the catechism:

> In this way they [preachers and pastors] would once again show honor and respect to the gospel, through which they have been delivered from so many burdens and troubles, and they might feel a little shame that, like pigs and dogs, they are remembering no more of the gospel than this rotten, pernicious, shameful, carnal liberty. As it is, the common people take the gospel altogether too lightly, and we accomplish but little, despite all our hard work. What, then, can we expect if we are slothful and lazy, as we used to be under the papacy?[14]

Particularly noteworthy is Luther's charge that the people are failing to hold the gospel with appropriate regard. It's possible to hear this complaint as evidence that Luther considered the people's moral lives to be included as an aspect of the gospel. David Yeago certainly understands Luther this way. "Even in the sixteenth century," he writes, "the Reformers were well aware that there is more to the gospel promise than assurance that we will not be damned."[15] The

---

12. Charles P. Arand, *That I May Be His Own: An Overview of Luther's Catechisms* (St. Louis: Concordia Academic, 2000), 172–76. See also Robert James Bast, *Honor Your Fathers: Catechisms and the Emergence of a Patriarchal Ideology in Germany 1400–1600*, Studies in Medieval and Reformation Thought 63, ed. Heiko A. Obermann (Leiden: Brill, 1997), 131–45.

13. "The Small Catechism (1529)" (hereafter SC), preface, 3, in *Book of Concord*, 348.

14. "The Large Catechism (1529)" (hereafter LC), longer preface, 3–4, in ibid., 380.

sense of Yeago's position seems reasonable enough and appears to cohere with Luther's words. There is no doubt that the moral life of common Christians was critically important to the reformer. It might be wiser and more faithful to Luther's teaching, however, not to include works within the gospel. To subsume an advocacy for Christian living within the "gospel promise" can unintentionally and tragically end in the very diminution and distortion of the gospel that prompted the Reformation.[16] This is obviously a significant recurring concern that will further occupy our attention as the present argument develops.

The catechisms indisputably demonstrate that Luther recognized a need not only for doctrinal education, but also for training in the fundamental duties and practices of simple Christian living. "Luther's catechisms," notes Yeago, "display a clear awareness that doctrinal catechesis is part of a larger whole."[17] He points out that the Small Catechism provides instruction in prayer and private worship practice—evidence of Luther's attention to the practices of the Christian life. Yeago neglects, though, to mention an aspect of the catechism that holds even greater relevance for the question of Christian living. Quite willing to address the routine aspects of ordinary life with explicit dos and don'ts, Luther appended a *Haustafel*, or "table of duties," to his shorter catechism.[18] The Large Catechism reflects the same appreciation for the necessity of offering plain instruction in moral behavior. Fully one half of the Large Catechism is devoted to a practical exposition of the Decalogue that is at times quite startling both for its insight into the intricacies of human relationships and for the precision and practicality of the advice offered. Examples abound on every page, but from the exposition of the Eighth Commandment, Luther counsels:

> Therefore, if you encounter someone with a worthless tongue who gossips and slanders someone else, rebuke such people straight to their faces and make them blush with shame. Then those who otherwise would bring some poor person into disgrace, from which

15. David S. Yeago, "The Promise of God and the Desires of Our Hearts: Prolegomena to a Lutheran Retrieval of Classical Spiritual Theology," *Lutheran Forum* 30, no. 2 (May 1996): 25.

16. As discussed in the previous chapter, this is precisely the problem that would argue against fully adopting Hauerwas's effort to bring justification under the umbrella of the Christian's journey toward ethical perfection.

17. David S. Yeago, "Sacramental Lutheranism at the End of the Modern Age," *Lutheran Forum* 34, no. 4 (Christmas/Winter 2000): 15.

18. For a detailed consideration of Luther's *Haustafel* and its significance in the Catechism, see Arand, *That I May Be His Own*.

one could scarcely clear one's self, will hold their tongue. For honor and good name are easily taken away but not easily restored.[19]

In the catechisms, Luther evinces his capacity for the practice of what might be called unvarnished moralism.[20] That is, Luther engages in the effort to shape character and behavior, as he considers the realities of life from the perspective of the Christian's responsibilities to the surrounding fellow creatures. This ethical emphasis of the catechisms will be considered more fully in a section to follow.

THE FORMULA OF CONCORD

Naturally, the Formula of Concord also turns its attention to the question of the Christian's life of good works. Article 4 specifically addresses the necessity of good works, affirming (among other theses): "We also believe, teach, and confess that all people, particularly those who have been reborn and renewed through the Holy Spirit, are obligated to do good works."[21] Article 6 touches on the Christian life after justification as it settles the issue of the third use of the law:

> We believe, teach, and confess that, although people who truly believe in Christ and are genuinely converted to God have been liberated and set free from the curse and compulsion of the law through Christ, they indeed are not for that reason without the law. Instead, they have been redeemed by the Son of God so that they may practice the law day and night (Ps. 119). For our first parents did not live without the law even before the fall.[22]

It is of some significance and a point that should not be overlooked, that this article argues not only the importance of a Christian's conformity to the law, but goes much further by asserting the believer's practice of the law as the very purpose of redemption. The importance of the Formula's "*so that* they may practice the law" will become apparent as the present argument unfolds.

---

19. *Book of Concord,* 422 (LC 10 Commandments, 273).

20. Of course, in today's theological climate, few criticisms are considered more disparaging or devastating than a charge of "moralism" (though "pietism" comes close!). This aversion to "moralism" is itself another symptom of the theological and ethical inadequacies of much contemporary Lutheranism.

21. "Formula of Concord (1577)" (hereafter FC) Ep 4, 8, in *Book of Concord,* 498.

22. Ibid., 502 (FC Ep 6, 2).

It should come as no surprise that throughout *The Book of Concord*, justification and the absolute worthlessness of good works in meriting righteousness before God actually drive the discussion and occupy the bulk of the text. Considering the historical context, however, this should be expected. The threat of Roman works righteousness still loomed large for the second generation of reformers. It is important to appreciate, nevertheless, that these men were also quite concerned as their teacher, Melanchthon, had been about the promotion of civil morality and Christian good works. Holsten Fagerberg recognizes that, for the reformers, "There was general agreement that an upright life was required of everyone."[23]

A quick foray through the Confessions offers ample evidence of a concerted effort to guard and promote the place of good works. Recognition of the Reformation's acclamation and endorsement of Christian good works certainly helps, but does not yet fully accomplish the present purpose of providing a solid ground for a Lutheran understanding of character formation. That the reformers were in favor of morality and good works should be obvious enough. Would they, however, have endorsed the sort of intentional training in virtuous works and deliberate cultivation of Christian character that is advocated by the supporters of virtue ethics? Is the exhortation to good works the same thing as the inculcation of virtue? Did the reformers approve the idea that individual Christian character could and should be formed through human effort as virtue ethics holds, or did they rely solely on the gospel's power of transformation? Was there a place within the Christian faith and specifically within Lutheranism for the teaching of virtue, or were Christian virtues the essentially automatic fruit of the gospel and justification? All of these questions need to be faced and answered, and in time, each will be addressed, but for the present we turn to the last of the list. To make a case for character within Lutheran theology, it is essential to reckon with the fact that faith simply and spontaneously producing good works is an idea the Confessions endorse.

Faith and the Spontaneous Production of Good Works

It is certainly true that there are passages in the Augsburg Confession and the Apology which advocate faith's spontaneous generation of good works. Immediately after insisting that it is "necessary to do good works," Melanchthon continues in article 20 of the Augustana: "Moreover, because the Holy Spirit is received through faith, consequently hearts are renewed and endowed with

---

23. Holsten Fagerberg, *A New Look at the Lutheran Confessions (1529–1537)*, trans. Gene J. Lund (St. Louis: Concordia, 1972), 103.

new affections so as to be able to do good works."[24] Here, it could be argued, Melanchthon is subscribing to the idea that the simple presence of the Holy Spirit in a believer's life accounts for a subsequent life of good works. The concluding sentence from the same article in the Apology lends more momentum to the force of this view: "For we do not abolish the law, Paul says, but we establish it, because when we receive the Holy Spirit by faith the fulfillment of the law necessarily follows, through which love, patience, chastity, and other fruits of the Spirit continually grow."[25] The critical word, of course, is *necessarily*. In what sense, exactly, can it be said that the fulfillment of the law necessarily follows the gift of faith? If Melanchthon meant that the production of good works happened automatically, as a sort of theological function (Holy Spirit in—good works out), then there would seem to be scant space for talk of growth in virtues or formation through habituation.[26] In other words, character formation would basically be ruled out.

Similarly, in his discussion on "Love and the Fulfilling of the Law" in article 4 of the Apology, Melanchthon states, "the Spirit reveals Christ. . . . Then he also brings the other gifts: love, prayer, thanksgiving, chastity, endurance, etc."[27] Do the fruits appear as simply as that? Does one merely preach the gospel and then expectantly and passively await the guaranteed harvest of Christian character and virtue? It is surely conceivable that these outtakes from the Confessions could foster such conclusions. Certainly, this is all the more probable in light of Luther's exuberant and unforgettable words about the nature of faith. They are significant enough to have found a place within the Solid Declaration of the Formula:

> Faith, however, is a divine work in us which changes us and makes us to be born anew of God. It kills the old 'Adam' and makes us altogether different people, in heart and spirit and mind and powers; and it brings with it the Holy Spirit. O, it is a living, busy, active, mighty thing, this faith. It is impossible for it not to be doing good works incessantly. It does not ask whether good works are to be

24. *Book of Concord*, 57 (CA 20).

25. Ibid., 237 (Ap 20, 15).

26. It is interesting to note that moral theologians in the Roman Catholic Church have encountered similar perplexities in engineering a rapprochement between the idea of habituation in character and the teaching of infused virtue. See Romanus Cessario, *The Moral Virtues and Theological Ethics* (Notre Dame, IN: University of Notre Dame Press, 1991), 94–125.

27. *Book of Concord*, 141 (Ap 4, 132).

done, but before the question is asked, it has already done them, and is constantly doing them.[28]

Of course, this is not the only instance where Luther seems to assert the ability of faith single-handedly to make a new human and unilaterally to produce good works.[29] Obviously, Luther could muster compelling scriptural support for his position, thus increasing its plausibility.[30] Such unqualified endorsements of faith's capacity to yield good works without the need for further exhortation or training seem to controvert the argument that character must be habituated and cultivated. Still, those insisting on the need for such habituation and training are certainly not without recourse to their own collection of supporting Scripture.[31]

Nevertheless, the issue at hand is not the scriptural record, but the Lutheran Confessions and the reformers who shaped them. If the Confessions themselves actually teach a Christian regeneration that excludes, whether explicitly or implicitly, all training or formation, then Hauerwas's criticism of Lutheranism traces to the reformers themselves. Furthermore, the detractors are quite right: Lutheranism does not have—indeed, *cannot* have—the ability to do the task of ethics. It can only wait for faith alone to produce what it will produce. The inevitable result is obvious: ethical instruction and even concerns about basic issues of morality are essentially removed from the purview of Lutheran theology—all that is really needed to help people to grow in virtue and Christian character, it seems, is faith. When character is lacking, or virtues few, the solution is simply to preach more gospel, strengthen faith, and patiently wait for the promised fruit. It should be clear by now, however, that this constrained interpretation of the Confessions is severely mistaken and that the characteristic scopes of virtue ethics and Lutheran theology are not de facto mutually exclusive. But such a bold assertion should not be made without supporting evidence, and for that we turn again to the Confessions. To discover within *The Book of Concord* themes and ideas that may be read in sympathy with the concerns of virtue ethics and the desire to cultivate character would certainly

---

28. Ibid., 576 (FC SD 4, 11).

29. Another example outside the confessional corpus is located in Luther's "The Freedom of a Christian": "As it is necessary, therefore, that the trees exist before their fruits and the fruits do not make trees either good or bad, but rather as the trees are, so are the fruits they bear; so a man must first be good or wicked before he does a good or wicked work, and his works do not make him good or wicked, but he himself makes his works either good or wicked." From *Career of the Reformer I*, vol. 31 of *Luther's Works*, ed. Harold J. Grimm and Helmut T. Lehmann (Philadelphia: Fortress Press, 1957) (hereafter cited as LW), 361.

30. John 15:1-8 and Matt. 3:10, among others.

31. 1 Timothy 5, 6, and Matthew 6 are representative of a potentially long list.

meet the criteria of supporting evidence. To accomplish the present purpose, it needs to be demonstrated that the theology of the Confessions provides at least the possibility—if not the outright endorsement—of the practice of habituation in virtue and formation of character.

Justified in Order to Fulfill the Law

An interesting confessional accent, which provides a promising entrée for the concerns of virtue ethics and character formation, can be discerned readily in the Augsburg Confession. As previously observed, article 20 of the Augustana discusses faith and good works, and seems to support the idea that once the Holy Spirit is received through faith, the flow of good works is released automatically and continually. Yet, the close of that same article provides another nuance that points in a different direction when it indicates that the gift of faith actually leads the believer back to the Decalogue in order to *fulfill* the Decalogue. "Hence, it is readily apparent that no one should accuse this teaching of prohibiting good works. On the contrary, it is rather to be commended for showing how we can do good works. For without faith human nature cannot possibly do the works of the First or Second Commandments."[32] Faith allows the fulfillment of the Decalogue. In fact, the working assumption of the Confession seems to be that the Christian is justified in order that his newly created faith will lead and empower him to keep the law. Or, simply stated, the believer is justified so that one might fulfill the law.

The assertion that God justifies in order that the justified may follow the law gains considerable momentum in the Large Catechism. As Luther introduces his teaching on the Apostles' Creed, he considers the propriety of locating the discussion of the creed immediately after the exposition of the Decalogue. This is a particularly significant passage from Luther that deserves careful attention:

> The Creed properly follows, which sets forth all that we must expect and receive from God; in short, it teaches us to know him perfectly. It is given in order to help us do what the Ten Commandments require of us. For, as we said above, they are set so high that all human ability is far too puny and weak to keep them. Therefore, it is just as necessary to learn this part, as it is the other so that we may know where and how to obtain the power to do this.[33]

---

32. *Book of Concord*, 57 (CA 20, 35 & 36).
33. Ibid., 431 (LC 2, 2).

Without equivocation, Luther declares that Christians are to be busy about doing the Commandments. Even more significantly though, he brazenly advances the idea that the creed actually serves the Commandments.[34] The creed enables the observance of the Decalogue, which shapes and directs life in the civil realm. So the creed, which Luther rightly identifies with the proclamation of the gospel, can in some sense actually be understood as an auxiliary of civil righteousness—or perhaps better—active righteousness.

Lest one suggest that perhaps this is an instance of Luther being somewhat careless with his choice of words, the reformer fortifies the point by reiterating the same message in the conclusion of his discussion on the creed.

> But the Creed brings pure grace and makes us righteous and acceptable to God. Through this knowledge we come to love and delight in all the commandments of God because we see here in the Creed how God gives himself completely to us, with all his gifts and power, to help us keep the Ten Commandments: The Father gives us all creation, Christ all his works, the Holy Spirit all his gifts.[35]

Considered in the context of the standing of the individual before God—that is, *coram Deo*—the creed is all about God's grace—justifying sinners and delivering the gifts of salvation. But, as Luther stresses, this is hardly the extent of the creed's purpose or application. The creed also serves the believer's growth in new obedience and good works by enabling and empowering the observance of the divine law, which provides certain and formative directions for the shape of the Christian life in this world, or *coram mundo*.

James Nestingen concurs with this reading of Luther's teaching on the Commandments, understanding the Decalogue in the context of creation. "In interpreting the commandments," he writes, "Luther attempts to read life from the bottom up, to get to the nonnegotiable requirements of the human condition."[36] Those requirements are articulated by the Creator in the form of

---

34. Though they provide no reference information, John C. Mattes and Michael Reu relate another relevant comment of Luther: "There are three things which everyone must know in order to be saved. First, he must know what he ought to do and what he must leave undone. Then, as he has discovered that it is impossible for him to accomplish either with his own strength, *he must know where to obtain, where to seek, and find the power that will enable him to do his duty*. And, in the third place, he must know how to seek and obtain that aid." John C. Mattes and Michael Reu, eds., *Luther's Small Catechism: A Jubilee Offering* (Minneapolis: Augsburg, 1929), 15 (emphasis added). Here again, Luther stresses the idea of the creed's enabling the fulfillment of the Commandments, which are understood as the duty of the responsible believer.

35. Ibid., 440 (LC II, 69).

the Ten Commandments. Using a phrase that will be more fully explored in a subsequent chapter, Nestingen intriguingly calls the Ten Commandments the "explication of the ineradicable minimums of creatureliness."[37] Later, he asserts further that, for Luther, Christ's work was "to restore us to the creatureliness lost in all of our attempts at self-transcendence."[38] Christ restores people to the life for which they were created—the life that is given its shape by the Commandments. Christians, then, are given the creed, that is, the gospel, specifically so that they may be able to fulfill the requirements of the law as spelled out in the Ten Commandments.[39] "Through the catechism," writes Charles Arand, "they [the reformers] laid a lasting foundation for shaping both the faith and piety of the people."[40] Concern for the shape of Christian lives was a consistent interest of the confessors. As they understood the Christian faith, justified people are those who delight in the grace of the gospel and live lives being conformed to God's will as revealed in the Decalogue. While the Spirit prompts good works, the Decalogue gives those works their direction, content, and shape. A Christian whose works are shaped by the Decalogue, then, must know the Decalogue. The believer must be taught, indeed, thoroughly indoctrinated, into the concrete and particular realities that spring from the Commandments.[41] Such indoctrination in virtuous living was a recurrent feature of Aristotle's ethical work. Hence, Melanchthon's approbation of

---

36. James Arne Nestingen, "Preaching the Catechism," *Word & World* 10, no. 1 (Winter 1990): 36.

37. Ibid.

38. Ibid., 37.

39. As noted above, this theme is reiterated in article 6 of the Formula: "We believe, teach, and confess that, although people who truly believe in Christ and are genuinely converted to God have been liberated and set free from the curse and compulsion of the law through Christ, they indeed are not for that reason without the law. Instead, they have been redeemed by the Son of God so that they may practice the law day and night." *Book Of Concord*, 502 (FC Ep 6, 2). While a substantial argument could be advanced for the role played by the third use of the law in the promotion of good works and virtuous activity—the concern addressed in article 6 of the Formula, such a pursuit lies outside the scope of the current investigation. For a study of the important debate over the third use of the law, see Scott R. Murray, *Law, Life, and the Living God: The Third Use of Law in Modern American Lutheranism* (St. Louis: Concordia, 2002).

40. Arand, *That I May Be His Own*, 81. See in particular pp. 133–36 for a more complete account of Luther's understanding of the relation between the Decalogue and the creed.

41. Another topic relevant to, yet beyond the parameters of, the present discussion is the anthropology of a Christian. Article 2 of the Formula invites further investigation affirming, as it does, the believer's active role in the attainment of the knowledge of God's will and its pursuit. "After this conversion the reborn human will is not idle in the daily exercise of repentance, but cooperates in all the works of the Holy Spirit which he performs through us. . . . The will not only accepts grace but also cooperates with the Holy Spirit in the works that proceed from it." *Book of Concord*, 494 (FC Ep 2, 17, 18).

Aristotle, even within the confessional corpus, warrants a close and careful investigation.

MELANCHTHON'S USE OF ARISTOTLE WITHIN THE CONFESSIONS

In the Middle Ages, and certainly even down to the present, the most influential advocate and teacher of an ethics that promotes and indeed requires the cultivation of virtue is the Greek philosopher Aristotle. Another hopeful point of connection between contemporary proponents of virtue ethics and the author of the Augustana and the Apology, then, is a mutual respect for Aristotle. Beginning with Alasdair MacIntyre, contemporary supporters of an ethics of virtue have regularly turned to Aristotle for insight and clarification and commended his work.[42] As nearly all theologians before him, Melanchthon also granted Aristotle a significant place in his ethical study. It will become clear that Melanchthon's approval of Aristotle fell within sharply proscribed limits. Still, the use of Aristotle in any capacity could be considered somewhat remarkable. Aristotle, or more accurately the misuse of Aristotle, was regularly subjected to ardent attack by the confessors. Luther's own assessment of the philosopher was memorably harsh. In 1520, Luther offered his thoughts on Aristotle in his open letter, "To the Christian Nobility":

> In this regard my advice would be that Aristotle's Physics, Metaphysics, Concerning the Soul, and Ethics, which hitherto have been thought to be his best books, should be completely discarded . . . . nothing can be learned from them either about nature or the Spirit. . . . It grieves me to the quick that this damned, conceited, rascally heathen has deluded and made fools of so many of the best Christians with his misleading writings. God has sent him as a plague upon us on account of our sins. . . . His book on ethics is the worst of all books. It flatly opposes divine grace and all Christian virtues, and yet it is considered one of his best works. Away with such books! Keep them away from Christians.[43]

Typically, Luther leaves little room for the reader to wonder what he really thinks about Aristotle.

---

42. Alasdair MacIntyre, *After Virtue: A Study in Moral Theory* (Notre Dame, IN: University of Notre Dame Press, 1981), 196–203.

43. Martin Luther, "To the Christian Nobility," in *The Christian in Society I*, ed. James Atkinson and Helmut T. Lehmann, LW 44 (Philadelphia: Fortress Press, 1966), 200–201.

The intervention of twenty-three years, however, mitigated Luther's evaluation considerably; or perhaps the context within which he was writing simply allowed a different expression of his sentiments toward the philosopher. Whatever the reason, by 1543 in an exposition of Isaiah 9, Luther could actually commend the book and author he had once so severely condemned: "Cicero wrote and taught excellently about virtues, prudence, temperance and the rest; likewise also Aristotle excellently and very learnedly about ethics. Indeed the books of both are very useful and of the greatest necessity for the regulation of this life."[44] The comment itself actually provides at least a partial explanation for the shift in Luther's estimation of Aristotle. Luther continues his exposition of the light dawning on "those walking in darkness" by contrasting the value of the best human philosophy with what it cannot give: freedom from sin, death, and hell; peace for an anxious conscience; and the ability to guide one to God's heavenly kingdom.[45] When it comes to an individual's standing before God, human philosophers have nothing to contribute. For Luther and the other reformers, the chief concern was always the encroachment of Aristotle into the *coram Deo* domain; the problem was not Aristotle or his teaching, per se. Within appropriate bounds, then—that is, when addressing questions of ethics or the Christian in his relationship with the rest of creation—Aristotle does have a place, even within the Confessions.

Philip Melanchthon, the *Praeceptor Germaniae* (teacher of Germany), was a student and instructor of Aristotle in the disciplines of dialectics, rhetoric, and ethics.[46] Quite understandably, then, his appreciation for Aristotle is also manifest in his regular use of Aristotelian vocabulary, terminology, and methodology even in a theological work like the Apology. For example, when clarifying the "real purpose" for Christ's life and passion as the forgiveness of sins, he employs a term from formal logic, calling forgiveness of sins the *causa finalis*.[47] Abraham Edel identifies this term as part of the technical terminology in Aristotle's use of "causes" as an aid to understanding whatever one is investigating. For Aristotle and his students, including Melanchthon, a thing should be considered from the standpoint of the material cause, the formal

---

44. *D. Martin Luthers Werke, Kritische Gessamtausgabe*, 58 vols. (Weimar: Hermann Böhlau, 1883) (hereafter cited as WA), 40:608.

45. Ibid.

46. Philip Melanchthon, *Orations on Philosophy and Education*, ed. Sachiko Kusukawa, trans. Christine F. Salazar (Cambridge: Cambridge University Press, 1999), xv–xvii.

47. "Thus it is not enough to believe that Christ was born, suffered, and was raised again unless we also add this Article, which is the real purpose [*causa finalis*] of the narrative: 'the forgiveness of sins.'" *Book of Concord*, 128 (Ap 4, 51).

cause, the efficient cause, and the final cause. "The *final cause* is the for-the-sake-of-which; health, for example is the final cause of surgery. It is the end or goal (*telos*) toward which the thing is working or moving."[48]

Again, Melanchthon readily turns to terminology employed by Plato and refined by Aristotle when he finds it useful in explaining the Mass and the concept of sacrifice in terms of genus and species: "What Is a Sacrifice, and What Are the Kinds of Sacrifice?"[49] Introducing Aristotle's *Topics*, Robin Smith writes, "From Plato's work and other sources, a certain standard structure for definitions can be inferred: a definition must locate the thing defined in its general class or type (its *genus*) and then specify what differentiates it from other things of that type (its *differentia*)."[50] Aristotle's ten categories brought the art of taxonomy to new heights, an art Melanchthon understood well, as evidenced by the very Aristotelian progression of his argument in Apology 24, 16-49, as he instructs his opponents about the true meaning of sacrifice. Indeed, perhaps the most telling evidence of Aristotelian influence on Melanchthon is the one easily overlooked. The very shape and method of Melanchthon's argument throughout the Apology conforms to the instruction in dialectic that Aristotle offers in his *Topics*.[51]

Neither does Melanchthon hesitate to use a favorite concept of Aristotle, the philosophical term *epieikeia*, that is, "fairness, equity, clemency, or goodness," in an effort to clarify what Peter meant when he taught that love covers a multitude of sins (1 Peter 4:8).[52] Aristotle and Stoic philosophers after him numbered *epieikeia* among the virtues. "It is not without reason,"

---

48. Abraham Edel, *Aristotle and His Philosophy* (London: Croom Helm, 1982), 62.

49. "But our opponents . . . hack to pieces the various parts of the concept 'sacrifice,' as our enumeration of the types of sacrifice will make clear. As a matter of course, theologians rightly distinguish between a sacrament and a sacrifice. Therefore, the genus that includes both of these could be either a 'ceremony' or a 'sacred work.'" *Book of Concord*, 260 (Ap 24, 16-17).

50. Aristotle, *Topics: Books I and VIII with Excerpts from Related Texts*, trans. Robin Smith, Clarendon Aristotle Series, ed. J. L. Ackrill and Lindsay Judson (Oxford: Clarendon, 1997), xxx.

51. For example, Aristotle instructs: "It is useful to have examined in how many ways a word is said both for the sake of clarity (for someone would better know what it is he is conceding once it had been brought to light in how many ways the term is applied) and in order to make out deductions concern the thing itself rather than being about a word." Ibid., 18. Melanchthon argues, "Now there are two, and no more than two, basic kinds of sacrifice [*sacrificii species*]. In this controversy and in other disputes, we must never lose sight of those two kinds of sacrifices, and we should take special care not to confuse them." *Book of Concord*, 261 (Ap 24, 19-20). Melanchthon's reliance on Aristotelian dialectic for the construction of his argument presents a fertile field for further and more complete investigation. At present, however, it is enough to recognize Melanchthon's readiness to follow the instruction of Aristotle.

Melanchthon notes, "that the apostles speak so often about this responsibility of love, which the philosophers call 'fairness' [*epieikeian*]."[53] When Aristotle's discussion of *epieikeia* in the *Nichomachean Ethics* is consulted, Melanchthon's application in the context of 1 Peter is reasonable enough. The man demonstrating *epieikeia*, says Aristotle, "is no stickler for his rights in a bad sense but tends to take less than his share though he has the law on his side."[54] Melanchthon recognized an affinity between Aristotle's description and Peter's exhortation.[55]

APPROVAL OF ARISTOTLE IN MELANCHTHON'S WRITING

Not surprisingly, Melanchthon's high regard for Aristotle's method and ethics is reflected most explicitly and pervasively in his academic work. Indeed, it would be difficult to exaggerate Melanchthon's appreciation for the peripatetic philosopher of Greece, who is consistently praised throughout the academic writings of Germany's own teacher. Commending the publications of a friend, Simon Grynaeus, Melanchthon admits his admiration of Aristotle: "For by your favour [sic] we have a more faultless and more refined Aristotle whom you know I admire, love and cherish greatly."[56] In a dedicatory letter for his own work on moral philosophy, Melanchthon supplies at least a partial explanation for his robust sanction of Aristotle.

> Therefore, since in choosing a type of teaching one has to choose what is correct, true, simple, steadfast, well ordered and useful for life, I believe that young minds need to be instructed chiefly with Aristotelian doctrine, which in these qualities surpasses all other sects. Why? Because Aristotle's Ethics should also be loved, because he alone saw and understood that the virtues are middle states. By that description he instructs us most learnedly that the impulses of the mind must be bent to moderation and held back.[57]

---

52. *An Intermediate Greek-English Lexicon: Founded upon the Seventh Edition of Liddell and Scott's Greek-English Lexicon* (Oxford: Oxford University Press, 1978), 291.

53. *Book of Concord*, 157 (Ap 4, 243). Melanchthon also uses the term in CA 26, 14, page 76 in KW.

54. Aristotle, *The Nichomachean Ethics of Aristotle*, trans. Sir David Ross (London: Oxford University Press, 1925), 134 (Book 5, 11).

55. This is not to suggest that Melanchthon considered Aristotle's understanding of *epieikeia* to be the definitive interpretation, much less the source, for Peter's exhortation.

56. Melanchthon, *Orations on Philosophy*, 112.

57. Ibid., 141. See Karl Gottlieb Bretschneider, Philip Melanchthon, and Jean Calvin, *Corpus Reformatorum*, 86 vols. (Halle: C. A. Schwetschke and Son, 1836), 3:362.

More than merely an example of Melanchthon's high regard for Aristotle, this passage also provides a significant insight into Melanchthon's understanding of virtue and its role in life. His approval of virtues as "middle states" will be explored more fully below.

The Wittenberg professor of Greek and philosophy was convinced that Aristotle rightly could be considered a divine gift to school and church. "Even though some splendid books of his [Aristotle's] have perished," he told a graduating class, "I nevertheless reckon that those that are left—which at any rate are most fitting for schools—were preserved by divine providence in order that succeeding generations could be taught more correctly."[58] Specifically, Melanchthon urged the use of Aristotle's dialectic as "very useful, not only in the forum and in trials, but also in the Church."[59] As previously noted, Melanchthon himself proved his point by his own practice.

Certainly, Aristotle was also recommended for his ethical insight. In 1531, Melanchthon wrote, "Aristotle rightly and wisely said that the middle in virtue is of geometric proportion not arithmetic."[60] While widely recognized as Aristotelian, the doctrine of the mean is nevertheless often misunderstood. Edel gives this helpful explanation: "The mean is a proper, just-right point between excess and defect. It is not an arithmetical mean but a mean relative to the individual. If ten pounds is too much for person to eat and two pounds too little, it does not follow that a trainer will recommend six for a particular athlete. It depends on the person and the purpose."[61] Melanchthon applies this same principle to ethics, concluding that Aristotle was correct in stipulating that what is ethically right for a given individual may vary from what is right for another person. Aristotle gives the example of the virtue of liberality. "The term 'liberality' is used relatively to a man's substance; for liberality resides not in the multitude of the gifts but in the state of character of the giver, and this is relative to the giver's substance."[62] Melanchthon, then, readily employed Aristotelian method in his theological work, using tools that were no doubt familiar and comfortable. Not only did he use Aristotelian method, but Melanchthon openly endorsed the philosopher, finding opportunities explicitly to praise Aristotle's contributions even while confessing the Lutheran faith. In

---

58. Melanchthon, *Orations on Philosophy*, 208.

59. Ibid., 86. Aristotle provided his most explicit teaching on the art of dialectic in his *Topics*.

60. Robert Kolb and James A. Nestingen, eds., *Sources and Contexts of The Book of Concord* (Minneapolis: Fortress Press, 2001), 140–43.

61. Edel, *Aristotle and His Philosophy*, 270.

62. Aristotle, *Nichomachean Ethics*, 81 (Book 4, 1). See also *Nichomachean Ethics*, 112–14 (Book 5, 3), for Aristotle's discussion about the geometric proportion.

the Apology, Melanchthon declares, "Aristotle wrote so eruditely about social ethics that nothing further needs to be added."[63] Aristotle is also noted as a worthy authority on things political. Referring to a letter sent by Aristotle to Alexander, Melanchthon comments: "This is a most respectable speech, and nothing better could be said about the public office of a great prince."[64]

Aristotle certainly had his place within Melanchthon's theological work, but within limits. In accord with Luther's practice, Melanchthon allowed Aristotle no place in discussions about humankind's relationship to God. In fact, for all his admiration of Aristotle, Melanchthon did not hesitate to criticize the philosopher when his teaching threatened theological veracity. In article 2 of the Apology, Melanchthon defends the reformers' doctrine of original sin against the attacks of the Roman Catholic opponents who argued that "nothing is sin unless it is voluntary."[65] Melanchthon traces the problem to the opponents' use of philosophy. "In the schools, however, they [Roman Catholic theologians] have taken over from philosophy the completely alien notions that our passions make us neither good nor evil, neither praiseworthy nor contemptible."[66] Melanchthon's identification of the source of his opponent's errant thinking was on the mark. In the *Nichomachean Ethics*, Aristotle makes the argument that Melanchthon recognizes in the Roman Catholic position:

> Now neither the virtues nor the vices are passions, because we are not called good or bad on the ground of our passions, but are so called on the ground of our virtues and our vices, and because we are neither praised nor blamed for our passions (for the man who feels fear or anger is not praised, nor is the man who simply feels anger blamed, but the man who feels it in a certain way), but for our virtues and our vices we are praised or blamed.[67]

Still, even in this instance, Melanchthon's quarrel is not so much with Aristotle, as with his opponents' inappropriate use of Aristotle. "These statements in the philosophers," Melanchthon asserts, "speak about the judgment of civil courts, not about the judgment of God." Then the reformer adds, "In its place, we do not object to this statement." The "place," of course, was in the civil realm, that is, *coram mundo*. The central issue for Melanchthon was that

---

63. *Book of Concord*, 122 (Ap 4, 14).

64. Ibid., 160 (Ap 4, 252).

65. Ibid., 119 (Ap 2, 43).

66. Ibid., 118 (Ap 2, 43).

67. Aristotle, *Nichomachean Ethics*, 36 (2, 5).

his opponents "improperly mingle[d] philosophical or social ethics with the gospel."[68] Aristotle was not the problem; it was the imposition of Aristotle into a question of theology *coram Deo* that brought Melanchthon's rebuke. Melanchthon understood the extent and the limits of Aristotle's usefulness. In questions about daily life in the world, Aristotle was a great teacher; but for questions regarding one's standing before God, Aristotle had nothing to say. Aristotle was excluded from the vertical realm of the individual's relationship to God.

Melanchthon was fond of Aristotle, and freely adopted what he had learned from the philosopher when it would benefit his theological work. This is not to say, however, that Lutheran theology is Aristotelian or that Luther was hypocritical to disparage the philosopher while his lieutenant continued to make ready use of him. Aristotle does not drive Lutheran theology, nor is he central to Lutheran thinking; he is merely one tool to be used in the practice of theology. One should not overestimate the point of Aristotle's place in the Lutheran Confessions—but neither should that place be overlooked or trivialized. The fact is that Aristotle and Aristotelian methods were embraced by Melanchthon and eventually commended even by Luther. The point for this argument is very simple: a shared appreciation for the work of Aristotle provides an interesting and potentially fruitful correlation between twenty-first-century advocates of virtue ethics and the Lutheran reformers. But how far does this agreement go? Did Melanchthon merely use and quote Aristotle in passing, or is there perhaps a more significant overlap in an affinity with Aristotle's ideas about virtue and its formation? Was Melanchthon or even Luther prepared to follow Aristotle's prescribed method of ethical training whereby virtuous people are made that way by the practice of virtuous acts? Does Melanchthon endorse the idea that virtue needs to be learned through the inculcation of habits and the repetition of regular disciplines? Today's virtue ethicists champion these teachings of Aristotle.[69] What of the author of the Confession? How did Philip Melanchthon treat habituation and the formation of character?

---

68. *Book of Concord*, 119 (Ap. 2, 43).

69. It should be noted that the adoption of Aristotle by any form of Christian virtue ethics requires judicious editing. Christians typically count humility and patience as virtues. "Yet," MacIntyre observes, "in the only place in Aristotle's account of the virtues where anything resembling humility is mentioned, it is as a vice and patience is not mentioned at all by Aristotle." MacIntyre, *After Virtue*, 177. The Christian use of Aristotle is, as a rule, probably more formal than material.

Civil Righteousness in the Augustana and Apology

Melanchthon's distinction between two kinds of righteousness is a promising place to begin a closer investigation of his views on habituation and character development.[70] There is a righteousness that is civil, the Confessions acknowledge, and a righteousness of faith. Only the righteousness of faith justifies before God, and it is wholly the work of God.[71] The righteousness of faith is righteousness before or in the presence of God, that is, *coram Deo*. This is the righteousness confessed in article 4 of the Augustana. Civil righteousness is concerned with the right actions of individuals in this world.[72] It is righteousness before or in the presence of humans, that is, *coram hominibus*, or, more broadly and helpfully, before the world or *coram mundo*. Melanchthon is neither faint nor grudging in his affirmation and praise of civil righteousness. Typical is his comment in article 4 of the Apology: "Moreover, we willingly give this righteousness of reason the praise it deserves, for our corrupt nature has no greater good than this, as Aristotle rightly said: 'Neither the evening star nor the morning star is more beautiful than righteousness.'"[73]

Still, the fact that Melanchthon readily endorses civil righteousness is not yet an alignment between Lutheran theology and the tenets of virtue ethics with the consequent capacity intentionally to shape character. While it is true that the scope and concerns of virtue ethics roughly mirror what Melanchthon names civil righteousness, the objective here is to argue that particular aspects of virtue ethics—specifically its insights and instruction regarding the process of character formation—can be rightly and beneficially appropriated by Christians, including Lutheran believers. It is not enough merely to call attention to Melanchthon's approbation of civil righteousness for the citizens of the world.

70. While some scholars have insisted that the two kinds of righteousness is a subset of the distinction between law and gospel (see Fagerberg, *New Look*, 109; and Edmund Schlink, *Theology of the Lutheran Confessions*, trans. Paul F. Koehneke and Herbert J. A. Bouman [Philadelphia: Muhlenberg, 1961], XXI), Charles Arand has argued convincingly that "law and gospel is a subset of the two kinds of righteousness." See Charles P. Arand, "Two Kinds of Righteousness as a Framework for Law and Gospel in the *Apology*," *Lutheran Quarterly* 15, no. 4 (Winter 2002): 22. See also the discussion in Robert Kolb and Charles Arand, *The Genius of Luther's Theology: A Wittenberg Way of Thinking for the Contemporary Church* (Grand Rapids: Baker Academic, 2008).

71. Even when Melanchthon does not explicitly reference the two kinds of righteousness, the distinction is determinative. Melanchthon's regular references to the Christian's being justified *before God*, for example, imply another realm (i.e., before humans) with its own kind of justification.

72. Within the Confessions, civil righteousness may be referenced with one of a host of synonyms that convey particular nuances of meaning; some of these include philosophical righteousness and the righteousness of the flesh, of reason, of the law, of works.

73. *Book of Concord*, 124 (Ap 4, 24).

It is further necessary to demonstrate that Melanchthon and the Confessions commend the pursuit of civil righteousness with its moral habits and learned virtues also in the lives of those who confess Jesus as Savior from sin and death. In other words, the Confessions must allow civil righteousness as specifically applicable not only to fallen mankind in general, but also to redeemed Christians in particular. Civil righteousness cannot be merely a restraint for those who know no better. It must be treated as a standard and norm also for the redeemed in Christ. It is necessary for the present argument that the Confessions permit a call for Christians to manifest civil righteousness by practicing virtues and thus cultivating character. The Apology provides the first supporting evidence. While they are not extensive, or expounded, there are, in fact, several instances in the Apology where Melanchthon includes the tasks of civil righteousness within the life of the believer. The references are distributed throughout the Apology.

In article 16, Melanchthon chastises his opponents for approving monasticism and teaching that the gospel is something external—that is, to be accomplished in a person's outward life. Encouraging people to forsake their civil ties and responsibilities for spiritual motives, he asserts that monasticism obscures the gospel by identifying it with a higher, more demanding "evangelical [that is, gospel] counsel" expected of those who are serious in their Christian faith. Of course, this amounts to a perversion of the gospel into a rarified law. Melanchthon counters, "For the gospel does not destroy the state or the household but rather approves them, and it orders us to obey them as divine ordinances . . ."[74] The problem, as Melanchthon assesses it, is that "they failed to see that the gospel brings eternal righteousness to hearts while outwardly approving the civil realm."[75] In other words, the gospel justifies before God and at the same time sanctions the believer's life in the world, where civil righteousness applies. Robert Kolb calls attention to the significance of this article for Melanchthon's doctrine of civil righteousness: "Melanchthon here established the civil or earthly realm squarely upon the doctrine of creation ..."[76] Thus Christians should conform to the dictates of the civil realm simply by virtue of their place within creation. As will become clear, this is an important idea with significant and wide-ranging implications.

74. Ibid., 231 (Ap 16, 5).

75. Ibid., 232 (Ap 16, 8).

76. Robert Kolb, "God Calling, 'Take Care of My People': Luther's Concept of Vocation in the *Augsburg Confession* and Its *Apology*," *Concordia Journal* 8, no. 1 (January 1982): 5. This foundation will help to form the basis for the framework developed in the next chapter.

The idea of the responsibility of Christians to fulfill their civil callings makes other appearances in the Apology. While expounding the difference between the two kinds of righteousness in article 18 on free will, Melanchthon also indicates that the expectations of the civil realm are relevant for believers: "Therefore, it is helpful to distinguish between civil righteousness, which is ascribed to the free will, and spiritual righteousness, which is ascribed to the operation of the Holy Spirit in the regenerate. In this way outward discipline is preserved, because *all people alike ought to know that God requires civil righteousness* and that to some extent we are able to achieve it."[77] No doubt Melanchthon's inclusive "all people" was intended to bring even unbelievers within the jurisdiction of civil righteousness. It is important, though, to remember that his "all" certainly would not exclude Christians.

In article 21, Melanchthon discusses the fitting role for the saints in the lives of Christians. In the course of his argument, Melanchthon grants three types of appropriate honor. The first is offering thanksgiving for the mercy of God displayed in the lives of these individuals. The second is the way that the saints' lives serve to strengthen members of the church militant. "The third honor," Melanchthon writes, "is imitation: first of their faith, then of their other virtues, which people should imitate according to their callings."[78] It should be noted that Melanchthon's endorsement of the imitation of the saints extends beyond the example of the saints' faith to include also other virtues evident in their lives. Stipulating that Christians practice these virtues "according to their callings" indicates an orientation to the "left-hand" realm, or first-article world of creation, where Christians fulfill their responsibilities toward the rest of the created realm. While Melanchthon does not specifically label this Christian pursuit of virtue as civil righteousness, it would certainly fit within the broad schema of righteousness before humankind with its distinct nuances. Melanchthon's approval of saintly imitation thus supplies another connection with virtue ethics. The advocacy of *imitatio sanctorum,* or imitation of the saints,

---

77. *Book of Concord*, 234 (Ap 18, 9) (emphasis added). Luther also taught a distinction between two kinds of righteousness. But, while Melanchthon typically distinguished civil righteousness from spiritual righteousness, Luther distinguished between active righteousness and passive righteousness. "But this most excellent righteousness, the righteousness of faith, which God imputes to us through Christ without works, is neither political nor ceremonial nor legal nor work-righteousness but is quite the opposite; it is a merely passive righteousness while all the others listed above, are active." *Lectures on Galatians 1535, Chapters 1–4,* ed. Jaroslav Pelikan, LW 26 (St. Louis: Concordia, 1962), 4. The similarities and differences between the two kinds of righteousness as taught by Melanchthon and Luther will be considered more fully in ch. 4.

78. *Book of Concord*, 238 (Ap 21, 6).

would obviously allow, if not demand, precisely the practices of habituation and character formation that are the driving concern of this text; but for the sake of a coherent argument, a fuller treatment must be deferred for the moment. At present, it is enough to recognize that the context of Melanchthon's comment makes it abundantly clear that this call for the practice of the inculcation of virtue is issued to Christian people. Finally, returning to the emphasis on the civil realm, it seems safe to conclude that as present saints imitate previous saints, their unique callings are fulfilled in the left-hand or civil realm where its corresponding righteousness prevails.

In article 27 of the Apology, Melanchthon addresses what he sees as the Roman opponents' erroneous interpretation of Jesus' command to the rich young man to "sell your possessions . . . and follow me" (Matt. 19:21). Correcting Rome's tendency to find in Jesus' words a prescription for all disciples, Melanchthon writes, "Callings are personal, just as matters of business themselves vary with times and persons; but the example of obedience is universal."[79] Melanchthon summarizes his discussion by returning the obedient Christian to his unique station in life, squarely within the created realm, where each calling is accomplished: "So it is perfection for each of us with true faith to obey our own calling."[80] Kolb recognizes the significance of this article as it "reinforces this focus on the connection between faith and daily life . . ."[81] In article 27, then, Melanchthon is insisting "that proper and God-pleasing lives flow from the recognition of God as the good Lord of human living."[82] The sphere of activity for the practice of the Christian's vocation ("human living") is the wide, richly variegated world of creation, including the civil realm. Thus, the civil realm cannot be set in false opposition to the realm of faith. Both exist together in a complementary relationship.

One final example of the Apology's approval of the civil realm surfaces in article 28, in which ecclesiastical power is discussed. The issue at stake for the reformers was the correct jurisdiction of ecclesiastical authority. Seeking to curtail the overextended powers of bishops, Melanchthon argues, "Bishops

---

79. Ibid., 285 (Ap 27, 50).

80. Ibid. "Perfection" here is drawn from and defined by the context—the encounter of the "rich young man" with Jesus (Matt. 19:21). As Melanchthon uses the term here, *perfection* is the fulfillment of God's will for an individual, or as Melanchthon summarizes, "to obey our own calling." The doctrine of vocation taught in this and the previously considered article will be important in the next chapter's development of an overall framework. For a definitive explication of the Lutheran doctrine of vocation, see Gustaf Wingren, *Luther on Vocation*, trans. Carl C. Rasmussen (Evansville, IN: Ballast, 1999).

81. Kolb, "God Calling," 8. The critical importance of this intimate connection will be considered more fully in the final chapter.

82. Ibid.

do not have the power of tyrants to act apart from established law, nor regal power to act above the law."[83] Correcting his opponents' erroneous, but oft-repeated, interpretation of Hebrews 13:17, "Obey your leaders," Melanchthon insists that the biblical text certainly does not establish a power of bishops beyond the scope of the gospel. Rather, "This statement requires obedience under the gospel; it does not create an authority for bishops apart from the gospel."[84] Melanchthon's immediate purpose undoubtedly is to limit the scope of ecclesiastical authority. Such authority is bound by the gospel: "Bishops must not create traditions contrary to the gospel nor interpret their traditions in a manner contrary to the gospel."[85] Of interest in light of the present discussion is the fact that Melanchthon correlates a life of obedience with the gospel. Melanchthon takes for granted that the life of a believer living under, or in relation to, the gospel will be characterized by obedience.[86] One may reasonably wonder, "Obedience to what?" Melanchthon does not bother to specify the sort of obedience he envisions. By definition, obedience is in conformity to God's will for God's creation, that is, the law. Thus the Christian lives in obedience to the righteousness of the law.

While it is not part of the confessional corpus, and so does not fall within the scope of the present chapter, it is worth noting at this juncture that in his Galatians commentary of 1535, Martin Luther also correlates obedience to the law with the gospel. As he develops his early argument, Luther subdivides the "many kinds" of righteousness by reeling off three representative varieties of righteousness in addition to the crowning righteousness of faith. The reformer distinguishes a righteousness that is political, one that is ceremonial, and "the righteousness of the law or Decalogue, which Moses teaches." About this last righteousness, Luther makes the significant comment: "We, too, teach this, but *after* the doctrine of faith."[87] In view of the way that Melanchthon correlates obedience (civil righteousness) to the gospel, it seems valid to hear Luther saying not only that the righteousness of the law is taught in *subordination* to the doctrine of faith (understanding *after* hierarchically), but, significantly, also that it is taught to those who have learned the doctrine of faith (understanding *after* temporally). One might reasonably conclude that for Luther political righteousness and righteousness of the law are not synonyms, but actually descriptions of two different kinds of righteousness, one that specifically directs

83. *Book of Concord*, 290 (Ap 28, 14).

84. Ibid., 291 (Ap 28, 20).

85. Ibid.

86. The Latin preposition *erga* can be translated as "towards" or "in relation to."

87. LW 26:4 (emphasis added).

vocations in relation to the state or city, the other that guides the lives of all believers. Whether both would fit beneath the umbrella of civil righteousness will be considered at greater length in a subsequent discussion. For now, it is enough to take note of Luther's own practice of positioning Christian obedience after the gospel.

It is true, of course, that Melanchthon does not use the explicit language of civil righteousness when discussing the Christian's life of new obedience. Civil righteousness, as Melanchthon uses the term in the Confessions, typically describes the earned righteousness that prevails in the world, in contrast to the God-given righteousness of faith. Nevertheless, the Apology definitely does not exclude the morality of civil righteousness from the Christian's life. And it is possible and perhaps quite likely that the authors of the Confessions simply assumed that civil obedience or moral righteousness would be characteristic of believers without the need of explicitly expressing the idea. Obviously, this civil or moral righteousness endorsed by the Confessions is precisely the purview of virtue ethics.[88] Contemporary proponents of virtue ethics and Melanchthon appear to occupy some significant common ground.

FORMATION OF CHRISTIANS IN THE CONFESSIONS

The confessors' recurrent emphases on the need to teach and encourage civil righteousness as well as the idea that the gospel leads Christians to an observance of the Decalogue both provide potentially fruitful linkage between the Lutheran Confessions and the concerns of virtue ethics. A still greater link is forged, however, when explicit talk of formation or habituation in virtuous practices can be discerned in the Confessions; and of this, there is ample evidence, beginning with the catechisms.

THE APOLOGY

While the brevity and focused purpose of the Augustana did not invite a consideration of the issue of character formation, the Apology does contain references to its importance. Certainly, there are theological as well as moral convictions at work prompting the Apology's explicit and frequent calls for

---

88. But those interested in virtue ethics are not concerned exclusively with moral righteousness *coram mundo*. Since it is God's justifying and redeeming work in the gospel that makes a Christian and gives that Christian a new narrative and with it new practices, most virtue ethicists are also quite interested in the believer's righteousness before God, or passive righteousness. A framework that attempts to integrate civil righteousness with a believer's standing *coram Deo* is an overarching concern and will be the subject of the next chapter.

faith to be "exercised" in good works. Having asserted in article 4 that after teaching the gospel, "later we add also the teaching of the law," Melanchthon provides even more encouragement for this work of formation in the Christian life. "Thus good works ought to follow faith as thanksgiving toward God. Likewise, good works ought to follow faith so that faith is exercised in them, grows, and is shown to others, in order that others may be invited to godliness by our confession."[89]

The Apology acknowledges that good works serve an outreach or evangelistic purpose—a function of good works readily embraced yet today. But Melanchthon contends that they also provide a more personal benefit. The active pursuit of good works, Melanchthon writes, helps to "exercise" faith. In other words, striving for good works helps to affirm and strengthen faith as the business of faith is practiced and demonstrated in concrete actions. Melanchthon offers the example of Abel and his God-pleasing sacrifice: "Indeed, he carried out that work in order to exercise his faith and by his example and confession to invite others to believe."[90] The pursuit of good works, or what might also be called striving to live virtuously, actually serves faith by exercising or demonstrating it. Faith is given tangible expression in God-directed actions, and with the practice of those actions, Melanchthon asserts, faith grows. This should not be construed as a version of "faith formed by love."[91] The Confessions are unwaveringly consistent and adamant that saving faith is delivered whole and complete, in need of no supplement. Nevertheless, for that faith to continue and to grow in a human heart still plagued by sin, Melanchthon agrees with Scripture that faith should be exercised, or expressed, in the practice of virtuous habits.

The same "exercise" terminology reappears later in the Apology in article 15 on human traditions. Melanchthon affirms the normative place of the dying-and-rising motif of the cross in the life of Christians, but then continues:

> Alongside this true putting to death, which takes place through the cross, a voluntary and necessary kind of exercise also exists, about which Christ says, "Be on guard so that your hearts are not weighed

89. *Book of Concord*, 150 (Ap 4, 188). Perhaps Melanchthon's comment that "later we add also the teaching of the law," should be read in concert with Luther's comment in his Galatians introduction about the righteousness of the law: "We, too, teach this, but after the doctrine of faith." LW 26:4.

90. *Book of Concord*, 151 (Ap 4, 188).

91. For a helpful discussion of this term, see Steven Ozment, *The Age of Reform 1250–1550: An Intellectual and Religious History of Late Medieval and Reformation Europe* (New Haven: Yale University Press, 1980), 239–44. Melanchthon confronts and refutes this notion, typical of the medieval church in Ap 4, 218-243, pages 153–57 in KW.

down with dissipation," and Paul says, "but I punish my body and enslave it. . . ." We should undertake these exercises not because they are devotional exercises that justify but as restraints on our flesh, lest satiety overcome us and render us complacent and lazy. This results in people indulging the flesh and catering to its desires. Such diligence must be constant, because God constantly commands it.[92]

Melanchthon saw the need for Christians to be involved in ongoing training, or exercising, of their faith. This exercise was undertaken in order to leash the flesh and would be practiced then, in the external affairs of life in the world—*coram mundo*. Without a doubt, works righteousness was a pernicious menace to Christian truth and faith; but so was its antithesis: complacency and laziness. Believers needed to be trained, to be shaped and formed in piety.

One of the most direct references to this need for ongoing training or formation was encountered already under the discussion of civil righteousness. In article 21 of the Apology, Melanchthon encourages appropriate veneration of the saints through imitation: "first of their faith, then of their other virtues, which people should imitate according to their callings."[93] This idea of *imitatio sanctorum* implies, even necessitates, the encouragement of habituation. Habituation is the practice of virtuous acts and the cultivation of pious habits. *Imitatio sanctorum* describes this exactly. The call to imitate the saints is a plea to practice holy habits, or holy activities that in turn will aid the formation of character.

This passage from article 21 affords an opportunity to address a question that by now has swollen to the point of becoming impossible to ignore, namely, What is the relationship between good works and virtue?[94] Melanchthon comments in the Latin text that imitation of the saints should be first of their faith, then "of their other virtues." This passage is translated from the German as "We honor the saints when we follow after their faith, their love, and their patient example."[95] In the German, the love and the patience of the saints are treated as synonymous with "other virtues." Thus love, which is regularly counted among good works, is also counted a virtue. While a case could be made that there is no real distinction between virtues and good works, it seems that a different nuance does exist. Good works are perhaps best understood as

92. *Book of Concord*, 230 (Ap 15, 46-47).

93. Ibid., 238 (Ap 21, 6).

94. Of tangential interest is the history of the rise and fall of virtue within Christian theology. Like others of his time, Melanchthon gives no indication of a particular reluctance to use virtue terminology.

95. *Book of Concord*, 238 (Ap 21, 6).

deeds done in obedience to God for the good of the rest of creation. Virtue, on the other hand, describes the imprint such repeated obedience leaves on an individual's character. Not every good work is an indication of virtue, but a true virtue cannot exist without its attendant good works. "Good works" describes what is experienced externally; "virtue" describes the state of the character internally. From the believer's perspective, the net result is essentially the same.

Another explicit endorsement of the pursuit of virtues appears in the discussion of monastic vows in article 27 of the Apology. In this article, Melanchthon decries the notion of the opponents that only the monastic life leads one to perfection.[96] The influence of Luther and his doctrine of vocation are easily detected in the shape of Melanchthon's argument.[97] This passage also reinforces that for Melanchthon there is a remarkable affinity, if not identification, between good works and virtue.

> But the opponents cunningly seek to give the impression that they are modifying the common notion about perfection. They deny that the monastic life is perfection and instead say that it is a state for acquiring perfection. . . . If we follow this, the monastic life will be no more a state for acquiring perfection than the life of a farmer or an artisan. These, too, are states for acquiring perfection. All people, whatever their calling, should seek perfection, that is, growth in the fear of God, in faith, in the love for their neighbor, and in similar spiritual virtues.[98]

To grow in virtues is to grow into the will of God, which encompasses the whole life of Christians, their faith as well as their relations to their neighbors. The growth follows a certain shape, given by the commandments of God, but also reckons with the unique contours arising from particular vocations.

Melanchthon's entreaty for a life marked by growth in virtues is not advice aimed only at the heathen in the civil sphere. Neither can this passage be understood as supporting the idea that good works are automatic and continuous in the life of a believer. Here, he is quite explicit. The spiritual

96. Again, as Melanchthon will shortly make clear, in this context, "perfection" means a life lived according to God's will.

97. For an excellent discussion of Luther's doctrine of vocation and its place in the Augustana and Apology, see Kolb's article "God Calling." Kolb writes, "Against most of the sacred works of the medieval church Luther set forth the godliness of the activities of the profane realm, when performed by the person of faith" (5). Of course, an even more complete treatment can be found in Wingren, *Luther on Vocation*.

98. *Book of Concord*, 283 (Ap 27, 37).

virtues are something to be sought. Included in Melanchthon's broad understanding of spiritual virtues is love for neighbor, which is manifested in the acquisition and increasing display of the classic virtues—cardinal and theological.[99]

THE CATECHISMS

Disheartened and angered by his firsthand experience of Christian ignorance and impiety in local congregations encountered during the Saxon visitation, Luther was compelled to compose his Small Catechism. His instructions for its use include heavy emphasis on thorough teaching. "Using such a catechism," Luther told the pastors and preachers, "explain each individual commandment, petition, or part with its various works, benefits, and blessings, harm and danger, as you find treated at length in so many booklets."[100] This teaching was to be carried out with diligence and with the aid of "many examples from the Scriptures where God either punished or blessed such people," so that the hearers would be "orderly, faithful, obedient, and peaceful."[101] The examples, the exhortations, the scriptural threats, promises, and repetition were all intended to direct and affect the hearers, in order that they might grow in Christian character. In short, the catechism was taught to the people in order to shape the people.

The preface to the Large Catechism contains similar language. Luther complains about the sorry state of affairs where even pastors, "like pigs and dogs . . . are remembering no more of the gospel than this rotten, pernicious, shameful, carnal liberty." Of course, the attitude of the clergy is reflected in the people they serve. "As it is, the common people take the gospel altogether too lightly, and we accomplish but little, despite all our hard work. What, then, can we expect if we are slothful and lazy, as we used to be under the papacy?"[102]

For Luther, the gospel and its way of life needed to be inculcated in the lives of the people. "Let all Christians drill themselves daily," he urges, "and constantly put it into practice."[103] That Luther intended the cultivation of Christian (or virtuous?) habits is evident from his admonition that his students should put into practice what they had gleaned from their study. About the outcome of these efforts, the reformer was confident: "If they show such diligence, then I promise them—and their experience will bear me out—that

99. Prudence, justice, fortitude, temperance, faith, hope, and love.
100. *Book of Concord*, 349 (SC preface, 17).
101. Ibid. (SC preface, 18).
102. Ibid., 380 (LC preface, 4).
103. Ibid., 383 (LC preface, 19).

they will gain much fruit and God will make excellent people out of them."[104] Luther was not so heavenly minded as to miss the importance of Christian formation in this life. Christians should desire and seek what God intends for them—that they attain the full potential for which they were created. Excellent people are people who are living as fully human, realizing in their own lives all that it means to live rightly before God and before humans.

Later in the text of the Large Catechism, Luther concludes his treatment on the Close of the Commandments with a reference to formative training:

> It is useful and necessary, I say, always to teach, admonish, and remind young people of all of this so that they may be brought up, not only with blows and compulsion, like cattle, but in the fear and reverence of God. . . . Therefore it is not without reason that the Old Testament command was to write the Ten Commandments on every wall and corner, and even on garments. Not that we are to have them there only for display, as the Jews did, but we are to keep them incessantly before our eyes and constantly in our memory and *to practice them in all our works and ways.* Each of us is to make them a matter of daily practice in all circumstances, in all activities and dealings, as if they were written everywhere we look, even wherever we go or wherever we stand.[105]

The inculcation of the Ten Commandments plays a critical role in the formation of Christians young and old, a role limited not simply to their second, or theological, use of exposing and condemning sin. The Commandments are to be urged, learned, and practiced so that Christians might become more nearly the kind of people that God wills them to be—internally or "in our memory," as well as externally. The goal is not mere outward conformity, but genuine inward renewal accomplished through repetitive practice and established habit.

In the Large Catechism, Luther's comments on the Second Commandment offer another outstanding example of his high regard for spiritual habits that contribute to the formation of Christian character. Within his pastoral exhortation, Luther extols the practices of piety. The remarkable extent and variety of habituation endorsed by Luther deserves measured consideration and warrants an extensive quotation:

---

104. Ibid. (LC preface, 20).
105. Ibid., 430–31 (emphasis added) (LC I, 330-332).

One must encourage children again and again to honor God's name and to keep it constantly upon their lips in all circumstances and experiences. . . . This is also a blessed and useful habit, and very effective against the devil, who is always around us, lying in wait to lure us into sin and shame, calamity and trouble. . . . For this purpose it also helps to form the habit of commending ourselves each day to God. . . . From the same source comes the custom learned in childhood of making the sign of the cross when something dreadful or frightening is seen or heard, and saying, "Lord God save me!" . . . Likewise, if someone unexpectedly experiences good fortune—no matter how insignificant—he or she may say, "God be praised and thanked!" . . . See with simple and playful methods like this we should bring up young people in the fear and honor of God so that the First and Second Commandments may become familiar and constantly be practiced. Then some good may take root, spring up, and bear fruit, and people may grow to adulthood who may give joy and pleasure to an entire country. That would also be the right way to bring up children, while they may be trained with kind and agreeable methods.[106]

Luther grants a hearty endorsement to habituation—the practices of piety designed to form and shape Christian character. It is a tenet of virtue ethics: right practices oft-repeated form habits that in turn serve to shape character. Luther describes it in different language: holy habits help the good to "take root, spring up and bear fruit," resulting in adults who bring joy and pleasure to a whole country. The terminology is different, but the idea is the same. The outcome of holy habituation is adults with good character.

Luther again makes it clear that he seeks more than outward conformity and is confident that what he seeks will be realized: "But this kind of training takes root in their hearts so that they fear God more than they do rods and clubs."[107] Through pious practices and holy habits, children are trained to obey the First and Second Commandments. Through this formation, they are shaped within—the training takes root in their hearts. Their character, or "what they are in their hearts," is stamped by this process of learned obedience to God's commandments. So shaped, these children exhibit this character throughout their lives; and all, especially neighbors and nation, reap the reward.

106. Ibid., 395–96 (LC I, 70-76).
107. Ibid.

THE FORMULA OF CONCORD

The second generation of confessors continued to affirm the validity and even necessity of Christian habituation and character formation, but did not limit its application to young believers. Curiously, one of the most ardent appeals to formation appears in article 11 of the Formula, on election:

> Next, the Holy Spirit dwells in the elect who have believed as he dwells in his temple and is not idle in them but impels the children of God to obey God's commands. Therefore, believers should in the same way not be idle either, much less resist the impetus of God's Spirit, but should practice all Christian virtues, godliness, modesty, moderation, patience, and love for one another—and should diligently seek to "confirm their call and election," so that the more they recognize the Spirit's power and strength in themselves, the less they doubt their election.[108]

For the framers of the Formula, to obey God's commands is to practice Christian virtue; and to practice virtue is to give confirmation of the Spirit's work within. The practice of virtue is of a piece with what it means to be Christian.

Article 2 of the Formula, on free will, also calls on the regenerate to be active in the pursuit of Christian works: ". . . after this conversion the reborn human will is not idle in the daily exercise of repentance, but cooperates in all the works of the Holy Spirit which he performs through us."[109] As the Confession affirms, Christians should be busy with the business of Christian living, practicing with diligence "all the works of the Holy Spirit which he performs through us." What can the practice of such Christian works mean but the ongoing task of learning and doing what is rightly named virtuous, in other words, habituation in Christian character? The reformers expected believers to be both obedient to God's commands and zealous in the production of Christian virtues. Virtue ethics would name this the cultivation of character. Clearly, from the Apology to the Formula, the Confessions recognize and encourage the need for Christians, all Christians, to be growing actively in their desire for and possession of virtues or moral habits, which in turn shape Christian character.

---

108. Ibid., 652 (FC SD 11, 73).
109. Ibid., 494 (FC Ep 2, 17).

SUPPORT FROM OTHER SOURCES

A wider reading of material from Melanchthon's pen serves to corroborate this study's reading of the Confessions as supportive of the concerns and objectives of virtue ethics vis-à-vis habituation and character formation. That Melanchthon was willing and, indeed, quite eager to employ Aristotle for academic and for civil purposes has been demonstrated previously. But there are further references worthy of attention. By 1524, Melanchthon was already making the sharp distinction between the two kinds of righteousness. This careful distinction permitted him, as it permits anyone who grasps it, to address two topics of perennial importance: the proclamation of justification by grace through faith and the exhortation to civil or moral righteousness in the affairs of this world. Melanchthon—like his theological mentor, Luther—was concerned above all to secure the undiminished comfort of the gospel for troubled sinners. This is evident in a succinct "Summary of Doctrine" that Melanchthon produced in 1524 at the behest of Philip of Hesse, who was eager to have the Wittenberger's opinion on the day's pressing theological topics. Predictably, Melanchthon begins with a celebration of the gospel:

> See, moreover, how much comfort there is in this proclamation for miserable consciences when they understand that it is the truest possible righteousness to believe that through Christ our sins are forgiven without our own satisfaction, without our own merits. I have known some who had clearly thrown away all hope of salvation before they discovered this teaching because their conscience could not be lifted by satisfactions and feigned works. These persons, after the Gospel had illuminated the world much more clearly, again with a strong spirit conceived the hope of salvation, and not only the hope but also the power or strength against sins.[110]

The gospel delivers inestimable consolation and assurance, lifting from troubled souls the burden of guilt and despair, assuring them of eternal salvation, and renewing them for life in the world. Certainly, it was Melanchthon's great delight to champion the pure comfort of the gospel.

Yet, this was not the end of the issue. Melanchthon was well aware that since faith, and therefore the righteousness of faith, is not the possession of all people, there remains a need also for the law. "Accordingly," Melanchthon instructs his reader, "besides Christian righteousness there is human

---

110. Philipp Melanchthon, *Melanchthon: Selected Writings*, trans. Charles Leander Hill (Minneapolis: Augsburg, 1962), 96.

righteousness, by which the wicked should be coerced."[111] Besides needing to establish the comforting work of the gospel, Melanchthon also needed to confront what Timothy Wengert calls "the theological aberration he most feared."[112] The Wittenberg theologian identified many of the same dangers the twenty-first-century theologians of chapter 2 describe:

> But many today are preaching evangelical righteousness in such a way that a new wickedness is being born. For some wicked persons are feigning faith and are glorying in the name of Christ and conceiving a certain kind of carnal security by which they are being precipitated into great crimes, and they think that they ought not to be coerced. Both the training of children is being neglected and other things of this nature, although God has nevertheless subjected to this schooling all who either are not in Christ or are weak, according to the position of Paul in Galatians 3 and 4.[113]

The church of the Reformation was plagued not only by the then freshly identified threat of people clinging to a righteousness of works, but also by the newly revived threat of people insisting that the gospel meant an antinomian variety of freedom which excused gross licentiousness. As the years elapsed, the latter threat, the antinomian abuse of the gospel, proved to be a perennial concern for the teacher and reformer.[114]

Even as Melanchthon allowed that civil righteousness served a thoroughly secular function as a hedge against impious people and immoral behavior, it is important to recognize that he also grasped the value of civil righteousness as a tool for spiritual pedagogy: "This training of the state is a certain righteousness which forms character and contains rites and human and civil duties. It accustoms children to the worship of God by teaching and exercise, and restrains foolish people from vices . . ."[115] As Melanchthon saw it, civil righteousness was not optional for Christians; more significantly, neither was it in any sense antithetical to the "spirit of the gospel." Civil righteousness served Christians by forming character, equipping worshipers with fitting habits, and

---

111. Ibid., 97.

112. Timothy J. Wengert, *Law and Gospel: Philipp Melanchthon's Debate with John Agricola of Eisleben over* Poenitentia (Grand Rapids: Baker, 1997), 102.

113. Melanchthon, *Selected Writings*, 97.

114. While Melanchthon's wrestling with these issues is not without significance, they lie just beyond the scope of this inquiry. Timothy Wengert provides excellent details of Melanchthon's lifelong struggle against antinomianism in *Law and Gospel*.

115. Melanchthon, *Selected Writings*, 97.

curtailing the casual practice of sin. Divinely ordered civil righteousness did not "merit grace or remission of sins," but it did "serve human need."[116] This service was reason enough for Melanchthon to encourage the clear teaching and practice of civil righteousness. Historical circumstances, however, made the encouragement of civil righteousness even more pressing. Throughout the 1520s, Melanchthon contended with elements of the radical reformation—those who had little use for the civil realm or political order. Sachiko Kusukawa summarizes Melanchthon's response: "Melanchthon saw poor education and confusion of philosophy and theology as the root of the problem. . . . He needed to establish the distinction between theological truths and truths attainable through human reason alone. . . . Above all, he needed to prove that everybody, both believers and unbelievers alike, had to obey civil authority."[117]

A decade later, Melanchthon continued to echo familiar themes, but went further by removing any lingering questions as to the place of civil righteousness in the life of a Christian:

> Moreover it is generally acknowledged that everyone needs some teaching on morals and a description of virtues, so that we understand in our manners and in judging about human business what is proper and what is not, what is done rightly and what is ill done. Accordingly, it is necessary to have forms and images of virtues, which we follow in all decisions and in our judgements [sic] on all matters. This teaching is strictly speaking to be called humanity, and it shows the way to live properly and as a citizen; those who do not know it are not very different from beasts.[118]

It was not complicated. Training in virtue was simply part of being human. As creatures of God lacking omniscience concerning God's will for their living, Christians, too, were in need of "some teaching on morals and a description of virtues." With his endorsement of the teaching of two kinds of righteousness and his advocacy of civil righteousness for all people, Melanchthon embraced many of the same interests and priorities as today's advocates of virtue ethics.

A final representative comment from the Melanchthonian corpus illustrates the extent of Melanchthon's support for the central concerns of virtue ethics. In thoroughly Aristotelian language, Melanchthon writes in his 1542 *Rhetoric*: "What is virtue? It is a habit of the will inclining me to be obedient to the

---

116. Ibid., 98.

117. Melanchthon, *Orations on Philosophy*, xvii.

118. Ibid., 80–81.

judgement [sic] of right reason."[119] While contemporary advocates of virtue ethics attempt more precise definitions, they should find little in Melanchthon's basic concept with which to quarrel.[120] Melanchthon was concerned as they are to foster the pursuit of habits that will influence behavior in the direction of obedience to the highest norm—helping humans to realize their telos.[121]

CONCLUSION

Stanley Hauerwas's charge that Lutheranism is incapable of presenting a viable Christian ethics may be substantiated when applied to some contemporary Lutherans. The sampling of material presented in this chapter, however, should provide ample evidence to support the contention that when the sixteenth-century reformers and their confessions are considered, the accusation becomes untenable and evaporates. The primary concern of the Confessions was obviously the defense of justification by grace through faith alone. The contemporary context demanded it.

> In former times, consciences were vexed by the doctrine of works; they did not hear consolation from the gospel. . . . Consequently, it was essential to pass on and restore this teaching about faith in Christ so that anxious consciences should not be deprived of consolation but know that grace and forgiveness of sins are apprehended by faith in Christ.[122]

Melanchthon fully grasped the necessity of guarding and extending the gospel's ability to proclaim pure grace and deliver an unencumbered and unmitigated word of absolution to a desperate sinner.

Still, this pervasive attention to the comfort and consolation inherent in a right proclamation of the gospel was not accomplished with a corresponding

119. Philipp Melanchthon, *Elementorum Rhetorices Libri Duo* 1542, trans. Mary Joan LaFontaine (n.p.: n.d.), 102. Aristotle wrote: "Virtue, then, is a state of character concerned with choice, lying in a mean, i.e. the mean relative to us, this being determined by a rational principle, and by that principle by which the man of practical wisdom would determine it." Aristotle, *Nichomachean Ethics*, 39 (2, 6).

120. Alasdair MacIntyre's thorough but unwieldy definition has been especially influential: "A virtue is an acquired human quality the possession and exercise of which tends to enable us to achieve those goods which are internal to practices and the lack of which effectively prevents us from achieving any such goods" (*After Virtue*, 191). See the discussion above in ch. 1.

121. Clearly, this statement raises a host of questions about humankind's telos and the best route to be followed there. A Christian perspective curtails the bulk of these questions with the ready answers found in the Bible.

122. *Book of Concord*, 55 (CA 20, 19 & 22).

neglect or diminution of other pressing theological questions. A wise and faithful theologian must not suffer a myopia that prevents him or her from seeing the breadth of the theological task. The men who penned the Confessions were such wise, faithful theologians. Indeed, it has been made clear that the author and supporters of the Augsburg Confession and its Apology demonstrated an intense interest in the believer's continual, intentional growth in good works and corresponding virtues. Nor were the reformers reluctant to place this responsibility squarely on the shoulders of believers. While the Holy Spirit worked a life-altering regeneration, the effective presence of the Spirit did not exclude the ongoing obligation of the believer to grow in Christian virtues or of the church to cultivate them. Spiritual formation and cultivation of Christian character were not and are not antithetical to the substance of the Confessions.

Not every aspect of contemporary virtue ethics is specifically articulated in the Confessions, of course. This is, however, hardly surprising, and certainly no detriment. What the Confessions do say sufficiently provides precisely what is needed for concerned believers seeking to address thetwenty-first-century manifestations of the same dangers that plagued the church five centuries before. The Confessions furnish the possibility and the justification for developing a theological frame wide enough to accommodate the concerns of faithful Christian people—even faithful Lutheran people—who, like Melanchthon, strive to retain the pure gospel while at the same time endeavor to advocate a Christian life that actively pursues the virtues and intentionally cultivates Christian character. A meaningful and effective theological framework that attempts to accomplish exactly this is the subject of the chapter that follows.

4

The Search for a Paradigm
Some Lutheran Efforts

Five hundred years after the Reformation, Lutheranism faces an ethical challenge. Neither a peculiar moral conundrum that perplexes Lutheranism nor a particular denominational behavior or practice that invites charges of corporate immorality, this more fundamental challenge is simply that of finding a way to teach and encourage Christian ethics among its adherents. Unable to address the basic question of the place of ethics, the further concern of character formation is thus all but ignored. The accusation that Lutheran theology is incapable of engaging in the tasks of Christian ethics in any significant or meaningful way derives in part from academia, with Stanley Hauerwas serving as a singularly articulate representative voice. Yet, the charge is leveled not only by those looking in at Lutheranism; even Lutheran theologians admit the inadequacy of contemporary Lutheranism's approach to the ethical endeavor.[1] More importantly, perhaps, the indictment of ethical irrelevance is substantiated, albeit unintentionally, by Lutheran laity, who attest to the meager ethical resources of their own confession by their ready consumption of the ethical and practical guidance that other Christian traditions furnish.[2]

Some trace Lutheranism's ethical difficulties—or perhaps deficiencies—directly to the Reformation, and conclude that Lutheran doctrine itself is at fault: the fundamental emphasis on justification by grace through faith alone is irreconcilably at odds with any notions of habituation, character formation, or ethical progress.[3] The previous chapter investigating the Lutheran

---

1. See ch. 2 for four representative Lutheran voices.

2. This can be seen in the steady popularity, among Lutherans intent on living the Christian life, of literature and programming deriving from "evangelical" sources such as Promise Keepers, Focus on the Family, and Fellowship of Christian Athletes.

Confessions and their stance toward righteousness in the affairs of this world attempted to refute this charge, contending that a careful reading of the Confessions reveals not an antipathy to ethics, but—within the arena of Christian living—a keen interest in the ethical task. The evidence simply does not support the charge that Lutheran doctrine is inherently opposed or even merely poorly disposed to the promotion and development of Christian ethics. The Confessions, in fact, allow ample space for the application and practice of the vital and active sort of ethical agenda typical of virtue ethics and the deliberate formation of character.

THE NEED FOR A FRAMEWORK

While the approval and even promotion of Christian ethics is not, as some may suppose, a concept or activity alien to the Lutheran confessions, it cannot be denied that it has yet to gain a secure footing in the practice of contemporary Lutheranism.[4] The reason for this detachment and disparity between Lutheran confession and Lutheran practice has been the subject of assorted studies. Suggested culprits range from Enlightenment philosophy to over-zealous orthodoxy; and of course, there are those who yet insist that the problem is intrinsic to Lutheran doctrine itself.[5] Fascinating as this question is, the issue

3. Gerald Strauss summarizes his research into educational efforts of early Lutheranism with an assertion that "fatal inner contradictions" doomed the success of the Lutheran efforts at pedagogy. "Preachers and catechists," argues Strauss, "had to steer cautiously through the perilous theological narrows separating man's fallen condition from the promise of his ultimate deliverance through no merit of his own." Strauss concludes, then, that the reformers were "torn between their trust in the molding power of education and their admission that the alteration of men's nature was a task beyond human strength." See Gerald Strauss, *Luther's House of Learning: Indoctrination of the Young in the German Reformation* (Baltimore: Johns Hopkins University Press, 1978), 208, 300. As noted in previous chapters, Hauerwas also seems to favor a version of this assessment, and Yeago and Hütter both recognize its manifestations in today's Lutherans.

4. This is not to say that Lutheran seminaries do not teach courses on ethics or even theological ethics. They do. It is, rather, to say that too often questions of morality and Christian living are perceived or conveyed as somehow out of place or inappropriate for authentically Lutheran men and women to consider. Reinhard Hütter has labeled this tendency "Protestantism's antinomian captivity." For a thoughtful treatment of this problem, see Reinhard Hütter, "(Re-)Forming Freedom: Reflections 'After *Veritatis Splendor*' on Freedom's Fate in Modernity and Protestantism's Antinomian Captivity," *Modern Theology* 17, no. 2 (April 2001): 117–61.

5. For a classic example of the latter, see the complete argument made in Strauss, *Luther's House*. For just cause, Strauss's study is not without its critics, but Strauss will be considered more thoroughly in the following chapter. An altogether different, though nonetheless equally provocative, investigation leads David Yeago to point the finger of blame at Werner Elert. See David S. Yeago, "Gnosticism, Antinomianism, and Reformation Theology: Reflections on the Costs of a Construal," *Pro Ecclesia* 2, no.

currently under consideration does not depend on an answer to the "Why?" question. The argument of this book does not necessitate an assessment of blame against either an individual or, as is more likely, a host of villains. The present task is simply to help contemporary Lutheranism find a way out of its ethical irrelevance—or, put less critically, to reflect on the ethical task in a distinctively Lutheran way, thus clearing the way for Lutherans and other conscientious Christians actively to engage the work of character formation. This can be accomplished without the distraction of attempting to assign blame for the unfortunate unraveling of ethical reflection within the Lutheran tradition.

Even the present modest effort simply to recapture ethical relevance is not without its hazards. Gilbert Meilaender supplies a forthright assessment of the dangers:

> The attempt to say something *uniquely* Lutheran sometimes succeeds but more often fails—and nowhere is that failure more likely or more costly than in ethics. Attempts to say a uniquely Lutheran word about the moral life are likely to end either in an ethics that concerns itself with motives alone and gives no guidance about what deeds ought or ought not to be done, or an ethic that leaves the wisdom found in the kingdom of the left hand entirely untransformed by the mind of Christ.[6]

Although I am cognizant of the perils, the compelling practical need to clear space for training in character requires that the task be shouldered and an attempt be made to chart a safe course between the Scylla and Charybdis that Meilaender identifies and, in the process, address both of his concerns.

Lutheran believers living in the twenty-first century need some means for thinking about ethics in a way that is, for their lives, practical, relevant, and significant—but above all, meaningfully related to the central doctrine of justification. What is needed is a framework that can account for the wide range of material found in the Lutheran Confessions that is at once doctrinal and ethical.[7] Such a frame, it is hoped, would enable Lutheran believers to

---

1 (Winter 1993): 37–49. Not surprisingly, David Scaer lays the blame at the feet of pietism. See his preface in Adolf Köberle, *The Quest for Holiness: A Biblical, Historical and Systematic Investigation*, trans. John C. Mattes (New York: Harper & Brothers, 1938; reprint, Evansville, IN: Ballast, 1998), ix. Perhaps the most balanced and compelling study is that of Reinhard Hütter, "(Re-)Forming Freedom."

6. Gilbert Meilaender, "The Task of Lutheran Ethics," *Lutheran Forum* 34, no. 4 (Winter 2000): 17 (emphasis in original).

understand, manage, and meaningfully relate both the doctrinal truths of their faith as well as the ethical implications which spring from that faith.[8] Put another way, this frame must be capable of managing both the centrality of justification by grace through faith alone, as well as the practically useful tools acquired from the insights of virtue ethics.

Eventually, of course, an effective frame must serve to diminish, or even altogether erase, the false and often disastrous divorce between doctrine and ethics identified by Hauerwas and others.[9] Ultimately, a valid frame should be recognizable by the fact that it does not unite disparate parts but merely provides the means for recognizing the unity and connections that preexist when all elements of the picture are rightly viewed within the context supplied by the appropriate frame. In this chapter, a frame equal to these demands will be presented. First, however, some important yet not wholly sufficient attempts to account for the data—particularly the seemingly disparate relation between justification and ethics—will be considered.

MOTIVATION AS A FRAMEWORK

One of the most enduring attempts at a rapprochement between justification and Christian ethics, or what is essentially nothing more or less than the Christian's daily life, is the suggestion that the two interests are joined by the link of motivation. The frame follows a logical or theological progression like this: God grants salvation purely by divine grace, and so overcome with the resultant gratitude is the redeemed person that the life of sanctification inevitably blossoms. This approach to relating doctrinal truth with ethical realities continues to enjoy wide popularity among Lutheran laity and theologians alike. Generations of young confirmands have received their pastor's painstaking instruction that "good works are your 'thank-you note' to

7. "Framework" is meant simply as a label for the process or method of understanding or synthesizing whatever data are encountered in study or experience. "Framework" is roughly synonymous with a structuring horizon within which to place the data. The objective is not to obscure, confuse, or efface the frame—or to assume the existence of a universally assumed frame already in place. Such assumptions do not serve the church. Rather, the goal must be to articulate and suggest a frame within which to understand the confessional data so far considered. Certainly, the proposed framework should be capable of managing data from the scriptural record as well; the consideration of that material, however, lies well beyond the current project.

8. Of course, putting the matter this way runs the risk of abetting the cleavage between doctrine and ethics that Hauerwas has insightfully identified as a significant factor in the demise of vital Christian ethics. The use of this terminology should be understood not as an endorsement but merely as an acknowledgment of the status quo.

9. See the discussion in ch. 1 as well as the discussion to follow in ch. 5.

God."[10] The widely held belief that gratitude for God's gift of salvation supplies the driving force and the lone link between God's work of justification and the Christian's daily life gains further support from within Lutheran academia.[11]

Despite its broad popularity, however, Robert Benne identifies this obsessive interest in motivation as one of the principle obstacles to be overcome by a viable Lutheran ethic: "A persisting tendency in Lutheran ethics, is to reduce the whole of ethical life to the motivation touched off by justification. Dazzled as they are by the wonder and profundity of God's justifying grace in Christ, Lutherans are tempted to think that the only really interesting ethical question is the motivational one."[12] In other words, since the gospel is so overpoweringly and delightfully liberating, it eclipses all else, including any discussion of a continuing role of the law in the process of formation and training in righteousness. Benne labels this error "a kind of soteriological reductionism that downplays the role of the First and Third persons of the Trinity."[13] Benne's observation is accurate, as is his conclusion that the ethics that result from this position lack substance. "The gospel forgives and motivates," Benne notes, "but from what and to do what?"[14] The problem is that when Christian ethics is confined only to a consideration of justification's motivation, Benne's penetrating rhetorical question, "from what and to do

10. For a concurring view spelled out in print, see Edward W. A. Koehler, *A Short Explanation of Dr. Martin Luther's Small Catechism with Additional Notes* (River Forest, IL: Koehler, 1946), 187.

11. Theologians loath to admit a third use of the law—that is, a post-repentance use of the law as guide—are typically among this number. See William H. Lazareth, "Foundation for Christian Ethics: The Question of the 'Third Use' of the Law," in *Confession and Congregation*, ed. David G. Truemper (Valparaiso, IN: Valparaiso University Press, 1978), 48–56, and the response by Theodore R. Jungkuntz which follows, 57–59. Though his account is rich in theological nuance and usefulness, a form of gospel reductionism supportive of a motivational framework can also be detected in the work of Gerhard O. Forde. See his contribution, "Eleventh Locus: Christian Life," in Carl E. Braaten and Robert W. Jenson, eds., *Christian Dogmatics*, vol. 2 (Philadelphia: Fortress Press, 1984), 395–469. For a good example of the gospel alone as appropriate motivation for Christian living in practical application, see Delbert Schulz, "Law and Gospel in the Classroom," *Lutheran Education* 124, no. 3 (January/February 1989): 151–56. A capable rebuttal is provided by S. Jay Lemanski, "The Law in the Christian's Life—A Response," *Lutheran Education* 125, no. 1 (September/October 1989): 43–48.

12. Robert Benne, "Lutheran Ethics: Perennial Themes and Contemporary Challenges," in Karen L. Bloomquist and John R. Stumme, eds., *The Promise of Lutheran Ethics* (Minneapolis: Fortress Press, 1998), 27.

13. Ibid. Though Benne does not elaborate on this comment, the context indicates that he has in mind those who reduce their Christianity to the salvific work of Jesus Christ to the exclusion, or neglect, of the equally significant work of Father and Holy Spirit within creation and specifically in the life of the believer.

14. Ibid., 28.

what?" elicits little more than vacant stares of incomprehension from those intent on doing ethics "from the Gospel alone."

The notion that the motivation sparked by justification is able adequately to account for the ensuing Christian life of good works or growth in character faces its greatest challenge not from theological arguments, however, but from reality. In Romans 7, the apostle Paul forthrightly admits his ongoing struggle to maintain a life of Christian character even after receiving the gift of justification.[15] Luther himself was compelled to reconsider his dreams of a gospel-induced revolution of Christian living after his eyewitness encounter with reality during the Saxon visitation.[16] Neither should one casually dismiss the testimony of countless multitudes of wise Christian parents who for generations have relied upon more than the "gospel motivation" of justification in rearing their children. Meilaender provides a blunt admission of this reality:

> The problem: Why do parents worry about where their children go to school, about their playmates and peers, about the ways they use their free time, about the television shows they watch? They worry because all of us know that Aristotle was—at least to some extent—right. Moral virtue *is* habit long continued. The inner spirit is shaped and developed by the structures within which we live, the things we see and do daily.[17]

It is fascinating, and extremely telling and relevant, to recognize that Luther, as a parent, also gave heed to this reality. The same week that the Augsburg Confession was presented to Emperor Charles, Luther penned a letter to his four-year-old son, Hans, in Wittenberg. Luther, of course, was confined to the relative safety of the Koburg Fortress while Melanchthon worked in Augsburg to craft the Confession, with much regular guidance from Luther via a vigorous written correspondence. During that busy time, Luther's thoughts turned toward home as he wrote to Hans. A full appreciation of Luther's parenting method and necessary theological underpinnings warrants quoting the letter in its entirety:

15. For an excellent account of Scripture's failure to conform to the notion that the motivation created by justification is sufficient to account for the whole of the ethical life, see Paul R. Raabe and James W. Voelz, "Why Exhort a Good Tree? Anthropology and Paraenesis in Romans," *Concordia Journal* 22, no. 2 (April 1996): 154–63.

16. See the discussion in the previous chapter, page 95.

17. Gilbert Meilaender, *The Limits of Love: Some Theological Explorations* (University Park: Pennsylvania State University Press, 1987), 36 (emphasis in original).

To my beloved son Hänschen Luther at Wittenberg

Grace and peace in Christ! My beloved son: I am pleased to learn that you are doing well in your studies, and that you are praying diligently. Continue to do so, my son [and] when I return home I shall bring you a nice present from the fair.

I know a pretty, beautiful, [and] cheerful garden where there are many children wearing little golden coats. [They] pick up fine apples, pears, cherries, [and] yellow and blue plums under the trees; they sing, jump, and are merry. They also have nice ponies with golden reins and silver saddles. I asked the owner of the garden whose children they were. He replied: "These are the children who like to pray, study, and be good." Then I said: "Dear sir, I also have a son, whose name is Hänschen Luther. Might he not also [be permitted] to enter the garden, so that he too could eat such fine apples and pears, and ride on these pretty ponies, and play with these children?" Then the man answered: "If he too likes to pray, study, and be good, he too may enter the garden, and also Lippus and Jost. And when they are all together [there], they will also get whistles, drums, lutes, and all kinds of other stringed instruments; and they will also dance, and shoot with little crossbows." And he showed me there a lovely lawn in the garden, all prepared for dancing, where many gold whistles and drums and fine sliver crossbows were hanging. But it was still so early [in the morning] that the children had not yet eaten; therefore I couldn't wait for the dancing. So I said to the man: "Dear sir, I shall hurry away and write about all this to my dear son Hänschen so that he will certainly study hard, pray diligently, and be good in order that he too may get into this garden. But he has an Aunt Lena, whom he must bring along." "By all means," said the man, "go and write him accordingly."

Therefore, dear son Hänschen, do study and pray diligently, and tell Lippus and Jost to study and pray too; then you [boys] will get into the garden together. Herewith I commend you to the dear Lord ['s keeping]. Greet Aunt Lena, and give her a kiss for me.

Your loving father Martin Luther[18]

18. From *Letters II*, LW 49, ed. Helmut T. Lehmann, trans. Gerhard A. Krodel (Philadelphia: Fortress Press, 1972), 323–24.

To say that Luther was willing to allow inducements toward the cultivation of good character other than simple appeals to the reality of justification by grace alone is a vast understatement. Luther actively employs the very best techniques of classic parental "bribery" with no hint of hesitation or embarrassment. Indeed, he employs them with such unabashed fervor and zeal that most modern Lutheran parents blush to hear them, and worry about Luther's ready willingness to tell a tall tale to his young son. For his part, Luther, it seems likely, would have offered his epistle as a concrete instance of the "playful . . . kind and agreeable methods" of childrearing he endorsed in lieu of beatings.[19] Five centuries removed from the Reformation, the prospect of a morning spent dancing would probably strike most young boys as a less-than-agreeable threat on a par with corporal punishment; but Luther's "fine sliver crossbows," it seems likely, would still serve as a remarkably effective "carrot" for young males even in the twenty-first century. More to the point, it is altogether intriguing that Luther has nothing to say to Hans about the child's baptismal identity or the wonderful gift of justification by grace alone that from Luther's perspective was his son's greatest possession. Apparently, these points were not particularly relevant in the composition of this letter. In the context of encouraging good behavior and cultivating character in his child, Luther employs techniques that he has learned to trust. To put it bluntly: he uses the law.

It is essential that there is no misunderstanding: there is certainly no intent on my part—or on Luther's part, for that matter—to denigrate the regenerative power of justification, or its ability to foster genuine conversions of character and behavior. The extraordinary message of the gospel does spark remarkable transformations—justification does motivate a zeal for increasing holiness.[20] The problem comes when the whole of ethics is reduced to the question of motivation—good works as the intuitive, inevitable, and automatic outcome of gospel proclamation. As the previous chapter revealed, the reformers themselves were well aware of this potential liability and so supplemented their ebullient praise for justification's life-altering power with concrete exhortations for the exceedingly practical, and often mundane, business of disciplined Christian living.[21] This is precisely what Luther is doing in his letter to young Hans. There is no indication whatsoever that Luther somehow feels constrained to

19. *Book of Concord*, 396 (LC I, 76).

20. A point made with unparalleled eloquence and verve by Luther in his Romans preface and quoted in the Formula: "It [faith] kills the old 'Adam' and makes us altogether different people. . . . O, it is a living, busy, active, mighty thing this faith." *Book of Concord*, 576 (FC SD 4, 10-12).

21. Of course, this is also the established pattern for the biblical writers, evident especially in the structure of Paul's letters.

make moral appeals based only on the gospel or to induce good behavior and actions motivated by the gospel alone. In fact, the opposite is the case.

The tendency to circumscribe Christian ethics exclusively within a motivation of gratitude is so prevalent among believers, particularly Lutheran believers, that it is helpful to consider another dissenting voice. Adolf Köberle's mid-twentieth-century Lutheran classic, *The Quest for Holiness*, is sometimes regarded as an affirmation of those who would curtail the role of intentional Christian ethics, making ethics simply the automatic fruit of justification. Without question, the first portion of Köberle's work makes the quintessential case for sanctification as fully the activity of God alone. Köberle continues his argument, however, by acknowledging and heartily affirming the scriptural emphasis on human responsibility for one's own morality and then warning his readers against any view of ethics that does not take this into account: "But to make ethics depend only 'on the slender thread of thankfulness' (Schlatter) would be to underestimate the terrible power of sin, whose nature according to the fine description of the Second Article of the Augsburg Confession consists in the lack of fear of God (*sine metu*), and so can be overcome only through the awakening of a holy fear."[22] In words that sound oddly un-Lutheran, Köberle bluntly recommends complementing the motive of gratitude with the less attractive, yet highly effective, motive of fear: "At the end of days the judgement [sic] will actually be passed on the works of the sinner and of the righteous, and so the fear of displeasing God must accompany even the life of the believer as a holy fear and as an aid in overcoming temptation."[23]

Köberle is confident that the creation of this holy fear can restore ethics to its rightful place within the Christian faith: "When men are unequivocally taught that the saving faith that has been given through Word and Sacrament will be lost if it be without the actual following of Christ in obedience and love, then the antinomian misunderstanding that has followed in the steps of the Gospel like some dark shadow, even to our own day, will finally be overcome."[24] Augmenting the motive of gratitude with the motive of fear provides a significant corrective for the moral laxity that can damn as capably as its antithesis, legalism. The Confessions themselves recognize the threat and make a similar claim:

22. Köberle, *Quest for Holiness*, 168.

23. Ibid., 166. Köberle's counsel is not so different from Luther's stern admonition in his explanation of what is termed the close of the Commandments: "God threatens to punish all who break these commandments. Therefore we are to fear his wrath and not disobey these commandments." *Book of Concord*, 354 (SC TC 22).

24. Köberle, *Quest for Holiness*, 246.

> For the old creature, like a stubborn, recalcitrant donkey, is also still a part of them [believers], and it needs to be forced into obedience to Christ not only through the law's teaching, admonition, compulsion, and threat but also often with the cudgel of punishments and tribulations until the sinful flesh is completely stripped away and people are perfectly renewed in the resurrection.[25]

As Köberle and the Formula of Concord both make clear, motivation is wholly inadequate as a framework within which to account for all that the Confessions, and for that matter the Scriptures, have to say about the Christian life. One significant problem is the subjective nature of the motivational emphasis. Whether the motivation is gratitude or even fear, the arena of ethics then hinges on internal psychological responses in the believer.

Stanley Hauerwas helpfully elaborates on this liability of the motivation scheme. When "religious beliefs," Hauerwas contends, "are relegated to the motivational or subjective side of the moral life . . . they can have no possible bearing on the way the moral life is conceived or lived."[26] In other words, when ethics is confined to the question of motivation, the Christian's faith is only able to speak about *why* that Christian should live a "holy life," but when asked *what* that life should look like, or *how* it should be cultivated, faith has nothing to say. All that matters is motive. As long as the motive has a divine source, the particular shape or content of the ethics must remain an open question, answered only according to the choices, or perhaps whims, of each individual. Overcome and displaced by the "why" of ethical behavior, the "what" of that behavior fades into insignificance and irrelevance. Preoccupation with the question of motivation leaves character formation eviscerated and those concerned with the formation of virtuous behavior with but one option: talk incessantly about God's unconditional love and hope for the best.

The question of motivation proves to be altogether inadequate as a comprehensive account of the task of Christian ethics. A Christian ethic founded only on motivation fosters an obsession with elusive internal responses and self-evaluations and tends to minimize external standards of behavior. To reduce the ethical question to one of motivation produces a framework that not only fails to account for the breadth of the confessional and experiential data, but in fact further complicates and distorts the picture.[27] The question of motivation has its place in ethical discussions, no doubt. Motivation speaks

25. *Book of Concord*, 591 (FC SD 6, 24).

26. Stanley Hauerwas, with Richard Bondi and David B. Burrell, *Truthfulness and Tragedy: Further Investigations in Christian Ethics* (Notre Dame, IN: University of Notre Dame Press, 1977), 42.

meaningfully to the relation between a Christian's standing before God and that Christian's responsibility within the created world. But this is only one part of the ethical picture. Much more remains to be said.

Law and Gospel as a Frame

The possibility of using the motivation initiated by the gospel as a framework for understanding the scope and location of Christian ethics has been considered as a distinct option and dismissed as insufficient. In truth, the motivational frame should be recognized as a subset of a somewhat broader framework: the dynamic of law and gospel. Of course, no theological frame is so characteristically Lutheran as that of the law/gospel dialectic. In our vertical relationship with God, the dynamic of the law that convicts, crushes, and kills, and the gospel that forgives, comforts, and makes alive is the distinctive Christian frame that defines all else.[28] Yet, in spite of its critical importance to the paramount question of one's standing before God, or *coram Deo*, the dialectic does not serve well as an all-encompassing frame into which everything in theology and life can be made to fit. The pressing problem is that the duality's undeniable beneficial aspects are forfeited when the tension is pushed into a negative versus positive polarity and applied indiscriminately in all of life's circumstances. At that point, the otherwise fruitful paradigm actually forces apart what must be kept together and declares one half of the duality to be essentially irrelevant—or worse. The reality of this threat and its significance as a genuine liability is better appreciated in light of the propensity of theologians, or perhaps human nature generally, to gravitate to one or the other of the poles. Indeed, Köberle accurately recognizes, "the painful impression that theological perception is apparently unable to apprehend or express more than one statement in its entirety."[29] In other words, theologians have a hard time adequately maintaining potent tensions. And as David Yeago argues convincingly, never is this inability properly to sustain the tension more in evidence than with the law/gospel duality.[30]

27. A motivational framework cannot make sense of Melanchthon's use of Aristotle or the confessional encouragement of habituation as considered in the previous chapter.

28. Hence, this frame is critically important in many situations of pastoral counsel where the need is the conviction of sin and then the proclamation of grace and forgiveness. This was also the driving concern of Melanchthon in article 12 of the Augustana and Apology. In the vertical dimension, it is the law's second, or theological, use that is in action. The law's third use, on the other hand, applies directly to the horizontal realm.

29. Köberle, *Quest for Holiness*, 208.

30. Yeago, "Gnosticism." See the full discussion in ch. 2.

The singular vulnerability of the law/gospel framework to be collapsed into an oppositional polarity has a host of underlying causes, led by the aversion of many to any understanding of a "third use" of the law. An exploration of this problem is certainly warranted and unquestionably fascinating; for the sake of the present argument, though, the temptation to pursue it must be resisted.[31] In the current discussion, it is enough to recognize the persistent problem that when a law/gospel polarity becomes the universal frame for all theological and ethical thinking, it inevitably succumbs in practice to the affirmation of one pole and the rejection of the other. The unintended fruit of a law/gospel framework may be either a legalistic absorption in self-justifying works (the loss of the gospel), or at the opposite extreme, the very licentious and antinomian attitudes that prompted this study (the loss of the law).[32] Again, for a variety of reasons, the duality proves exceptionally difficult to maintain in practice; the balance is tipped, frequently, in one direction or the other, with predictable results.

While few Lutherans are foolhardy enough to subscribe openly to legalistic or antinomian theories or theologies, practical legalists and practical antinomians abound. The theologians considered in chapter 2, particularly David Yeago and Reinhard Hütter, provide compelling accounts of the current consequences of the misuse and misapplication of the potent dialectic of law and gospel. Their analysis is clear: the balance today is tilted sharply in the antinomian direction. This current problem is far from novel. Indeed, it is intriguing to note the remarkable correspondence between the assessment of today's church offered by Benne, Hütter, Meilaender, and Yeago, and Köberle's evaluation of the Western church of the 1930s. Köberle wrote:

> Today, in view of the crass weakness and unbridled license in nation and Church, at home and in heathen lands, the danger of luxury and debauchery must appear much greater than its legalistic opposite. The number of those destroyed by the mad zeal of monastic methods of seeking sanctification is small compared with the millions who are the victims of the lowest defilements of the flesh. A one-sided opposition that is directed exclusively against work-righteousness cannot for the time being be the task of theology.[33]

---

31. Fortunately, that study has already been undertaken and accomplished successfully. See Scott R. Murray, *Law, Life, and the Living God: The Third Use of Law in Modern American Lutheranism* (St. Louis: Concordia, 2002).

32. The history of Lutheranism provides examples of both extremes, with the law-consumed pietists of a past era contrasting with today's gospel-cloaked antinomians.

Despite the significant shortcomings of the law/gospel framework for ethical thinking, there are nevertheless no shortage of those who promote or at least assume the adequacy of the dialectic as the ultimate and final structuring frame for Christian doctrine and life. While he does not employ the framework vocabulary, Carter Lindberg essentially argues for the sufficiency of the law/ gospel dialectic. In an article specifically addressing the Lutheran relationship between justification and sanctification, Lindberg concludes:

> Do Lutheran theologians shout justification, but whisper sanctification? No. Their rejection of any concept of sanctification apart from justification is loud and clear. Leading contemporary Lutheran theologians follow Luther in rejecting all forms of theology per *modum Aristoteles*. The Christian life is not a progress from vice to virtue but a continual starting anew by grace, *simul iustus et peccator*.[34]

In Lindberg's view, the Christian life—justification along with sanctification—can be fully explained and subsumed within the dynamic of law and gospel. Considered from a perspective *coram Deo*, Lindberg is right. But this is only one perspective, and neither the complete portrait nor full story. By addressing the question of sanctification without also taking into account *coram mundo* realities of ethics and character, Lindberg gives tacit endorsement of the sufficiency of law and gospel as an overall framework. And by his summary dismissal of the pursuit of virtue he provides a vivid illustration of the inability of this paradigm to speak to questions of habituation and character formation.

Gerhard Forde can be similarly understood. He states, "If justification is unconditional and total, it explodes into love and good works."[35] Again, this is indisputably true—as far as it goes. But it does not go far enough. Whether he intends it or not, Forde can be heard as underwriting the idea that little or no further training or instruction in Christian living is necessary or even desirable. While both Lindberg and Forde offer important and accurate arguments for the centrality of the gospel and its role in the Christian's life, especially within the *coram Deo* relationship, their positions cannot account for all of the data compiled in the previous chapter's investigation of the Confessions.[36] Although the law/gospel dynamic might be assumed to be the authentically Lutheran

---

33. Köberle, *Quest for Holiness*, 194.

34. Carter Lindberg, "Do Lutherans Shout Justification But Whisper Sanctification?" *Lutheran Quarterly* 13 (Spring 1999): 15.

35. Forde, "Eleventh Locus," 434.

framework, it is not only incapable of managing all the realities and challenges of life and doctrine but, used as an overall framework, it is finally detrimental to the vitality of Lutheranism.[37]

Two Kinds of Righteousness as a Frame

The challenge of proposing a system of Christian ethics that a Lutheran can embrace with confidence is finding a way to express a meaningful and dynamic understanding of the Christian's life that takes character formation into account and yet remains vitally connected to the great truths of the gospel without in any way diminishing those truths. Two typical answers to this challenge have been considered and found wanting. The motivation answer (a new motivation sparked by the gospel simply produces good works) conveys elements of truth and accords with some scriptural and confessional statements, particularly the image of a good tree bearing good fruit. Still, it does not account for all the data revealed in a brief survey of the Confessions. Likewise, the law/gospel dialectic is good and right in its appropriate sphere—*coram Deo* issues of soteriology—yet quite inadequate when pressed into service as a norming frame for all doctrinal thinking and ethical living. Neither of these frames, for example, is able to provide a place for Melanchthon's approval and use of Aristotle. Another considerably more suitable frame derives from another great duality within Lutheranism: the two kinds of righteousness.[38]

As the previous chapter demonstrated, the duality of two kinds of righteousness was critically important for Melanchthon and the other reformers. This twofold understanding of righteousness provides a much more effective framework within which to consider the complexities of faith and life than does the law-and-gospel dialectic just considered. As a framework, the two-kinds-of-righteousness paradigm is also much less vulnerable to the ill effects of misconstrual than the classic law/gospel paradigm. Expressing the distinction between the righteousness of faith and the righteousness of the law, as well as the legitimacy of both, helps to expand the theological and ethical horizon beyond solely *coram Deo* questions to include also the concerns of living *coram*

---

36. For example, the exhortation in the Apology: "All people, whatever their calling, should seek perfection, that is, growth in the fear of God, in faith, in the love for their neighbor, and in similar spiritual virtues." *Book of Concord*, 283 (Ap, 27, 37). See the full discussion in ch. 3.

37. This was the crux of Yeago's important argument already considered above in ch. 2.

38. Luther is generally credited with formulating this distinction. His sermon, "Two Kinds of Righteousness," from 1519 provided the terminology of "alien righteousness" and "proper righteousness," distinguishing between the righteousness passively received by the believer and the subsequent righteousness of life actively pursued by the believer. LW 31:297–306; WA 2:145–47.

mundo. In particular, the recognition of the propriety of civil righteousness within the horizontal realm provides a vantage point for the consideration of life and activity in the realm of the left hand where Christians actually live and function.[39] The left-hand realm with its civil righteousness is certainly within the purview of ethics—Christian ethics, as well as non-Christian ethics.

Luther testified to the significance and usefulness of the duality of two kinds of righteousness in the preface to his 1535 Galatians commentary. In keeping with his historical context, Luther uses the distinction primarily to extol the wonder and glory of the righteousness of faith. "It is a marvelous thing and unknown to the world," he declares, "to teach Christians to ignore the Law and to live *before God* as though there were no Law whatever."[40] Before God, not the law, but grace prevails. In the world, however, Luther knew that it was a different matter altogether: "On the other hand, works and the performance of the Law must be demanded *in the world* as though there were no promise or grace."[41] Two different realms require two different understandings of righteousness. There is one kind of righteousness *coram Deo* and another *coram mundo.* Luther's preferred terminology in his Galatians introduction is to name the Christian's righteousness before God as passive, while the righteousness necessarily pursued before humans in this world he labels active.[42]

Robert Kolb was among the first contemporary theologians to grasp the scriptural basis and rich theological potential in Luther's too-often overlooked and undervalued distinction of the two kinds of righteousness.

39. Along with his two kinds of righteousness, Luther also taught the need to discern between two kingdoms or realms: one, the realm of divine realities and justifying faith, or the right-hand realm; the other, the realm of the created world, or the left-hand realm. A Christian inhabits both realms under the jurisdiction of both authorities. The definitive treatment remains Luther's treatise, "Temporal Authority: To What Extent it should be Obeyed," in LW 45:81–129. The subject is also handled admirably by Robert Benne, *The Paradoxical Vision: A Public Theology for the Twenty-first Century* (Minneapolis: Fortress Press, 1995).

40. LW 26:6 (emphasis added).

41. Ibid. (emphasis added).

42. Ibid., 4–5. Luther's enumeration of the varieties of righteousness, not atypically, is somewhat less than thoroughly systematic. While he distinguishes two kinds of righteousness throughout the introduction, in the opening discussion he suggests the existence of many additional varieties of righteousness: "For righteousness is of many kinds. There is political righteousness. . . . There is ceremonial righteousness. . . . There is, in addition to these, yet another righteousness, the righteousness of the Law or the Decalog, which Moses teaches. . . . Over and above all these there is the righteousness of faith or Christian righteousness, which is to be distinguished most carefully from all the others" (LW 26:4). The possible implications of these other righteousnesses will be considered later in this chapter.

In developing this contrast between passive righteousness—which expresses itself in faith—and active righteousness—which expresses itself in performing the deeds of God's plan for human life—Luther was bringing to light a fundamental distinction that had escaped articulation by most theologians since the time of the apostles. This distinction recognizes and rests upon Christ's observation that human life consists of two kinds of relationship, one with the author and creator of life, the other with all other creatures (Matt. 22:37-39).[43]

The value of Luther's distinction is not lost on Kolb, who indicates the ability of the two kinds of righteousness to serve as a frame not only for theological endeavor but thinking about all of human existence.

God's human creatures are right—really human—in their vertical relationships because their faith embraces the God who loves them through Jesus Christ with the reckless trust of total dependence and reliance on him which constitutes their identity. They are right—really human—in their horizontal relationship with God's other creatures when they live a life which is active in reflecting his love through the deeds that deliver his care and concern.[44]

The teaching of two kinds of righteousness as articulated by Luther and further elaborated by Kolb addresses fundamental questions about human existence, purpose, and relation to God. This teaching provides a rich understanding of human life lived both *coram Deo* and *coram mundo*. Indeed, the kind of substantial treatment that Kolb gives the topic very nearly provides precisely the kind of frame that will be sufficient for the development of a specifically Lutheran Christian ethic.

Nevertheless, an attempt to employ the two kinds of righteousness as a norming frame for all of theology and the Christian life is not without its difficulties. The previous chapter's reading of the Confessions revealed that while Melanchthon commended the teaching of civil righteousness along with the righteousness of faith, at times his presentation can be read as limiting the application of civil righteousness solely to the unregenerate.[45] Civil

---

43. Robert Kolb, "Luther on the Two Kinds of Righteousness: Reflections on His Two-Dimensional Definition of Humanity at the Heart of His Theology," *Lutheran Quarterly* 113, no. 4 (Winter 1999): 452.

44. Ibid., 453.

45. For example: "Therefore it is helpful to distinguish between civil righteousness, which is ascribed to the free will, and spiritual righteousness, which is ascribed to the operation of the Holy Spirit in the

righteousness seen as strictly an application of the law's first use fails to embrace adequately all aspects of the believer's new life—particularly one's *coram mundo* responsibilities. Nor does it create space for talk of growth in holiness or the cultivation of holy habits leading to the cultivation of Christian character. Kolb avoids this criticism by following Luther in developing the distinction in terms of passive and active righteousness. *Active* righteousness provides a wider and so more inclusive term than does *civil* righteousness. The dichotomy of active righteousness and passive righteousness is, then, better able to handle both the *coram Deo* elements as well as the *coram mundo* aspects of the Christian's life. A strict emphasis on civil righteousness versus the righteousness of faith—as Melanchthon sometimes treats it—however, runs the risk of encouraging a rift between doctrine and ethics. Civil righteousness could be perceived as unspiritual, something exclusively for those without faith, thus lending credence to the unfortunate notion that Christians need not, indeed *should* not, concern themselves with ethics.[46]

Talk of two kinds of righteousness, then, is burdened with a certain amount of ambiguity, an ambiguity exacerbated by the multiplication of synonyms for the various types of righteousnesses produced by both Luther and his younger colleague. One could easily compile a list of a score of righteousnesses named by the two reformers. A way out of this difficulty begins by recognizing a distinction between Luther's "righteousness of the law" and Melanchthon's "civil righteousness." The civil righteousness Melanchthon endorses in the Apology is rightly understood in its most natural sense—a righteousness governing the behavior of all humanity, redeemed and otherwise. Melanchthon followed this distinction in his 1524 "Summary of Doctrine," where he wrote: "Accordingly, besides Christian righteousness there is human righteousness, by which the wicked should be coerced."[47]

Luther's references to righteousness of the law, on the other hand, are best interpreted in terms of the Christian who already possesses the righteousness of faith, or Christian righteousness. Consider the subject of the righteousness of the law in Luther's Galatians discussion:

regenerate. In this way outward discipline is preserved, because all people alike ought to know that God requires civil righteousness and that to some extent we are able to achieve it." *Book of Concord*, 234 (Ap 18, 9).

46. This was the danger highlighted by Meilaender, as noted as the outset of this chapter. See Meilaender's comments in "Task of Lutheran Ethics," 17.

47. Philipp Melanchthon, *Melanchthon: Selected Writings*, trans. Charles Leander Hill (Minneapolis: Augsburg, 1962), 97.

We set forth two worlds, as it were, one of them heavenly and the other earthly. Into these we place these two kinds of righteousness, which are distinct and separated from each other. The righteousness of the Law is earthly and deals with earthly things; by it we perform good works. But as the earth does not bring forth fruit unless it has first been watered and made fruitful from above—for the earth cannot judge, renew, and rule the heavens, but the heavens judge, renew, rule, and fructify the earth, so that it may do what the Lord has commanded—so also by the righteousness of the Law we do nothing even when we do much; we do not fulfill the Law even when we fulfill it. Without any merit or work of our own, we must first be justified by Christian righteousness, which has nothing to do with the righteousness of the Law or with earthly and active righteousness.[48]

It seems clear that Luther's "we" is referring to Christians, to whom active righteousness applies. Though the label "two kinds of righteousness" applies to the distinctions of both Luther and Melanchthon, it does not consistently mean the same thing for both. It is also wise to remember that Melanchthon and Luther chose their particular twofold distinctions in light of their respective occasions for writing. Melanchthon sought to defend the Lutheran teaching of justification against charges that it bred moral laxity. Luther's distinction was made for the benefit of the Christian readers of his commentary. The lack of consistency in the use of terms and the consequent potential for confusion remains, nonetheless.

THREE KINDS OF RIGHTEOUSNESS: LUTHER AND MELANCHTHON

One could endeavor to distinguish these two varieties of "two kinds of righteousness" by labeling one as Luther's and the other as Melanchthon's. This would not be entirely accurate, however, since at times, either can operate within the other's parameters.[49] A better way to clarify the issue might be to impose a more precise systemization and speak of three kinds of righteousness. Conveniently enough, Luther does exactly this in a sermon from 1518: "Three

48. LW 26:8.

49. Also in his Galatians commentary, Luther writes, "Christian righteousness applies to the new man, and the righteousness of the Law applies to the old man, who is born of flesh and blood" (LW 26:7). While this distinction does not exclude Christians from the righteousness of the law, neither does it exclude unbelievers. Melanchthon's use of categories later endorsed by Luther will be examined in what follows.

Kinds of Righteousness." In this sermon, the reformer pairs three kinds of sin (criminal, original, actual) with three respective kinds of righteousness (apparent, alien, active). The first category, apparent righteousness, has nothing to do with Christians: "Secondly, it serves not God, but itself, nor is it the righteousness of sons, but of slaves, nor is it a particular characteristic of Christians, but of Jews and gentiles, nor will Christians be exhorted to it, because it results from fear of punishment or from love of what is convenient for oneself, not from love of God."[50] This first righteousness is the kind encountered in the civil world that operates without concern or regard for the Triune God. The second two kinds of righteousness, on the other hand, are strictly for Christians. Luther pairs the second kind of righteousness with essential or original sin and names it appropriately: essential, original, or alien righteousness.[51] Luther describes the unique aspects of this righteousness: "This [righteousness] becomes ours through faith. . . . This [righteousness] is imputed through Baptism, this is characteristically how the Gospel announces, and is not righteousness of law, but righteousness of grace."[52]

Luther next expounds his sermon's third kind of righteousness, the one that corresponds to actual sin: "The righteousness over against this [actual sin] is actual, flowing from faith and essential [or alien] righteousness."[53] Thus the third kind of righteousness has its source in the second kind of righteousness and describes the believer's growth in holiness: "Because that third righteousness is sought for nothing other than that original sin be overcome and the body of sin be destroyed."[54] The third kind of righteousness, actual righteousness, flows from the faith characteristic of the second righteousness and so is unique to believers, as they alone possess faith. Why Luther later advocated two kinds of righteousness rather than three is a matter of speculation. However, the explanation could be as simple as addressing the need of the moment. Speaking to Christians, Luther may have considered it unnecessary to discuss the first and, in his thinking, irrelevant kind of righteousness. It is interesting, however, that in his Galatians introduction, with its passive and active division, Luther first recognizes the existence of "many kinds" of righteousness.[55] One could easily group the first two examples in his list (political and ceremonial) within the first category of the threefold division

---

50. WA 2:43 (the translations of these sermon excerpts are my own).

51. Ibid., 44.

52. Ibid., 45.

53. Ibid.

54. Ibid., 47.

55. LW 26:4.

advanced in his sermon from 1518. It is possible, then, to detect a threefold division of righteousnesses even in his most explicit endorsement of a twofold division.

Thirteen years later, it was Melanchthon who set forth a similar distinction of three kinds of righteousness in his disputation, "We Are Justified by Faith and Not by Love": "There are three kinds of righteousness. The first is that which is derived from reason. The second is that which conforms to the law of God. The third is that which the Gospel promises."[56] Before considering fuller definitions of each kind of righteousness, is should be noted that neither Melanchthon's terminology nor his order precisely coheres with that of Luther in his 1518 sermon. Melanchthon elaborates on each kind of righteousness as the disputation progresses. "The righteousness of reason," he writes, "is the righteousness of works, and reason produces it."[57] While people could understand the righteousness of reason, they could not comprehend the righteousness of the law that "consists of love toward God and neighbor."[58] The gospel's righteousness is that which justifies: "It is certain that we are justified neither by reason, nor by the law, but by the Gospel."[59]

In this disputation, Melanchthon recognizes a distinction between the righteousness of reason and the righteousness of the law. The latter depends on the righteousness of the gospel:

> The promise is received by faith. For that reason we are first justified by faith, by which we receive the promise of reconciliation by faith. Thereafter we keep the law. Nevertheless, since we are born anew by faith and have received the Holy Spirit, the righteousness of the law is present in us, namely, love for God and neighbor, fear of God, obedience toward governmental authorities and parents, patience, and similar virtues.[60]

56. Robert Kolb and James A. Nestingen, eds., *Sources and Contexts of The Book of Concord* (Minneapolis: Fortress Press, 2001), 141 (thesis 6); Johannes Haussleiter, ed., "Melanchthons *loci praecipui* und Thesen über die Rechtfertigung aus dem Jahre 1531," in *Abhandlungen Alexander von Oettingen zum siebenzigsten Geburtstag gewidmet von Freunden und Schülern* (Munich: Beck, 1898), 252.

57. Kolb and Nestingen, *Sources and Contexts*, 141 (thesis 10); Haussleiter, "Melanchthons," 252.

58. Kolb and Nestingen, *Sources and Contexts*, 141 (thesis 13); Haussleiter, "Melanchthons," 252.

59. Kolb and Nestingen, *Sources and Contexts*, 141 (thesis 7); Haussleiter, "Melanchthons," 252.

60. Kolb and Nestingen, *Sources and Contexts*, 142 (theses 17 & 19). Haussleiter, "Melanchthons," 253. Immediately before these two theses, Melanchthon wrote: "It is necessary, therefore, for the righteousness of the promise to be present before the righteousness of the law or reason" (thesis 16). It is altogether curious that Melanchthon added "or reason" since this seems to deny his earlier comment that the righteousness of reason could be apprehended by human beings even without knowledge of the gospel,

The righteousness of the law excels that of reason, in that it includes also love of God and higher standards of obedience. The Christian virtue of humility, or the rule of love for one's enemy, are both good examples of standards stemming from the law that surpass what can be expected from a standard founded on reason alone. And while Melanchthon relates the righteousness of the law to the righteousness of the gospel, he maintains a stringent distinction between them:

> James rightly teaches, "We are justified by faith and works," because works justify according to the righteousness of the law, which certainly ought to follow faith. Nevertheless, this righteousness of the law is not righteousness *in God's sight* except on account of faith.

> And the resulting works, because they please God on account of faith, are also meritorious, not for righteousness or eternal life but for other blessings of body and soul.[61]

The difference is grounded in the recognition of the different realms within which the Christian functions: *coram Deo* and *coram mundo*. Righteousness of the law is specifically concerned with a Christian's life in relation to *coram mundo* realities.

Both Luther and Melanchthon, each in his own way, work to make an absolute separation between the righteousness of faith, which justifies before God, and the other kinds of righteousness, which are interested in the concrete realities tied to living in the created realm. Both reformers also take the additional step of carefully distinguishing between two kinds of this-worldly righteousness: the one that is achieved by pagans seeking to live uprightly before others, and the other that is manifest in those who are justified by Christ and by faith living according to the dictates of God's revealed law. Using this rich teaching of Reformation theology as a foundation, it is time to return to the task of constructing a workable framework that will allow for a robust teaching of ethics—including the intentional inculcation of virtues and the resulting formation of character.

---

and it hardly seems likely in view of his careful distinction between law and reason that he means them here to be understood as synonyms. It seems highly likely from the standpoint of consistency within Melanchthon's argument that the variant reading, which omits "*aut rationis*" ("or reason"), should be preferred.

61. Kolb and Nestingen, *Sources and Contexts*, 143 (theses 33 & 34; emphasis added); Haussleiter, "Melanchthons," 254.

THREE KINDS OF RIGHTEOUSNESS: TOWARD AN EFFECTIVE FRAMEWORK

As a framework, the two-kinds-of-righteousness paradigm is more than adequate for distinguishing the difference between human righteousness *coram Deo* and human righteousness *coram mundo*. A two-kinds-of-righteousness frame is particularly useful in highlighting the spiritual realities of the human creature's relationship with the Creator while still making room to address concerns that are more earthbound. The advantage of a framework built on three kinds of righteousness is that it makes it possible to clarify further the differences within the horizontal or this-world righteousness, however it is named. Recognizing three kinds of righteousness obviously distinguishes the unique place of righteousness before God over against righteousness before humanity; but it has the added benefit of bringing greater clarity to the latter by accenting the distinction between the *coram mundo* righteousness of believers and that of unbelievers. The importance of this asset becomes immediately apparent when confronting the criticism that the two-kinds-of-righteousness paradigm eliminates the unique aspects of the Christian life and equates the morality of a "righteous pagan" with that of a faithful follower of Christ. Without a doubt, the life of a faithful Christian is different—a point enthusiastically made by the apostle Paul with some regularity—and, following both Luther and Melanchthon, by recognizing three kinds of righteousness, allows the differences to be highlighted and explored. More will be said about this in the next chapter.

Of course, establishing the value and desirability of a threefold framework does not yet provide the particular details of that framework. Exactly how the three kinds of righteousness should be described is a matter for some consideration. Luther and Melanchthon offered two versions of three kinds of righteousness, with noteworthy differences. It is difficult to settle on one as superior. Both Luther's and Melanchthon's threefold divisions offer useful aspects, and favoring one over the other risks forfeiting the other's strengths. Starting with a righteousness common to all people, then considering a person's righteousness before God, and concluding with the Christian's righteousness before humanity—Luther's order follows a familiar chronology of the salvation experience. Melanchthon's account—beginning with the righteousness of reason, then taking up the righteousness of Christians conforming to the law, and concluding with the righteousness of the gospel—has the strength of clarity and precision, particularly in distinguishing the righteousness of reason from the righteousness of the law. Well aware of the hazards of innovation, it is helpful, nonetheless, to draw on the careful thinking of both Luther and

Melanchthon, and offer a nuanced and fresh presentation of three kinds of righteousness suited for contemporary use.

My threefold division will follow both reformers. The sequence is Luther's, but the precision of distinction derives more directly from Melanchthon. For the sake of convenience and clarity and to avoid identification or, more likely, confusion with the familiar but sometimes ambiguous labels employed by the reformers, the three kinds of righteousness proposed here, at least initially, will be designated with a system as unimaginative as it is obvious—the simple ordinal numbers, first, second, and third, will provide a reasonable and prudent way to begin.

In the three-kinds-of-righteousness framework that I am suggesting, the first righteousness is the righteousness that applies to all people, regardless of a person's standing before God, whether justified *coram Deo* or not. A key aspect of the first kind of righteousness is its grounding in the recognition that God's will (that is, the law) has been revealed and is still present throughout all of creation. This first kind of righteousness is roughly parallel to what Luther called apparent righteousness, and what Melanchthon labeled righteousness of reason. The second righteousness is the righteousness of salvation that comes from outside, through faith. What is being called here the second kind of righteousness, Luther named, among a variety of other terms, alien righteousness. Melanchthon termed it the righteousness of the promise and considered it third. The third kind of righteousness in this threefold framework is the righteousness that is evident in the godly lives and good works of Christians as they function within the created world. In Luther's sermon from 1518, this pious Christian activity was labeled as actual righteousness, and Melanchthon designated it as the righteousness of the law. The order follows what is presumably the experience of a typical adult convert to the Christian faith: to begin, the individual lives in this world in accordance with the dictates of the first righteousness. Subsequently, by grace and the work of the Holy Spirit through the means, the new believer experiences the wonder, comfort, and joy of the second righteousness that bestows salvation. Now a member of Christ's church and a citizen of God's kingdom, the fresh convert sets out to live a new life in conformity with God's will and reflective of what it means to be a member of the body of Christ. The new Christian now pursues the third righteousness.

A moment of directed reflection would likely lead most readers to the observation that the order as well as the respective purview of what is here being called the first, second, and third righteousnesses very closely correspond to the first, second, and third uses of the law (curb, mirror, and guide). While not intentional or deliberate, it seems likely that this is no coincidence. The three uses of the law is interested in considering the impact that the law has on human beings, and the three kinds of righteousness is interested in a comprehensive understanding of the way that people are to live and function as creatures. Both threefold frameworks reflect the reality of the Creator's intentions and interactions with the fallen creation. Both "firsts" (first function of the law and the first kind of righteousness) share a scope as wide as all creation and speak to all humans, even those living apart from the gospel. The "seconds" are alike in narrowing the interest to a person's standing before God and the double reality of humans' abject inability and God's perfect provision. Finally, the "thirds" similarly focus on the believer's ordinary life in light of justification, and speak to God's directions for those redeemed people. The three uses of the law is somewhat limited in its application, dealing as it does only with the law—and is burdened with an unfortunate excess of negative baggage.[62] The three kinds of righteousness, then, provides a fresh framework that still coheres with God's reality as reflected in the three uses of the law.

Another moment of yet more carefully directed refection will probably lead a few readers to another observation that also seems to be no coincidence: the first, second, and third kinds of righteousness mesh rather well with the first, second, and third articles confessed in the Apostles' Creed. The overlap is broad and hardly subtle. The creed's first article, of course, centers on the reality and work of the Father who creates; accordingly, the first kind of righteousness is interested in the way that all creatures conform to God's will—even unwittingly and unwillingly. Of course, the second article proclaims salvation through Christ—precisely the interest of the second kind of righteousness. Along with sacramental sustenance and eschatological consummation, the third article is typically associated with the Spirit's sanctifying activity in the Christian person, which is essentially also the object of the third kind of righteousness. The importance of the creedal framework and its relation to a paradigm that allows and encourages character formation will be explored more fully below. For now it is enough to recognize that this rough parallel between the three kinds of righteousness and the articles of the creed, taken together with the overlap between the three uses of the law and the three kinds of righteousness, bolsters the argument that the three-kinds-of-righteousness paradigm is not so much innovation as clarification and illustration. It resonates with other doctrinal

---

62. The negative baggage is associated almost exclusively with the third function of the law, of course. Murray's book, *Law, Life, and the Living God*, competently explains the unwarranted, yet persistently dubious, reputation of the "third use."

formulations, simply highlighting and sharpening an aspect of Christian truth that has always been confessed but not always recognized or appreciated.

While the ordinal numbers seem to be sufficient as labels for each kind of righteousness, it may be helpful to ascribe further, somewhat more descriptive, monikers for each. The participles *governing*, *justifying*, and *conforming* can be appended, with a defensible rationale, to the simpler designations of first, second, and third, respectively. These participles point to the activity—and the subject of the activity who is always and only God alone—involved in each kind of righteousness. As participles they also encourage a sense of movement forward to the outcome of each kind of righteousness: a governed creature, a justified penitent, and a conformed believer. It should be understood, however, that these designations are provided only for the sake of understanding with no intention of reconciling or coinciding with the preferred and sometimes ambiguous terms used by the reformers.

The paradigm of three kinds of righteousness provides an effective framework within which to understand the data from the Confessions and their contexts related in the previous chapter, as well as other statements encountered in Scripture and theology. There is a righteousness based on God's will, governing righteousness, which rules and directs all of life in this world, and those who adhere to it attain a certain degree of righteousness according to the world. The second righteousness, justifying righteousness, is entirely distinct from governing righteousness and for the sake of Christ delivers salvation to the wholly passive recipient. Justifying righteousness flows (through new and heightened "Christian" motivations of love for God and concern for neighbor) into the third kind of righteousness, conforming righteousness, which in its expression often seems to the outward observer quite similar to the governing righteousness. It is unique, however, in its intimate relationship to justifying righteousness, and in its deliberate striving to emulate, or be conformed to, the example of Christ.

There are clear relationships between the three righteousnesses. The simple figure below may prove useful as a way to visualize the way that the different kinds of righteousness relate and connect—or fail to connect. As noted, in many respects, the third righteousness resembles the first as both are guided by the Creator's will for this world; thus, in the diagram (chart 4.1), governing righteousness and conforming righteousness are parallel and oriented horizontally. Both are concerned primarily with horizontal relationships; that is, they are occupied with the inescapable realities of mundane creaturely existence in this world. Their driving concern is *coram mundo* relationships between creatures. In addition to the obvious common ground between governing

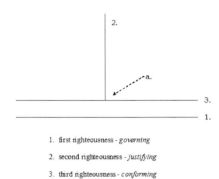

1. first righteousness - *governing*

2. second righteousness - *justifying*

3. third righteousness - *conforming*

a. the connection between 2. & 3.

Biermann Chart 4.1

righteousness and conforming righteousness, another close relationship exists between the second and third kinds of righteousness. This is indicated in the figure by the fact that the representative lines for justifying righteousness and conforming righteousness actually come into contact with one another. Justifying righteousness is concerned with *coram Deo* realities, describing the vertical relationship between God and the individual—a relationship of grace through faith. As expected, then, the line for this second kind of righteousness is oriented vertically, and the word *God* could even be added to the top of that vertical line to emphasize that this is the righteousness concerned with the creature's relationship to the Creator. In the realm of justifying righteousness, God alone is subject and actor, and the creature is the passive recipient of all that God graciously delivers. Still, conforming righteousness is intimately connected to the righteousness that justifies and is possible only because of the reality of the second, justifying righteousness. They are both, in a sense, the righteousness of Christians: the second or justifying righteousness is the righteousness that is passively received; the third or conforming righteousness is the righteousness that is actively lived. So, while the first and third kinds of righteousness—governing and conforming, respectively—are parallel and similar, they are marked by different motivations, a different understanding of the goal and standard, and, most significantly, by the unique activity of the Holy Spirit in the life of the believer—a gift unknown to the unbeliever living only according to the basic dictates and norms of governing righteousness.

The figure makes it impossible to miss the inextricable link joining justifying righteousness to conforming righteousness—a link that once recognized leads invariably, it seems, to a desire to explore the connection between them. While the urge to explain the interaction between the two is undeniably compelling, it is an urge that is best resisted. In the realm of theology, it is too often the case that attempts at explanation end badly—merely spawning misleading or false doctrine. Two ready examples of this tendency are the *crux theologorum* and the attempts at theodicy.[63] Similarly, any effort to elaborate on the interaction between justifying righteousness and conforming righteousness is an ill-advised adventure since it always forces the would-be teacher into the role of innovator. Scripture says very little about the inner workings of the relationship between justification and a life of good works, and the Confessions are similarly all but silent about *how* justification and new obedience are related. The two are related—period. Indeed, the authors of the Confessions demonstrated little interest in explaining how the Christian's righteousness before God and the Christian's righteousness before the world actually intersect and interact; they appeared to be altogether content simply to recognize that the connection involved new motivations for the Christian along with the indwelling activity of the Holy Spirit. Of course, the reformers also made clear that the conforming righteousness of the believer could contribute nothing to the God-worked reality of what is given in the kind of righteousness that justifies before God. For Christians, both realities hold and they themselves embody the intersection and interrelation between their vertical righteousness before God and their horizontal righteousness before the world.

While the three-kinds-of-righteousness framework does capably manage significant concerns and nuances of Lutheran theology, it also provides a connection with the insights and interests of virtue ethics and with the effort to instill and encourage worthy character in those who profess faith in Christ. Alasdair MacIntyre highlights the importance of community, narrative, and practices for understanding ethical questions. He argues convincingly that the particular narrative of the community in which one is operating or living determines the desired outcomes or goods for that individual and so dictates the kind of practices (both activities and patterns of thinking) that will concern and direct that individual so that the goods may be realized. The three-kinds-of-righteousness framework can readily incorporate the insight that there are a great many narratives in which people operate and so a wide variety of

63. The false doctrine in each case results when an attempt is made to explain what is inexplicable: why a sovereign God saves some creatures with a bound will while others are lost, and why a benevolent and omnipotent God coexists with evil, respectively.

practices that potentially may direct individuals. Luther also acknowledged this truth, naming political and ceremonial as two of the many possible kinds of active righteousness.[64] MacIntyre and the virtue ethics he espouses might extend the list begun by Luther to include also the practices intrinsic to such diverse activities as football, environmental activism, or membership in a monastery. The frame of a threefold righteousness as represented in the above figure accepts this truth, placing these multiple narratives of assorted communities within the first category of governing righteousness as coplanar subsets. To represent accurately the manifold forms that the first kind of righteousness can take, it would be necessary to create a three-dimensional figure with these righteousnesses and their attendant practices all occurring within a single plane. Naturally, these different narratives sometimes compete and conflict as they inevitably cross one another or make opposing claims on their adherents. Nevertheless, they all function within the common plane of governing righteousness and offer guidance for meaningfully negotiating life in this world.

Parallel to the plane representing governing righteousness, yet separate from it, is the plane that represents conforming righteousness, which is connected to the perpendicular and only vertical element in the suggested image: the line labeled justifying righteousness. The existence of multiple narratives, each with distinct practices, characterizes the plane of governing righteousness and also marks the plane of conforming righteousness. Each possible understanding of conforming righteousness constitutes one of the traditions or narrative communities within Christendom that suggest specific and sometimes contradictory guidance on what comprises the faithful Christian life. Of course, all of these possible conceptions of what constitutes a Christian life rightly lived would share at least an inseparable union with the vertical reality of justifying righteousness. The existence of multiple, yet coplanar, narratives and practices is the commonly experienced reality of different Christian traditions providing more or less accurate accounts of the narrative of the Christian life, yet with distinct nuances and emphases. Some center around the liturgy, some champion learning and doctrine, others focus on contemplative prayer, still others promote a busy life of service—but all celebrate the centrality of vertical righteousness: God's justifying work in Christ. This variety within the category of conforming righteousness should be expected and even welcomed. Within the fold of Christendom, many particular narratives are possible and good—as long as they remain tightly bound to the righteousness that justifies by grace through faith alone.

---

64. LW 26:4.

CONCLUSION

The strength of a framework utilizing three kinds of righteousness is the ability it possesses to handle the diverse assortment of confessional and scriptural data—a *sine qua non* of an effective framework. The three-kinds-of-righteousness framework allows the central truth of justification by grace through faith in Jesus Christ alone to be clearly articulated. Additionally, it can accommodate and make sense of such confessional teachings as the civil righteousness of unbelievers and the new life of obedience of believers, realities also borne out by common Christian experience. The framework provides an effective and useful tool, then, equal to the demands of confessional fidelity, doctrinal accuracy, and ethical relevance. All three aspects are vital, of course, but for the purpose at hand—advocacy of character formation—it is the capacity of the three-kinds-of-righteousness paradigm to move confidently into the ethical realm that holds the most potential for useful service.

The advantages of a three-kinds-of-righteousness framework are many, yet it is possible to enrich and strengthen them by recognizing that this paradigm is actually grounded in another crucial framework. Indeed, whether one subscribes to the argument that has been made and embraces a threefold understanding of righteousness or elects to operate with the simple distinction of two kinds of righteousness, the framework of different kinds of righteousness is significantly enhanced when placed within the grounding framework of the Christian creed. Predictably, but appropriately, precisely this endeavor will occupy the investigation of the next chapter.

5

A Creedal Framework

A Proposal for the Reclamation of Ethics within Lutheranism

A directing premise of this brief study has been the desirability of being able to locate within Lutheran theology a place for the concerns, insights, and even practices of an ethics of virtue, thereby making possible the work of intentional character formation. The present chapter will endeavor to synthesize what has gone before and offer what fruit this investigation has to yield. In other words, the time has come to develop and defend a viable framework that opens working space for the practice of an ethics of virtue within Lutheranism while maintaining doctrinal positions distinctive to Lutheranism. A significant element of the proposed framework, the three kinds of righteousness, was introduced in the previous chapter. That aspect of the overall paradigm will be elaborated and supplemented as it is grounded in the fundamental framework provided by the church's creed, whether confessed as the Nicene Creed or the Apostles' Creed.

The Creedal Frame

The quest for a framework within which to proclaim the truths of the gospel and to address seriously the needs of Christian living, while at the same time taking into account the interrelationship between both, has proven to be a greater challenge than most might have expected. The hope, of course, is that such a frame will serve the rejuvenation and development of Lutheran ethics and allow for a concerted effort at character formation among the people of today's church. Sadly and—at least from the perspective of the church's vitality—tragically, typical and well-known Lutheran frames (gospel motivation, law and gospel, and spontaneous production of good works, and even some aspects of two kinds of righteousness) have been found, in varying degrees, not entirely satisfactory. An acceptable frame worthy of use and promulgation must be equal to the needs of contemporary Lutheranism while at the same time relatively familiar and so readily accessible to all Christians. In addition to the framework of three kinds of righteousness, the complementary component of this study's suggested framework is discovered by considering some of the most basic features of the theological landscape.

A theological frame that can accommodate the scope of Lutheran theology along with the significant practical concerns of virtue ethics is founded upon and shaped within what is perhaps the most expansive yet inclusive of all possible frameworks: the fundamental form of the church's creed. After considering the benefits of thinking of the creed in terms of a paradigm, I will then describe a single guiding frame that adopts the three-kinds-of-righteousness framework and then roots that framework within the basic creedal paradigm. As the argument unfolds, it should become clear that this newly described framework is able to receive, accommodate, and make sense of the sometimes disparate data that are encountered in Scripture, the Confessions, and Christian experience. For the sake of convenience, this framework of three kinds of righteousness grounded in a creedal paradigm will be designated simply as the creedal framework. This means that references to a creedal framework should not be construed as another competing frame over against the three-kinds-of-righteousness framework. Rather, the three kinds of righteousness frame is grounded within and drawn from the creedal frame. Taken together, the depth and richness of the creedal basis and the precision and ready application of the three kinds of righteousness offer a potent and helpful framework within which to think and live faithfully as a disciple.

Unencumbered by the propensity toward polarization inherent in all dualities, nor beguiled by the errant attempt to make motivation say everything of interest about the Christian life, and making use of language and concepts immediately recognizable to all Christians, a creedal framework offers much to commend its adoption as the fundamental and norming frame for faithful Christian reflection and action. The church's creed, whether expressed as the Nicene Creed or the Apostles' Creed, provides a view comprehensive enough to encompass all of theology and all of life. Justification *coram Deo* and the Christian's life in the world *coram mundo* are not placed in polarity to one another, nor are they collapsed into a unity. Both are rightly understood as aspects of God's larger work of creating, redeeming, and restoring. The great strength and advantage of this frame is that it is founded upon and reflects the work of the Trinity itself—not the ineffable, transcendent intra-trinitarian works of the Godhead, but the work of the economic Trinity on behalf of humankind and creation—and the salvation of both.

The Trinitarian Basis

Robert Benne suggests that to overcome its infamous ethical irrelevance, "Lutheran ethics will have to be more trinitarian."[1] Obviously, a creedal framework for doctrine and ethics is a significant move in a trinitarian direction. A healthy dose of caution and clarification is in order at this point. The linking of the Trinity and ethics is hardly novel; indeed, it has become an exceedingly popular pursuit among Christian thinkers of all kinds. It would be a mistake, however, for the reader to identify the creedal framework being proposed here with the kind of thinking that typically operates under the heading of trinitarian ethics. Having imbibed much of what can be recognized as the spirit of Jürgen Moltmann, trinitarian ethics as practiced today has developed into a specific approach to Christian ethics with distinct characteristics, some of which are altogether at odds with my purpose.[2] Noteworthy among these is the assumption, widespread among many doing Christian ethics, that the Trinity, especially the intra-trinitarian relationship, is somehow normative for Christians and their ethical life. L. Gregory Jones furnishes a representative example:

1. Robert Benne, "Lutheran Ethics: Perennial Themes and Contemporary Challenges," in Karen L. Bloomquist and John R. Stumme, eds., *The Promise of Lutheran Ethics* (Minneapolis: Fortress Press, 1998), 28. Benne's essay, unfortunately, does not elaborate on what he thinks a more trinitarian Lutheran ethics might entail. That he intended the direction that I will take certainly is not assumed; nevertheless, his observation is relevant to the present investigation.

2. Jürgen Moltmann espouses the "social doctrine of the Trinity" and reaches several conclusions that might be summarized: (1) The Trinity must be understood in the sense of community; (2) the monarchical view of God must be eliminated; (3) "Almighty" must be understood as a reference to God's love; and (4) the doctrine of the Trinity requires that the church be "free of dominion." See Moltmann, *The Trinity and the Kingdom: The Doctrine of God*, trans. Margaret Kohl (New York: HarperCollins, 1991), viii, 197–202. In recent history, liberation theologians, such as Leonardo Boff, have capitalized on Moltmann's work: "The community of Father, Son and Holy Spirit becomes the prototype of the human community dreamed of by those who wish to improve society and build it in such a way as to make it into the image and likeness of the Trinity" (Boff, *Trinity and Society*, trans. Paul Burns [Kent, UK: Burns & Oates, 1998], 7). Moltmann's social doctrine of the Trinity as articulated by Boff is now widely accepted by contemporary theologians as the norm for theology and society: "Christian ethicists as well as theologians speculating on the meaning of divine and human personhood must deliberate on the social order. To do any less undermines the point of a trinitarian doctrine of God." See Catherine Mowry LaCugna, *God for Us: The Trinity and Christian Life* (New York: HarperCollins, 1991), 288.

Instead, the moral life, understood most adequately in terms of Christian life, should be lived in the mystery of the Triune God. From such a perspective, I suggest that the moral life involves an ongoing "perichoretic dance." Such a dance, grounded in the perichoretic relations of God's Trinity, requires and enables people to discern the overall pattern their lives are to take, to puzzle with others about what that patterning entails concretely, and to question received claims to truth from the standpoint of the Gospel.[3]

Regardless what Jones may have intended, this line of thinking too often leads to the endorsement and encouragement of a host of practices diametrically opposed to scriptural revelation and the church's time-honored interpretation of that record. Some familiar and obvious examples might include the acceptance of pre-marital sex, the denigration of parental or pastoral authority, the celebration of same sex unions, and an "everybody wins" attitude that eschews all competition.

Beneath the acrimony and distress fomented by either the advocacy or the dread of such contentious social issues, lies a more fundamental and genuinely worrisome problem. A central flaw in the kind of "trinitarian ethics" that Jones and others promote is that it too easily degenerates into a subjective, or at best, an anthropocentric ethic as people "puzzle" together about how exactly a trinitarian-shaped life should look. If trinitarian ethicists such as Moltmann and his successors are any example, it does seem that the answers that eventually emerge from such puzzling usually bear a remarkable resemblance to the prevailing ethical sensibilities of society's most enlightened (that is, Enlightenment-bred) thinkers and eventuate in the predictable progressive endorsements previously noted.[4]

---

3. L. Gregory Jones, *Transformed Judgment: Toward a Trinitarian Account of the Moral Life* (Notre Dame, IN: University of Notre Dame Press, 1990), 4.

4. For example, David S. Cunningham concludes that a truly trinitarian view of the Christian life will lead "pastors and congregations . . . to demonstrate their willingness to provide the same kinds of pastoral care to committed same-sex relationships as they do to opposite-sex couples" (Cunningham, *These Three Are One: The Practice of Trinitarian Theology* [Oxford: Blackwell, 1998], 303). Thomas Marsh critiques this tendency, observing that those who advocate social and political action based on the Trinity may have allowed "their own notion of an ideal human society to influence their understanding of the Triune God" (Marsh, *The Triune God: A Biblical, Historical, and Theological Study* [Mystic, CT: Twenty-Third Publications, 1994], 186). About Moltmann, Alan J. Torrance concludes: "The tendency in Moltmann is for his theology to be shaped by a prior personalist, indeed socio-political, ontology" (Torrance, *Persons in Communion: An Essay on Trinitarian Description and Human Participation* [Edinburgh: T&T Clark, 1996], 249).

Tempting as it is to devote more time and attention to a fuller consideration of "trinitarian ethics," the topic as usually construed is not directly relevant to the task at hand. One final thought, though, is in order. It is a near-universal assumption that intra-trinitarian relationships, or the Trinity itself is (or *should* be) normative for human relationships, organizations, and society. This is the case even among those considered to be conservative and evangelical thinkers. Stanley Grenz once asserted, "In this manner the Christian vision of God as the social Trinity and our creation to be the *imago Dei* provides the transcendent basis for the human ethical ideal as life-in-community. Consequently the reciprocal, perichoretic dynamic of the Triune God is the cosmic reference point for the idea of society itself."[5] But the obscurity and debate that continue to surround the *imago Dei* or "image of God" hardly serve as conclusive proof that God intends the divine reality and being somehow to be normative for humanity. Mercifully, not all theologians have adopted this misuse of the trinitarian reality. Richard Bauckham quite rightly observes that "true human community comes about not as an image of the Trinitarian fellowship, but as the Spirit makes us like Jesus in his community with the Father and with others."[6] The hard fact is that neither Scripture nor the Lutheran Confessions ever offer the mystery of the trinitarian Godhead as the model or even *a* model for Christian living or the shape of Christian life. As the saying goes, "God is God, and you're not."[7] The Christian life is shaped not by God's trinitarian nature as model, but by God's revealed word and work in us.[8]

Trinitarian ethics aside, the efficacy of a creedal framework stems from its recognition of and grounding in the all-encompassing work of the Trinity. The framework presented here advocates not an emulation of perichoretic intra-trinitarian relations, but an appreciation for the extent of God's activity as creator, redeemer, and sanctifier. From the perspective of contemporary Lutheranism, the appropriation of a creedal frame points especially to a renewed appreciation for the importance of God's first-article work of creation. The creedal frame asserts that all of life and theology fit into the universal scheme of God's creative task. Once again, the idea of using a creedal framework is not

---

5. Stanley Grenz, *The Moral Quest: Foundations for Christian Ethics* (Downers Grove, IL: Intervarsity, 1997), 238.

6. Richard Bauckham, "Jürgen Moltmann's *The Trinity and the Kingdom of God* and the Question of Pluralism," in *The Trinity in a Pluralistic Age: Theological Essays on Culture and Religion*, ed. Kevin J. Vanhoozer (Grand Rapids: Eerdmans, 1997), 155–64, at 162.

7. With thanks to my colleague, Joel Okamoto.

8. Ethics, then, is not concerned with the *opera divina ad intra* (intra-trinitarian works of God), but with the *opera divina ad extra* (the works of God directed toward things outside the Godhead).

generated de novo. The precedents for this creedal, creation-affirming solution to the Lutheran dilemma are many.

MELANCHTHON AND LUTHER AND THE CREEDAL EMPHASIS

In his 1521 *Loci Communes*, Melanchthon recognized the importance of sustaining a theological perspective wide enough to include creation. He offers a rather insightful and charming image for the right understanding of earthly activity and good works: "In moral works too we have to be on our guard so that just as you do not eat and drink in order to be justified, you do not give alms for your justification. But just as you eat and drink in order to provide for your bodily needs, you should give alms, love your brother, etc., in order to provide for the common need."[9] Christian faith and life are not simply a "third-article" personal appropriation of the universal redemption in Christ proclaimed in the second article of the creed. Rather, the redeemed and sanctified individual who has been thoroughly blessed with all the gifts of salvation is sent back again into the created realm to exercise and distribute those gifts. By virtue of the first article, Christians have a responsibility to care for the other members of the creation into which they have been placed. For Christians, then, service *coram mundo* is tied at least as closely to the first article as it is to the third.

When Melanchthon turned his attention to the arena of moral philosophy, his affirmation of the created realm became even more pronounced. Reformation researcher Sachiko Kusukawa observes, "For moral philosophy, Melanchthon used parts of Aristotle's *Nichomachean Ethics* (especially book V) in order to argue that humans were created for a purpose and that that purpose was to obey the divinely instituted order, such as civil governments."[10] Evidence supporting Melanchthon's eager willingness to make use of Aristotle was presented already in the previous chapter. Another significant reference, however, is quite appropriate here:

> Since Christians should cherish and support this civil society, this teaching of civic morals and duties has to be known by them. It is not piety to live like Cyclopes, without justice, without laws, without teaching, or without any of the other things helpful for life that are contained in literature. Therefore those who disparage

9. Philipp Melanchthon, *"Loci Communes Theologici,"* in *Melanchthon and Bucer*, The Library of Christian Classics, vol. 19, trans. and ed. Wilhelm Pauck (Philadelphia: Westminster, 1969), 126.

10. Philipp Melanchthon, *Orations on Philosophy and Education*, ed. Sachiko Kusukawa, trans. Christine F. Salazar (Cambridge: Cambridge University Press, 1999), xviii.

philosophy not only wage war against human nature, but they also severely injure the glory of the Gospel, which commands that men be restrained by civic discipline; and nature decorates with the highest prizes the honourable [sic] institutions that contain the civil society of men.[11]

There is no question that Melanchthon fully understood and greatly appreciated the importance of the realm of creation and its purposeful maintenance. He was quite able to coordinate a consuming concern for *coram Deo* questions of justification with a keen interest in the *coram mundo* realities that surrounded him in the mundane processes of life.

Of course, Luther also cherished the gifts of creation and, like Melanchthon, recognized people as the fitting objects of our good works. With his understanding of two kinds of righteousness near at hand, Luther declares in his fuller explanation of the Fourth Commandment, "In God's sight it is actually faith that makes a person holy; it alone serves God, while our works serve people."[12] In the preface to his 1535 commentary on Galatians, Luther again affirms the Christian's responsibility to serve the rest of creation. In this important passage, Luther roots the redeemed Christian firmly in the created realm. It is here in the concrete realities and responsibilities of ordinary life that the believer's faith is given explicit and specific shape.

> When I have this [passive] righteousness within me, I descend from heaven like the rain that makes the earth fertile. That is, I come forth into another kingdom, and I perform good works whenever the opportunity arises. If I am a minister of the Word, I preach, I comfort the saddened, I administer the sacraments. If I am a father, I rule my household and family, I train my children in piety and honesty. If I am a magistrate, I perform the office which I have received by divine command. If I am a servant, I faithfully tend to my master's affairs. In short, whoever knows for sure that Christ is his righteousness not only cheerfully and gladly works in his calling but also submits himself for the sake of love to magistrates, also to their wicked laws, and to everything else in this present life—even, if need be, to burden and danger. For he knows that God wants this and that this obedience pleases Him.[13]

11. Ibid., 81.
12. *Book of Concord*, 406 (LC I, 147).

Made right in the heavenly kingdom, *coram Deo*, the justified Christian is returned to "another kingdom," the kingdom of the left-hand world, the world of the created realm, *coram mundo*, and is busy there with the varied and demanding affairs of "this present life." Such obedient work, Luther asserts, is God-pleasing as it conforms to God's will and desire for the creature. Yet such work is not in any way salvific—the passive righteousness of salvation has already been fully accomplished in Christ quite apart from the believer's performance of service to the neighbor.

It is vital to note that there is no conflict or tension between the two realities. Once believers have the passive righteousness of faith, *coram Deo*, they invariably and quite naturally return to doing the work that they have been given to do within their earth-bound responsibilities. Neither does Luther make any effort to explain the interrelationship between vertical righteousness and horizontal righteousness. While they are altogether distinct, they exist together quite compatibly in the life of the believer. Of course, all of this can be expressed in terms of the trinitarian creed. The redemption accomplished in the second article of the creed leads the believer back into the first-article world of creation, there to follow the lead of the Holy Spirit, who carries out the third-article work of restoration and fulfillment. Both Luther and Melanchthon operate quite naturally within a broad creedal framework. It is not difficult to see how their two kinds of righteousness distinctions, or my own suggested threefold format, can be anchored within the creedal framework. This will be explored in more depth presently; for now it is sufficient to note that the practice of the reformers supports my own creedal proposal.

Gustaf Wingren and the Importance of the Doctrine of Creation

Moving from the sixteenth century to the twentieth, it is possible to trace a renewed and increasing appreciation for the sort of creedal grounding that the reformers seem to have employed as a given. While, in the eyes of many, his legacy within the church is somewhat dubious, the early work of Gustaf Wingren does much to recapture the importance of the first article for both theology and living. Wingren develops the idea that creation is the ground for all of theology and that redeemed humanity is being restored to God's original creative intent.[14] With determination, the Swedish theologian defines the results

---

13. LW 26:11-12. This passage is but one among many that could be harvested from the considerable corpus of Luther's writing. The theme of service to the neighbor as the purpose of our lives in this world and the reason for our being appears in Luther's thinking with unfailing consistency.

of faith not merely in terms of spiritual realities, but according to the doctrine of creation: "Faith means a recovery of man's original and natural position, for which both he and Creation alike were destined and equipped."[15] And Wingren draws the good works of humans into the same material frame: "The purpose of all human work is man's continued 'conformation' to the destiny which has been appointed for him in Creation."[16] This earth-bound "destiny" emphasizes and reinforces the fact that civil righteousness—the setting for all work—is *human* righteousness. God's plan for human creatures is that each one should take his or her place within creation as a full human, not that the creature should become divine.

Wingren's talk of destiny is significant and should not be too quickly passed over, providing as it does, an opportunity to digress briefly into a consideration of human purpose. To speak of humanity having a destiny obviously assumes a goal, purpose, and end to his life, or, in the language of ethics, a telos to it all. And, as Hauerwas points out, the telos of life has everything to do with the ethics of life: "Ethics is a function of the telos, the end. It makes all the difference in the world how one regards the end of the world, 'end' not so much in the sense of its final breath, but 'end' in the sense of the purpose, the goal, the result."[17] Speculation about the existence and identity of a telos for humanity has been a hallmark of philosophic argument since pre-Socratic days. Actually, it might well be regarded as a required activity for any rational being—at least once in a lifetime. With the realization of individual self-awareness, the search for individual purpose begins—and then, in the face of too many dismissive and even angry responses to the inevitable hard questions that are asked by the newly aware, it grinds to a halt, more often than not, without resolution. No doubt, there are many who would applaud the unfinished pursuit as a hallmark of our brave new world and summarily dismiss any notion of an objective, universal telos for humanity as yesterday's quaint idea now wholly vacated by the scientific and societal triumph of evolutionary theory and cultural relativism. On the other hand, theology, at least theology

14. Though his own argument begins in a different place and develops in reaction to the work of Iris Murdoch, it is worth noting that Hauerwas also contends for the importance of the doctrine of creation for ethics. He is sure of "the difference the Christian account of creation ex nihilo makes for the Christian moral life." Stanley M. Hauerwas, *Wilderness Wanderings: Probing Twentieth-Century Theology and Philosophy* (Boulder: Westview, 1997), 157.

15. Gustaf Wingren, *Creation and Law*, trans. Ross Mackenzie (Philadelphia: Muhlenberg, 1961), 52.

16. Ibid., 153.

17. Stanley Hauerwas and William H. Willimon, *Resident Aliens: A Provocative Christian Assessment of Culture and Ministry for People Who Know That Something Is Wrong* (Nashville: Abingdon, 1989), 61–62.

that might be reckoned as orthodox, must continue to affirm the scriptural truth: humankind has a God-ordained telos. This telos, or destiny, Wingren argues, is intimately bound to each individual's place as a creature within creation. Simply put, human destiny, our telos, is to be all that God designed and created us to be—in other words, to be fully human.

Whether or not Wingren's contention is obvious, his idea that human destiny is bound to the created realm has important implications. Kolb connects this understanding of humanity's telos to Luther's explication of the two kinds of righteousness. "Also central to Luther's 'evangelical breakthrough,'" Kolb writes, "was his discovery of what makes the human creature 'righteous' or right, that is, truly human."[18] To be righteous is to be all that one was intended and designed to be. Thus fulfillment of humanity takes place on two planes: passively before God, and actively before humans. Kolb puts it this way: "Luther realized, however, that what made him genuinely right in God's sight had to be distinguished from what made him truly human—genuinely right—in relationship to other creatures of God."[19] True humanity is realized when individuals receive the passive righteousness of faith, and then conform to the Creator's will for this life. That will of God is clearly revealed in the divinely delivered law that is recorded in Scripture. Ivar Asheim reaches a similar conclusion: "The commandments of God set before us as normative in Scripture have as their aim the maintenance of humanity among men. The goal of ethics can therefore be defined as the *achievement of humanity*."[20] Emphasizing the doctrine of creation in the way of Wingren clarifies the simplicity and significance of humanity's telos, stemming as it does from the person's place as creature within creation.[21] This digression is sufficient for now; the question of humanity's destiny or telos will be taken up again in a subsequent section.

Not only does Wingren champion a fresh and vigorous appreciation for the first article's doctrine of creation, he also outlines explicit connections

18. Robert Kolb, "Luther on the Two Kinds of Righteousness: Reflections on His Two-Dimensional Definition of Humanity at the Heart of His Theology," *Lutheran Quarterly* 113, no. 4 (Winter 1999): 450.

19. Ibid., 451.

20. Ivar Asheim, ed., *Christ and Humanity* (Philadelphia: Fortress Press, 1970), 15 (emphasis in original). This is true, of course, in the appropriate realm, *coram mundo*.

21. While not explicitly disagreeing with Wingren's stress on the importance of reestablishing the priority of the first article, Fagerberg finds fault with Wingren for minimizing the role of God's commandments in shaping life in creation. "In Wingren one searches in vain for this direct connection with the word of Scripture, with him the command is a general demand for love of one's neighbor . . . " Holsten Fagerberg, *A New Look at the Lutheran Confessions (1529–1537)*, trans. Gene J. Lund (St. Louis: Concordia, 1972), 288. This legitimate observation illumines Wingren's rejection of a third use of the law as well as his equivocal reputation.

between all three articles of the creed highlighting the centrality of divine monergism—that is, God's exclusive activity through the Spirit to bring individuals to salvation without their cooperation—in every aspect of salvation history. The first and second articles are united by God's thoroughly consistent work on behalf of humanity, which is fulfilled in the person of Christ Jesus: "When it [the law] passes judgment upon me, it reveals throughout what I ought to have been. It bears in itself the image in which I have been created, and even as it accuses contains the original purity of Creation. The image of the law points forward to Christ, who is the image of God, and who can therefore make me human again."[22] God's activity in creation is not to be separated from God's continuing work of redemption. More than that, it should be seen as consonant with God's third-article work of restoration and fulfillment. God's work in and through Christ is central throughout.

> But Creation at the beginning was Creation in Christ. Before He came in the flesh, man was created and destined for Him. This does not mean that the doctrine of Creation can be derived from the Gospel of Christ, crucified and risen. It means that God's work of Creation is continued in His work of Redemption, and that this work of Creation is perfected in the Incarnation and the fulfillment of God's mighty works which are described or awaited in the second and third articles.[23]

Though it is not a prominent theme in this work, Wingren does indicate his appreciation for the eschatological element of God's plan for this world. At the eschaton, God brings to glorious completion all that originally had been envisioned for the creation. And the glory and wonder of the fulfillment exceeds that of the first creation. Humanity's redemption in Christ is not merely a return to prelapsarian conformity with God's will. In Christ, God's creation is raised to a higher plane. In Christ and in his gifts delivered in and through material realities, the restoration is begun, yet the full splendor is still being "awaited" as the church confesses in the third article. Wingren writes: "As we saw earlier, Christ in His restoration of man is more than man. The new life which He brings is raised and heightened, as well as restored . . ."[24] With admirable zeal Wingren invites his readers to recognize and to treasure the

---

22. Wingren, *Creation and Law*, 181–82.
23. Ibid., 161.
24. Ibid., 61.

primacy of creation as it is conceived, redeemed, restored, and finally glorified by God.

SUPPORT FROM LUTHERANS AFTER WINGREN

Wingren's high regard for the doctrine of creation and the theological framework of the creed is reflected in the work of a number of subsequent Lutheran scholars. The Norwegian Luther scholar Ivar Asheim is among those who realize the necessity of the doctrine of creation for a right understanding of Lutheran theology and ethics:

> To define the *content* of ethics we have to turn to the reality of the world around us. In the New Testament, the human relationships and social structures unquestionably presupposed, for instance, in the so-called Tables of Duties, are treated seriously and their particular importance even stressed in the name of Christ. In and through these relationships and structures Christians are to perceive God's demands. But the claim of the reality of the world upon Christians is not to be seen as Christ's hidden presence within the various human relationships and social structures. The basis for this claim, rather, is the fact that in the concrete reality of creation man as such is confronted by his Creator.[25]

As Asheim sees it, creation itself with its inherent responsibilities provides the Christian with the necessary ethical context and direction. Asheim later strengthens this idea of the claim of creation by relating it to God's commandments: "The commandments of God set before us as normative in Scripture have as their aim the maintenance of humanity among men."[26] Asheim affirms the necessity of a setting that begins in and extends to all of creation, and then uses the articles of the creed to provide more clarity to his argument. Seeking to direct a believer's Christ-won freedom back into the world, Asheim states, "Ethics must be firmly rooted in both the first *and* the second articles of the Creed, in the doctrine of creation and in the doctrine of Christ."[27] The ethical implications of the "doctrine of Christ" Asheim identifies as "liberation from all legalistic ideals as well as from all utopian dreams of social order and personal conduct. It thus enables us to accept the world for what

---

25. Asheim, *Christ and Humanity*, 12 (emphasis in original).

26. Ibid., 15.

27. Ibid., 14 (emphasis in original).

it really is. True, Christian freedom is freedom *from* the world. But precisely because it is, it is also at the same time freedom *for* the world."[28] Christians, according to Asheim, live in a unique relationship with the world—no longer bound by its misdirected and idolatrous goals and standards, they are nevertheless intimately connected to and invested in God's created world.

Lutheran systematician Friedrich Mildenberger also recognizes the central importance of the doctrine of creation for understanding human living. In the context of the transformative work of the gospel, the Tübingen scholar commends a deliberate move toward a creation-oriented understanding of humanity's responsibilities and challenges in this world: "The gospel reshapes the human will and establishes it on a new basis. In this new form, the will to live fits into the kind of human-being-in-the-world defined by God's activity and expresses its new orientation to the God-willed good works that we encounter in the doing and suffering that comes to us in the unavoidable realities of life."[29] Life grounded in the created realm, then, becomes the impetus and, in a least some sense, even the motivation for good works. The daily needs and occasional emergencies of creaturely existence, most especially the needs of fellow creatures, provide the arena, the drive, and the direction for the practice of a virtuous Christian life—in other words, the exercise of Christian ethics. As Mildenberger puts it, "Living in this world is all that we need to require us to do what will support life."[30] A Christian ethic, then, is not complicated. Simply being a part of creation with its routine and required tasks is sufficient to provide the essential outline and content.

Two more Lutheran theologians who have done much to advance a renewed appreciation for the significance of a creedal framework and the importance of the doctrine of creation for a rightly ordered theology are colleagues at Concordia Seminary in St. Louis, Charles Arand and Robert Kolb. Arand calls attention to a consistent emphasis on creation in the work of Luther. More than a peripheral aspect of Luther's writing, Arand notes that a creedal framework actually accounts for the overarching structure of the Small Catechism. "By tying the Ten Commandments to the First Article and the Third Article to the Lord's Prayer, Luther has brought the three chief parts into a thoroughly Creedal and Trinitarian framework. In doing so, he has provided a way for Christians to make sense of their lives with God in light of the Baptismal Creed and the triune salvific work in creation and history."[31] Once

---

28. Ibid. (emphasis in original).

29. Friedrich Mildenberger, *Theology of the Lutheran Confessions*, trans. Erwin L. Lueker, ed. Robert C. Schulz (Philadelphia: Fortress Press, 1986), 167.

30. Ibid., 168.

again, as Arand makes clear, we see the creed supplying a frame sufficiently expansive to contain what needs to be said about faith and life while yet holding the different aspects together in a meaningful and consistent relation.

Like Arand, Kolb discerns the importance of the doctrine of creation for Luther, rightly connecting the doctrine of creation with the reformer's teaching on vocation. "For Luther," Kolb writes, "the situations and responsibilities which structure human life are part of the doctrine of creation."[32] Luther's comments in the introduction to his 1535 commentary on Galatians fully corroborate Kolb's claim. Creation provides the rich setting within which human beings live out their lives according to God's plan—a plan wired into the very structure and interrelationships of creation. But Kolb also places the events of the second and third articles within the frame of creation.

> First, faith recognizes that God is a good and loving Lord. In sin we regard His will as our enemy, for His Law only condemns and curbs us. In faith we regard Him no longer as our enemy but as the loving Father and Friend who has beneficially created and ordered our existence. We embrace Him once again as the loving Creator whose wisdom for human living is reflected in the commands of His Law and in His Son's earthly life. We recognize His lordship by responding with a God-pleasing lifestyle which reflects our faith's conviction that He is our God.[33]

All of theology fits within the vast frame of creation. The law/gospel dynamic is played out within this structure, likewise the Christian's new life of obedience. Justification and the active pursuit of a virtuous, God-pleasing life are fully compatible elements within this frame.

A Proposed Framework

As noted at the outset of this chapter, the valuable framework of a threefold righteousness considered in chapter 4 is fully compatible with—indeed grounded in—the paradigm of the trinitarian creed. Taken together, these two approaches provide the framework that has been the object of this investigation: a framework that can preserve the doctrine of justification while also affirming

31. Charles P. Arand, *That I May Be His Own: An Overview of Luther's Catechisms* (St. Louis: Concordia Academic, 2000), 136.

32. Robert Kolb, "God Calling, 'Take Care of My People': Luther's Concept of Vocation in the *Augsburg Confession* and Its *Apology*," *Concordia Journal* 8, no. 1 (January 1982): 6.

33. Ibid., 10.

the place of a Christian's ethical pursuit—a frame broad enough to handle the whole of theology. It may be helpful to provide a presentation that is not only verbal but also visual (see chart 5.1).

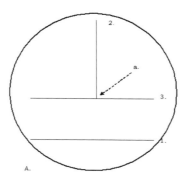

1. righteousness one (governing)

2. righteousness two (justifying)

3. righteousness three (conforming)

A. realm of creation

a. the connection between 2. & 3.

Chart 5.1

In the diagram, the three kinds of righteousness are again present. Righteousness 1 is governing righteousness, the morality of all people *coram mundo*, and finds its foundation in God's action of creation. Righteousness 2 is justifying righteousness. It is here, in the vertical dimension, *coram Deo*, that the reality of the law/gospel duality reigns alone. This vertical righteousness is declared by the creed's second article and bestowed in the third. Righteousness 3, conforming righteousness, grows out of God's monergistic action of righteousness 2 and must be joined to it. The conforming righteousness is uniquely Christian and driven by the truths of the second article yet led back into the created world of the first article. Here the Christian pursues a virtuous life *coram mundo*, but one that is also certainly God-pleasing. Thus love of God and the need of neighbor are both recognized as legitimate and appropriate sources of motivation. Finally, surrounding the entire scheme is the realm of creation, or the first article. The encompassing sweep of the circle is meant to convey the truth that *all* of the righteousnesses are accomplished or practiced within the structure of God's created world.

It is important that the creedal frame not be regarded as an innovation but as an attempt to articulate and commend a directing paradigm that, consciously or not, has long guided much theological thinking. A Lutheran Church—Missouri Synod study document on spiritual gifts furnishes one example of the creedal framework's effectiveness in addressing fundamental questions of theology and practice. In this document, produced by the Synod's Commission on Theology and Church Relations, a creedal frame is used extensively to offer a creation-based understanding of the charisms of the Holy Spirit. Particularly important for the purpose of the project of this book, however, is the document's use of and insight into the general need and value of a creedal view for theology.

> At times Christians may give the impression that they are "Second or Third Article people" who are only concerned with "personal salvation" and the life hereafter or those matters that pertain only to the realm of the church. As a result, the First Article and its implications for life in this world recede into the background of Christian thought and practice. When this happens the danger arises that one not only distinguishes between the works of God but actually separates them from each other. The end result is that the gifts and works referred to in the First Article have little to do with the works of God presented in the Second and Third Articles and vice versa.[34]

In a similar way, it is precisely this exaggerated separation between God's various works outlined in each of the articles that has wreaked havoc on Lutheranism's ability to grapple with questions of Christian ethics.

The study document successfully demonstrates a lively understanding of the importance and interrelation of all three articles of the creed, or more accurately, the work of God confessed in each of the articles. As the document addresses the question of spiritual gifts, it is the often undervalued or overlooked first article that receives significant and appropriate attention. Most importantly, though, the document demonstrates the close interrelationship that exists

---

34. The Lutheran Church—Missouri Synod, *Spiritual Gifts: A Report of the Commission on Theology and Church Relations of the Lutheran Church—Missouri Synod* (St. Louis: The Lutheran Church—Missouri Synod, 1995), 46. Though study documents issued by the CTCR are officially documents by committee and never specify an author, it is hardly surprising to any careful reader to learn that Charles Arand played a key role in the production of this particular document.

between each of the articles. For instance, the document makes clear that it is *through* creation, not in opposition to creation, that God redeems humanity.

> As he worked through creation to give us life and sustain our lives, so God redeems and sanctifies us through the elements of creation, through the incarnation of Christ, through water, and through bread and wine. Thus creation serves redemption and redemption fulfills creation. This means that one article of the Creed, in this case the First Article, informs and shapes the other two, which build upon it.[35]

This reaffirmation of the created realm and its close relation to God's work of redemption not only assists in an understanding of spiritual gifts but, as discussed above, holds great promise for the challenge of providing a meaningful place for ethics in relation to the doctrine of justification.

The third-article work of the Spirit is not to overthrow, displace, or supplant creation, but to restore it to God's original creative intent. "As the forgiveness of sins and Baptism restore us to our proper place before God and place us under one head, Jesus Christ, they also free and recreate us to live as God intended."[36] While it may be obvious, it bears stating nonetheless: it is within the created realm that Christians live and serve. God does not redeem people from creation, but for creation. "The Third Article sends us back into our daily lives within the First Article so that we may begin to live our lives as God intended his creation to work."[37] As the study document demonstrates, the creedal framework is remarkably capable and versatile at relating the depths and heights of theological thought with the concrete and practical concerns of ordinary life.

Before turning to the task of relating the creedal framework specifically to the challenges and needs posed by virtue ethics, it should be noted that the creedal frame readily accommodates essential aspects of eschatological truth. The believer's restoration for and into the created realm should not be understood as the return arc of a closed circle that merely deposits church and creation back into Edenic existence. Luther acknowledged the continuity, yet at the same time heightening implicit in God's plan of salvation: "For this is the righteousness [alien, justifying] given in place of the original righteousness lost in Adam. It accomplishes the same as that original righteousness would have accomplished; rather it accomplishes more."[38] God's creation is moving

35. Ibid., 46–47.
36. Ibid., 56.
37. Ibid., 68.

not back to the garden, but forward to the eschaton. "Therefore, the law is not destroyed by Christ, but restored, so that Adam might be just as he was, and even better."[39] With the incarnation, God's plan for creation was elevated and expanded in ways that could not have been anticipated by Adam—even in his state of perfection. Similarly, creation awaits still greater imagination-defying wonders as God's creative intentions blossom at the parousia. While there is continuity between the articles as God relates to the created world, there is also purposeful, linear movement aimed at a definite goal as all of creation is swept up into God's unfolding master plan of creation, restoration, and consummation.

VIRTUE ETHICS WITHIN THE CREEDAL FRAME

The creedal framework, including the distinction of the three kinds of righteousness as just outlined, is exactly the sort of tool needed to help Lutheranism overcome its longstanding difficulties with Christian ethics. Lutheran theology is neither inherently nor by definition incapable of addressing ethical questions in vital ways. Indeed, Lutheran theology, and Lutheran thinking grounded in that theology, is quite capable of providing a meaningful connection between its theological convictions and both the cultivation of character and the pursuit of virtue integral to the practice-oriented interests of virtue ethics. The concerns and tenets of Lutheran doctrine and virtue ethics can be related meaningfully and powerfully in the paradigm provided by the creed.

Christians have long regarded the virtues with keen interest, recognizing in them potential allies in the task of cultivating Christian character.[40] It is hardly surprising that Aristotle and his ethics were received by the medieval church with such interest. The great Greek philosopher was, as Charles Arand notes, "looked upon as the philosopher who had come the farthest with respect to ethical questions."[41] Aristotle offered practical ideas and lofty goals that Christians could embrace. Moreover, Aristotle presented a system for the

---

38. LW 31:298–99.

39. WA 39/1:354. This translation is by James Arne Nestingen, "The Catechism's Simul," *Word & World* 3 (Fall 1983): 364–72.

40. See Josef Pieper, *The Four Cardinal Virtues: Prudence, Justice, Fortitude, Temperance* (Notre Dame, IN: University of Notre Dame Press, 1967), xi. Of course, Pieper also admits "It is true that the classic origins of the doctrine of virtue later made Christian critics suspicious of it. They warily regarded it as too philosophical and not Scriptural enough." See also the discussion in ch. 1.

41. Charles P. Arand, "Two Kinds of Righteousness as a Framework for Law and Gospel in the *Apology*," *Lutheran Quarterly* 15, no. 4 (Winter 2002): 422.

attainment of moral excellence that was both reasonable and workable. Arand succinctly and fairly summarizes Aristotle's program this way: "What we do determines who we are. Worthwhile activities make our lives worthwhile. By practicing virtue, we become virtuous."[42] So taught Aristotle, and so believed the church's teachers at the time of the Reformation.

While Melanchthon could agree with his contemporaries and affirm the legitimacy and value of Aristotelian philosophy, Aristotle's usefulness was always confined to the sphere of civil righteousness. This is a crucial limitation. For Melanchthon, Arand observes, "a righteousness of works or virtuous habits could shape the conduct of a person, but not change the heart."[43] From Melanchthon's perspective, the mistake of the medieval church was obvious. As Melanchthon saw it, "His opponents thus conceived of life not in terms of two perpendicular axes, (two different bases for two different kinds of righteousness), but as a single vertical continuum by which we ascend from this world to God. They had turned the horizontal axis onto its head and made it into a vertical ladder by which one ascended from earth to heaven."[44] The two distinct righteousnesses had been collapsed into one. Aristotle and his practical truth had been adopted as the single structuring frame for all of life. The Christian ideal of love, which transcended any standard advocated by Aristotle, was nevertheless fit into the philosopher's system. With the two kinds of righteousness having been reconfigured into one single kind of righteousness, the cultivation of the habit of love became the established route for the justification of the individual *coram Deo*. This was the faith-destroying error Luther and Melanchthon each endeavored to correct with their individual emphases on two kinds of righteousness.

The error of the medieval church, however, does not necessarily negate the validity or the usefulness of Aristotle's thinking on virtue and its cultivation.[45] Aristotle's observations and conclusions about human character and its development are founded in his study of the tangible realities of God's creation. The insights of a philosopher or a student of nature into some aspect of creation

---

42. Ibid., 428. See Aristotle, *The Nichomachean Ethics of Aristotle*, trans. Sir David Ross (London: Oxford University Press, 1925), Book 2, 4.

43. Arand, "Two Kinds," 435.

44. Ibid., 428.

45. Josef Pieper notes that by the time of Socrates, thinkers "took for granted not only the idea of virtue, which signifies human rightness, but also the attempt to define it in that fourfold spectrum [prudence, justice, fortitude, and temperance]" (*Four Cardinal Virtues*, xi). Nevertheless, Aristotle is typically singled out because of his extensive writing on the subject, and his subsequent influence in Western civilization, especially within the church.

are not nullified when it is revealed that in another sphere, *coram Deo*, they are not only wrong, but damnably dangerous in that they obscure Christ and his redeeming work. What is true remains true—within the appropriate sphere—much as the "truth" or rules for a game of croquet cannot be applied to a game of golf without the result being general chaos and mischief. The truth of each game holds within the sphere of that particular game.

The judicious and salutary course, then, is to fit Aristotle's teaching about the importance of virtue and the cultivation of character—observations confirmed by thinkers in virtually every subsequent generation—into a distinctively Christian frame expansive enough to accommodate these truths. This avoids two grave mistakes: either forcing Christian truth into Aristotle's frame as the pre-Reformation church had erroneously done, or summarily rejecting Aristotle's truth as a contradiction and danger to Christian faith as some Lutheran thinkers recently have done. The Christian creed provides the ideal pattern. The medieval church erred when it treated Aristotle as normative. Christian doctrine—whether the triumvirate of virtues of faith, hope, and love, or the crucial issue of one's justification before God—was forced and sometimes twisted into the Aristotelian pattern. Some of today's Lutherans have observed that thinking about virtue in the way of Aristotle is antithetical to a Christian confession of salvation by grace through faith alone, and wrongly conclude (by action if not by profession) that virtue has no place in Christian thinking. Instead, the creed should be established as the normative, regulating frame, and Aristotle's contribution given its place as one aspect of the overall Christian pattern supplied by the creed.[46]

The reformers did not attempt to correct their church's errant teaching by replacing the narrow *coram mundo* frame (supplied by Aristotle and promoting a life of virtue and merit) with an equally narrow *coram Deo* frame (focused only on the proclamation of the gospel of divine monergism and grace). Either frame, when made normative for all of human life and experience, collapses the two distinct righteousnesses into one and ends in error. The truth of both aspects must be maintained within the wider creedal frame that reflects God's will and activity on behalf of humanity in all areas of life. When a creedal framework is employed, it is immediately apparent that pursuing virtue and intentionally cultivating character are absolutely appropriate activities for Christians. The pursuit of virtue sustains the pursuit of righteousness *coram*

46. Certainly, as previously noted, the process of fitting Aristotle into a Christian—specifically a creedal—frame will sometimes require that Aristotle's contribution be trimmed or otherwise adjusted to square with the norming frame. The example of humility as a virtue presents itself as one case when this would be necessary.

mundo, a pursuit that is thoroughly God-pleasing and in conformity with Christian truth.

One of the strengths of the creedal framework is the compelling and frankly convincing answer that it offers to the question of mankind's purpose or telos. Though the idea of a human telos of any sort will be disputed and denounced by consistent evolutionary agnostics and atheists, most observant and reflective people still yearn for some answer to one of life's enduring big questions: What is the point of it all? The need to supply a reasonably satisfying answer is recognized by most thinkers, and even those not accustomed to thinking directly about such things would probably find themselves eventually agreeing with Aristotle that discerning the purpose of a thing is rather important for determining or evaluating the right actions of that thing. Aristotle concluded that *eudaimonia* was humanity's telos. Finding a worthy translation for *eudaimonia* is difficult. It means "pleasure"; but more than merely pleasant experiences, the word conveys a sense of contentment and an "all is well with me and the world" kind of existence. It is a deep, steady, settled happiness that endures. Aristotle was no hedonist. He understood this kind of happiness to be "activity in accordance with virtue," the best of which was the "life according to reason," or the contemplative life.[47] Based not on human reason, but on divine revelation, the creed provides a profoundly more fundamental, truthful, encompassing, and even practical telos than Aristotle's insightful yet reason-bound conclusions.

The creed takes into account humanity's purpose from a divine as well as a human perspective and binds them both under a singular goal: to become fully human. To be fully human, the creed teaches, is to be righteous before God and before humanity; that is, to be fully human is to be rightly related to God and to humanity, to Creator and to creation. Reinhard Hütter expresses the idea perfectly with his simple, yet powerful, definition of "genuine humanity" as "the truthful enactment of created existence."[48] This enactment takes place as people become all that God intends them to be in their creaturely relationships *coram Deo* and *coram mundo,* which, of course, is precisely what it means to be fully human. Thus, righteousness may be understood correctly as a synonym for genuine humanity or being fully human. When one becomes all that God intends, either *coram Deo* or *coram mundo*, then one has righteousness in that particular sphere.

47. Aristotle, *Nichomachean Ethics*, Book 10:6, 7.

48. Reinhard Hütter, "(Re-)Forming Freedom: Reflections 'After *Veritatis Splendor*' on Freedom's Fate in Modernity and Protestantism's Antinomian Captivity," *Modern Theology* 17, no. 2 (April 2001): 119, 130.

Aristotle's insights into human life and the role of virtue certainly are not denied by the creedal telos. Rather, the creedal frame actually permits Aristotle's ideas to operate freely—within their fitting sphere. The activity of striving to attain virtue, the creedal framework would allow, is part of what it means to become fully human according to God's intentions for the created world. Asheim argues that "God's will expressed in the concrete demand bound up with particular situations, enable[s] us to define ethical action as being laid upon us in and with our existence as human beings."[49] The virtuous individual is the one who is living, at least *coram mundo*, as truly and fully human—that is, according to God's will for God's creation.

Incidentally, it is worth noting that this application of the creedal frame provides a reasonable way of reading the potentially enigmatic reference in article 6 of the Augustana to good works "on account of God's will," or "for God's sake": "Likewise, they teach that this faith is bound to yield good fruits and that it ought to do good works commanded by God on account of God's will . . . It is also taught that such faith should yield good fruit and good works and that a person must do such good works as God has commanded for God's sake . . ."[50] Good fruit is produced by a good tree. Virtuous people produce virtuous acts. The fruitful living of Christians simply accords with the will of God for all of the whole of creation whether yet redeemed or not. This is why the good works are commanded "on account of God's will." Nestingen concurs: "That the Ten Commandments were given to Moses, that they are in the Bible, that they are understood in the Old Testament as torah—all of this is incidental to their explication of the ineradicable minimums of creatureliness."[51] God's commandments are "hard wired" into the universe; thus, fruitful living in conformity to those commandments is the only option for those desiring to live rightly, that is, virtuously. Those who are rightly related to God by grace through faith will also certainly conform to God's will for the right functioning of creation. The pursuit of virtue, then, is the pursuit of God's will for the creation.

To pursue virtue is to pursue the restoration of God's creation, the very reason for God's work of justifying fallen humans. Christians strive to grow in virtues and the consequent production of good works for their fellow creatures simply because this is their appropriate work as redeemed creatures—it is what they have been put here to do. Melanchthon concurs by providing an interesting correlation of the notion of duty with the idea of virtue: "It is

49. Asheim, *Christ and Humanity*, 15.

50. *Book of Concord*, 41, 40 (CA, 6, 1).

51. James Arne Nestingen, "Preaching the Catechism," *Word & World*, 10, no. 1 (Winter 1990): 36.

the duty of virtue to do what is right and be of use to others, even though the multitude may be ungrateful."[52] Indeed, it is the appropriate work of all creatures to seek this kind of virtue; Christians enjoy the advantage of being rightly related to the Creator, enabling them to live virtuously *coram mundo* with greater intentionality and understanding about what it is that they should be doing. This connectedness is visually illustrated in the figure by the connection between righteousness 3 and righteousness 2. Righteousness 3 runs parallel to righteousness 1. They are similar in that both conform to the same will of God for the entire realm of creation and in that both have reference to the *coram mundo* realm. Yet, there is a difference between these two righteousnesses. Because of their greater awareness of the divine source and reason for the arrangements of the horizontal realm, Christians will strive for standards that are at times higher and more intentionally in agreement with God's revealed commandments. Thus righteousness 3 functions in its own distinct plane above the righteousness common to unregenerate humanity. Of course, it is also distinct, in that the one who strives for conforming righteousness lives rightly related to God, and so ideally would pursue horizontal righteousness with motivations altogether foreign to one who does not know vertical righteousness.

For Christians, the expectation or perhaps even necessity that they pursue civil virtue, or virtue *coram mundo*, subtracts nothing from God's *coram Deo* decree of forgiveness and righteousness. The quest for virtue is part of the reality of life in God's created realm. In this realm, Christians would do well to heed Aristotle and the wise counsel of his students in subsequent generations, as well as other moralists and teachers with insight into the realities of human life and relationships as they offer guidance in the way of *coram mundo* righteousness.[53] Aristotle's place is in the first article (specifically, according to chart 5.1, Aristotle's place is in *both* the parallel lines of righteousness 1 and righteousness 3), where understood within the creedal frame he poses no theological threat and actually can be pressed into the service of the third article. Aristotle does not

---

52. Melanchthon, *Orations on Philosophy*, 138. Melanchthon's juxtaposition of duty and virtue is interesting in that philosophical ethics, especially Christian ethics, has traditionally held duty and virtue as almost antithetical ways of approaching the Christian life. See Pieper, *Four Cardinal Virtues*, xi–xii.

53. Of course, as previously noted, the pursuit of a peculiarly Christian telos will necessitate the adoption of a corresponding set of peculiarly Christian virtues. Some of these will neatly correspond to the virtues enumerated by Aristotle, while others may gain definitions other than those intended by Aristotle, and still other Christian virtues will be altogether at odds with some listings in Aristotle's catalog of virtues.

supply the frame. God does. Yet, within God's creedal frame there is an essential place for the Aristotelian tools known today as virtue ethics.

A Practical Illustration

The creedal framework as it has been presented with its distinction between three kinds of righteousness is quite adept at clarifying and conveying different aspects and emphases of theology. It has been demonstrated that creation, soteriology, eschatology, and the new obedience each has place within the frame; but other theological loci not yet specifically discussed also fit with comparable ease within the creedal frame. Another test remains: the frame's capacity for accurately and usefully handling the realities and experiences of actual life in light of the context of theological truth. In other words, can the proposed framework shed theological light on the sort of experiences and questions encountered in the course of ordinary life? A fictitious long-haul truck driver will serve as a helpful example.[54] My imaginary middle-aged laborer is not a Christian. Nevertheless, he is, from the perspective of all who know him, an upright, good, and moral man, raised to place a premium on personal honor, small-town kindness, and southern hospitality. These admirable traits are part of his character by virtue of the ceaseless training and example of parents, teachers, and peers who made up his community. Naturally, this driver regularly displays his noble character by stopping to aid distressed motorists, dealing honestly with business associates, looking out for fellow drivers, and obeying what he considers to be the spirit of the laws governing his industry. He is a "stand-up" kind of a guy. In the horizontal realm, *coram mundo*, the driver is doing it right. In fact, he is righteous. He has a righteousness according to the first distinction, governing righteousness. Without realizing it, he is fulfilling a God-given calling within the first article, conforming to the Creator's will for creation. Indeed, by ably fulfilling his vocation he is serving God's creation—he aids in the delivery and distribution of goods, thus contributing directly and indirectly to the welfare of others.[55] Nonetheless, in the vertical realm, *coram Deo*, he yet remains a condemned sinner—lost in spite of the many virtues in evidence in his life. He is, quite literally, good and damned.

54. Admittedly, there is good Lutheran precedent for using either a butcher or a cobbler as a generic example of an ordinary man living within the creation, but in the twenty-first century, a truck driver seems a more readily accessible representative figure.

55. Through this unbeliever who possesses governing righteousness, God is preserving and protecting God's creation, an example of God's *opera ad extra*.

One evening, however, the driver's life is dramatically changed during a break at a "Christian truck stop." Confronted with God's word, delivered through the means of a fellow driver, our imaginary unbeliever recognizes himself as a sinner and realizes the inadequacy and filthiness of even his greatest acts of kindness. Through the work of the Holy Spirit, he receives forgiveness in Christ and the multitude of blessings that come with faith. Of course, in time and in the context of continued catechesis, these gifts of forgiveness, faith, and divine adoption will be grounded and founded in the flood of baptism. Through the means of word and sacrament, the Holy Spirit does God's work. That evening, the word works. That evening, *coram Deo,* the driver is fully righteous and rejoices in the truth of God's work of salvation. That evening, *coram mundo,* he is still the same driver with the same virtues, though internally he is now reluctant to accept the world's judgment of his righteousness, aware as he is of a higher standard for his life in the world, a standard that far excels his own performance. The work of God the Holy Spirit according to the third article has brought the man to Christ, restoring him according to the divine intention for creation. Through faith, the driver is now rightly related to his Creator. God has accomplished the work of redemption and restoration; the driver now has justifying righteousness—vertical righteousness before God.

Genuinely converted—indeed, a "good tree" before God—he begins to produce good fruit, and the driver joins the fellowship of other Christians and worships with them. He steadily learns new aspects of what it means to be a Christian, one who is righteous *coram Deo.* At the same time, the driver strives to conform more fully to God's vision for humanity as revealed in the Scriptures, beginning with the Decalogue. Of course, as one who had previously lived as a righteous man *coram mundo,* this is not an altogether new activity. Before becoming a Christian, he had sought, albeit in a limited sense and unwittingly, to conform to God's will for humanity because he had been formed and shaped to do so by his community. Now, as a believer, he continues the endeavor but with new understanding and with new purpose—and a new community, the community of believers, the church. Indeed, our new believer eagerly pursues a new life, the third or conforming righteousness, similar yet completely different from the righteousness he once sought as an unbeliever. Part of this conformation to a new way of living will be the sometimes difficult task of forsaking old habits antithetical to his new identity (such as a penchant for off-color jokes and conversation), while simultaneously striving to acquire new habits of holiness (such as daily Scripture reading and prayer). Now, his compelling desire is to be what God created him to be—fully human, a creature rightly related to God through faith and eager to demonstrate love for his fellow creatures. By striving to be fully human, he follows the pattern of the one who fully accomplished God's will for humanity. Intentionally, he seeks a character more like that of his Lord, Jesus.

Digressing for a moment from the illustration of the converted truck driver, it is worth noting that both Hauerwas and Wingren, each in his own way, of course, endorse this tight connection between living as fully human and seeking to follow Christ. Hauerwas makes the connection this way: "Furthermore, to be a Christian is not principally to obey certain commandments or rules, but to learn to grow into the story of Jesus as the form of God's kingdom. We express that by saying we must learn to be disciples; only as such can we understand why at the center of creation is a cross and resurrection."[56] Gustaf Wingren considerably elaborates this link between Christ and God's intentions for creation and substantiates his claims with an appeal to the New Testament texts.

> The Creator who lets man live and who thereby creates him, creates him in His image (Gen. I.26 f.), and this image in which every man has been created is Jesus Christ, who is "the image of the invisible God, the first-born of all Creation" (Col. I.15). The "new Man" whom the believer in Christ "puts on" (Rom. XIII.14; Gal. III.27) is Christ Himself. This is what God the Creator intended man to be in Creation. To become like Christ, therefore, is also to conform to God's will in Creation and to receive "life" (cf. Col. III.10; Eph. IV.24).[57]

The insights of both theologians as recorded here conform to the Lutheran way of thinking we saw evidenced in the *Book of Concord*, and so fit easily and comfortably within the creedal framework.

Meanwhile, our newly reborn truck driver learns about his Lord and follows him by doing the things that Christians do. He joins himself to a faithful congregation, participates in the church's worship, and attends a Bible class. He begins to memorize Scripture and the catechism. He initiates the habit of personal devotions centered on Scripture and prayer. He reads Christian literature. He engages in dialogue with other believers. In short, he avails himself of the blessings of word and sacrament that constitute the community that is the church. He works to practice the virtues that typify and define this

---

56. Stanley Hauerwas, *The Peaceable Kingdom: A Primer in Christian Ethics* (Notre Dame, IN: University of Notre Dame Press, 1983), 30.

57. Wingren, *Creation and Law*, 35.

community. Consequently, his character, his guiding and directing morality, and what is in truth his *self*, is further shaped. Obviously, the pursuit of the Christian virtues certainly influences the cultivation of individual character. Roman Catholic moral theologians have long recognized this fact. An excellent representative, Romanus Cessario, sums up the connection quite well: "Virtue realizes a deliberate and efficacious modification of a person's capacity for performing well. It consists both in qualifying a person for the business of being human and a Christian for the business of being a Christian."[58] While our driver is certainly working to live a more virtuous life, in another sense, it is all the work of God through the third article that shapes his character in these new ways. His new way of living and being is worked by the Spirit and complements and fulfills what had already been put in place via the first-article training he had received even before becoming a Christian—and yes, some parts of that character marred and deformed by sin need to be cut away by the Spirit's transforming and conforming work.

L. Gregory Jones, scholar and professor at Duke Divinity School, corroborates this idea that Christian faith may well build on foundations already established, thus bringing about the *trans*formation of a person's existing character. He offers this insight:

> The new convert does not begin de novo. That is to say, she comes to Christianity as a person already habituated in certain perspectives; whatever else it is, the Christian context should not be described so much as moral formation as moral transformation. It is a reconstruction of humanity, a reorientation of moral perspective. . . . The Christian stake in moral formation is centered in the belief that formation can help to render a person's transformations intelligible and desirable.[59]

The character transformations brought about through God's third-article activity in the context of saving faith do not only or necessarily oppose, but in some ways actually complement and fulfill, what was already accomplished through God's first-article activity even before conversion. Indeed, the formation peculiar to the community of the church takes the individual to a higher, yet parallel plane; according to the three-kinds-of-righteousness frame, the person moves from governing righteousness to conforming righteousness.

58. Romanus Cessario, *The Moral Virtues and Theological Ethics* (Notre Dame, IN: University of Notre Dame Press, 1991), 54–54.

59. Jones, *Transformed Judgement*, 114.

Certainly, there will be an abundance of occasions when God's activity in the life of a believer will generate internal oppositions and conflict as the Old Adam resists the coming to life of the new man. Hauerwas may have been aiming his comment, "at the center of creation is a cross and resurrection," at the totality of creation that finds its meaning and purpose only in the cross, but it is also true of the individual's creation and recreation.[60] A central reality of conversion in Christ is the death of the old human and the coming to life of the new. Following Christ, the disciple *will* die to self and rise to a new life, and the cost of following could even demand a literal giving of physical life. Short of that complete sacrifice, every believer experiences many little deaths in the daily fight to drown the old man who is slow to die and, like the archvillain in a bad horror movie, notoriously unwilling to stay dead. The image of the Christian's dying and rising provides an important description of God's activity in the life of the believer.[61] The observation that there are likely many continuities between a person's virtues before and after conversion should not be construed as a denial of the validity and usefulness of the dying-and-rising motif. In truth, the process of refining and enhancing existing virtues and practices may at times be experienced as a process of dying and rising. The focus of this book's argument is to describe and emphasize, more specifically, how this dying and rising is made concrete in the life of a follower of Christ as she is formed by the community of faith and her character is more fully conformed to that of Christ.

Practicing virtues, whether old or new, the believer continually adds fresh and excellent contours to her own character. It is vital to keep in mind that vertical (divine monergism) and horizontal (human responsibility) realities are at work concurrently in this process of character formation. The Christian's character is fully shaped by God even through the habits that the individual is most certainly learning and the deeds that the same individual is definitely performing. The good works that were done before—good in the *coram mundo* sense of human interaction and evaluation—are still being done; only now, these good works are expanding in ever-increasing number, range, and quality. Now these good works are linked to the reality of the believer's second kind of righteousness, that is, passive justification *coram Deo*. The linkage is neither overly complicated nor amenable to much scrutiny or explanation. Christians simply live in the exhilarating and unspeakably comforting wonder of divine forgiveness and freedom even as they simultaneously strive to grow in good

---

60. Hauerwas, *Peaceable Kingdom*, 30.

61. See Gerhard Forde's thorough treatment, "Eleventh Locus: Christian Life," in Carl E. Braaten and Robert W. Jenson, eds., *Christian Dogmatics*, vol. 2 (Philadelphia: Fortress Press, 1984), 395–469, esp. 406–412.

works and character. True, new motives will be at work as they pursue lives of virtue, both love of God and concern for neighbor, yet the presence of new motives is, in a sense, almost incidental. More significant is the believer's possession of a new character, or more precisely, the same character now made, and being made, complete in Christ. The believer then lives accordingly, at once vigilantly active in the world of the first article, blessedly aware of the salvific truths of the second article, and eager for the consummation promised in the third article—the joyful day when that believer's standing *coram Deo* and *coram mundo* will become identical and all things, including the character of each individual Christian, will be fulfilled.

CONCLUSION

The framework provided by the church's creed and the three kinds of righteousness accommodates both the concerns and contributions of virtue ethics as well as the truths of Lutheran theology. Using the perspective provided by the creedal framework, it is readily apparent that Lutheran theology and virtue ethics are not mutually exclusive but are actually complementary. This suggested framework for theological thinking and Christian doing also provides a significant challenge to the conventional wisdom about Lutheranism's ethical disability. The notion that the Lutheran emphasis on justification by grace alone through faith disallows any possibility of producing or practicing a viable ethics is blunted, indeed invalidated, by Lutheran theologians who simply embrace the doctrine of their confessional heritage. Such students of the Confessions are able to follow the example of the reformers. They can retain the central and attendant articles of their faith, even as they utilize the tools and practice the arts supplied by virtue ethics. The creedal framework outlined in this chapter is sufficiently wide to encompass all that is involved with both Christian doctrine and Christian living. Indeed, as the next chapter will elaborate, a creedal framework does much to heal the disease that continues to infect much of Christendom—that is, the breech between doctrine and practice. As this unfortunate and debilitating division is made right, the way will also be made clear for the active and intentional cultivation of Christian character.

6

An Ethic for the Church
The Place of Character Formation

The death of character as eulogized by James Davison Hunter seems to be an altogether modern—or perhaps some would argue, postmodern—problem.[1] In many ways, of course, it is. Economic, societal, academic, and psychological forces have collided if not conspired to create the normal nihilism and therapeutic culture that now define Western civilization.[2] But the final passing of character after a long but precipitous decline has not provoked the shedding of tears or the founding of memorials. Besides some who make it their business to worry, few notice and few seem to care, which is not surprising given the realities of the sort of world in which the would-be mourners live. Christians, however, do care—or at least they should. Christians care about character because character is the reflection of a person who is living in tune with the Creator's will. Character is a living profession of the basic truth of this world's inherent, God-given order. Hunter is quite right: "To have a renewal of character is to have a renewal of a creedal order that constrains, limits, binds, obligates, and compels."[3] A pluralistic, therapeutic world of normal nihilism scoffs at the idea of a comprehensive order that directs all things, but the church

---

1. James Davison Hunter, *The Death of Character: Moral Education in an Age without Good or Evil* (New York: Basic Books, 2000), xiii–xv. Admittedly, Hunter wrote not a sympathetic eulogy but, rather, a more sober and factual yet no less passionate postmortem for character.

2. The amount of material written on the contemporary situation and its causes is bewildering. But one would be well served by considering James C. Edwards, *The Plain Sense of Things: The Fate of Religion in an Age of Normal Nihilism* (University Park: Pennsylvania State University Press, 1997); and Philip Rieff, *The Triumph of the Therapeutic* (Chicago: University of Chicago Press, 1966). Also worth consideration are two from Peter Berger: *The Heretical Imperative* (New York, Anchor, 1979) and *The Sacred Canopy* (New York: Anchor, 1967).

3. Hunter, *Death of Character*, xv.

embraces it. The culture cannot cultivate character. It is simply incapable of the feat. But the church can. In fact, the church is ideally suited for the task of character formation—that is, if the church can come to terms with the idea that training in character is not somehow antithetical to its own essence or raison d'être. This challenge is hardly a new one. The end of character as a viable cultural objective may be a new phenomenon, but the church's struggle rightly to locate the place of moral training and formation in character is very old, indeed.

If Lutherans Can Do It, Anyone Can

While even the book of James can be read as an effort to inculcate moral virtue among people saved by grace, it is enough for the present purpose to go back in church history only half a millennia and pick up the saga of the church's effort to understand the place best to fit character formation with the advent of Lutheranism. Since the beginning of the Reformation, of course, Lutherans have championed the foundation of justification by grace through faith alone. This doctrine remains, quite rightly, a central hallmark of Lutheran theology. Nevertheless, even the earliest Lutheran theologians were aware of the potential hazard of a lackadaisical licentiousness that abuses the central doctrine and makes a mockery of the Christian life. The relentless tug of sinful appetites is, as James and the other scriptural authors amply attest, simply a reality of life in a fallen world. The struggle against the temptation to sinful indulgence is challenge enough, though, without the complication of a doctrinal position that, intentionally or not, actually serves the cause of sin by denigrating God's law. Whether in the name of crass immoral license, human freedom, individual autonomy, or even the protection of the gospel, theologians commit a serious error when they endorse an antinomian spirit that in any way disregards or diminishes God's commandments.

Well aware of the gravity of this errant move, the first generation of reformers resisted the antinomian incursion, with both Luther and Melanchthon involved directly in the fighting. Reinhard Hütter considers this battle to be a significant shift in the course and emphasis of the Reformation: "It is important to at least explicitly acknowledge Luther's clear awareness of how radically the context in the course of the Reformation problematic changed from anxiety-driven works-righteousness to self-confident moral libertinism and indifferentism."[4]

---

4. Reinhard Hütter, "(Re-)Forming Freedom: Reflections 'After *Veritatis Splendor*' on Freedom's Fate in Modernity and Protestantism's Antinomian Captivity," *Modern Theology* 17, no. 2 (April 2001): 140. See

The challenge did not abate during the next generation, and the framers of the Formula of Concord were compelled to devote two full articles (four and six) and portions of others to the defense of orthodoxy against antinomian interests and influences. The confessors suffered no illusions as to the significance of the threat:

> For particularly in these last times it is no less necessary to admonish the people to Christian discipline and good works and to remind them how necessary it is that they practice good works as a demonstration of their faith and their gratitude to God than it is to admonish them that works not be mingled with the article on justification. For people can be damned by an Epicurean delusion about faith just as much as by the papistic, Pharisaic trust in their own works and merit.[5]

Notwithstanding such pointed admonitions endorsing the necessity of good works, while condemning the danger of a licentious Epicurean delusion, the antinomian foe demonstrated tremendous resilience. In whatever fresh form it was given, the question about the law and its relation to the believer would be visited and revisited with remarkable regularity in subsequent generations. Indeed, the debate has become so closely associated with Lutheranism that it is sometimes considered to be a defining characteristic of Lutheran theology.

In the early decades of thetwentieth century, this old Lutheran concern received renewed attention and enjoyed a fresh and extensive treatment in Adolf Köberle's thorough study known in English as *The Quest for Holiness.* Köberle left no doubt about his motivations for writing. The same antinomian spirit that had troubled the Reformation church was a compelling concern in Köberle's penetrating work, and he advocated an ambitious inculcation of morality intended to stem the tide of societal license:

> When, as at the present time, the desecration of Sunday is regarded as unblameworthy and a matter of course, when the proprieties in the relations of the sexes have ceased to exist and the fashions have become boundlessly indecent, such degeneration cannot be

also Luther's 1537 Theses against the Antinomians in WA 39/1, 342–58; and Timothy Wengert, *Law and Gospel: Philipp Melanchthon's Debate with John Agricola of Eisleben over* Poenitentia (Grand Rapids: Baker, 1997).

5. *Book of Concord,* 499 (FC Ep 4, 18). For a discussion of the Formula's suggested motivation for ethical behavior, see ch. 4. It is worth noting that the word translated "discipline" (*Zucht*) can also be translated "rearing" or "cultivation."

overcome by a single outburst of moral indignation. For custom whether it be noble, dead or repulsive always exerts a compelling influence over the collective consciousness of men; it has the power of producing an atmosphere by which thousands are consciously or unconsciously affected. It is always more powerful than a passing changing word. And, as Bruno Gutmann has correctly stated, "Only evil customs grow by themselves," while good customs need continual fidelity and renewed inculcation.[6]

Not only is the quotation relevant to the discussion at hand, but it is also a pointed reminder that no Christian generation is immune from the pressures of a faithless culture. While comparisons between eras and generations are invariably a perilous undertaking, it seems safe to say that Köberle's observation and exhortation is as relevant in the twenty-first century as it was in 1936 when his book was first published.

The intentional cultivation of Christian character is, then, an objective well within the purview of Christian faith and Lutheran confession. As the expression of an individual's creaturely identity, character indicates the manifestation of an individual's self in personal relations and activities *coram mundo*. Thus deliberate character development can be an effective corrective against the danger of the licentious attitude that currently pervades Western culture. From Köberle's perspective, this formation of character was, unquestionably, the business of the church: "Because customs always possess such an overmastering and formative influence, that is so much stronger than mere admonition, it remains as an essential task of the Church to use the power of custom in her constructive work that it may here serve to overcome the evil spirits and bring a blessing, as there it serves to destroy."[7] A "single outburst of moral indignation" is insufficient—an occasional stiff blast from the pulpit will not accomplish what needs to be done. The cultivation of character and the inculcation of admirable virtues require constant and consistent modeling, training, and practice. Köberle understood what Luther and Melanchthon recognized: the inculcation of righteous character necessitates purposeful and intentional formation and habituation.

6. Adolf Köberle, *The Quest for Holiness: A Biblical, Historical and Systematic Investigation*, trans. John C. Mattes (New York: Harper & Bros., 1938; reprint, Evansville, IN: Ballast, 1998), 202.

7. Ibid.

THE PLACE OF CHARACTER FORMATION

The effort of this book has been to demonstrate that Lutheran theology is able to provide a way to encourage habituation of character without undermining the doctrine of justification by grace through faith alone. Formation in character is not antithetical to the doctrine of justification. Shaping character through intentional inculcation of virtues is simply giving a God-directed form to the believer's life. Hütter correctly identifies this as a genuinely Lutheran position, since Luther himself did "not hesitate to put forth the Decalogue as the blueprint for the *gestalt* of Christian freedom."[8] What God declares, Christians live out. Directed and encouraged by the Holy Spirit, believers actively pursue God's intent for humanity. "It might come as a surprise to many," observes Hütter, "but clearly Luther assumes the original unity of Gospel and Law, of a creaturely freedom in communion with God that is practiced in obedience to God's commandment and thereby precisely receives its creaturely form."[9] Human beings are created to be shaped by God's law or commandment; Christians learn this and embrace it as the compelling and satisfying telos of life.

Martha Stortz provides additional support for a thoroughly Lutheran concept and practice of character formation. Like Hütter, she founds her argument on the writing of Luther himself, examining Luther's understanding of the appropriate relation between justification and the cultivation of character. Though it is commonly known that Luther was fond of the image of a good tree automatically bearing good fruit, Stortz calls attention to Luther's recognition of its limitations:

> In his catechetical material Luther trades organic metaphors for direct instruction. People are not plants; they both need and desire concrete ways of responding to divine initiative. In his pastoral counsel he exhorts pastors in their instruction to "lay the greatest weight on those commandments or other parts which seem to require special attention among the people where you are." Instruction and exhortation replace organic necessity.[10]

Formation is not automatic or self-fulfilling, but requires deliberate and directed effort toward a goal. Stortz discerns a threefold approach to formation in

8. Hütter, "(Re-)Forming Freedom," 138.

9. Ibid., 143.

10. Martha Stortz, "Practicing Christians: Prayer as Formation," in Karen L. Bloomquist and John R. Stumme, eds., *The Promise of Lutheran Ethics* (Minneapolis: Fortress Press, 1998), 59. Stortz quotes Luther from the preface to the Small Catechism.

Luther's work, referring to worship, catechesis, and individual prayer as "a three-legged stool on which Luther's approach to formation rests."[11] In another place, she terms this triumvirate "a trinity at the heart of Luther's work on formation."[12]

Stortz has no difficulty identifying examples of Luther's interest in formation and is satisfied that the evidence confirms what she regards as "Luther's obvious efforts in the work of formation."

> Rather than recruiting Aristotle in this enterprise, Luther turns to the practices of Christian discipleship or, in his own words, to the "marks of the church." These practices shape person and community for worship and witness. Virtues like responsiveness, gratitude, modesty, and joy come to characterize people and communities who engage in the practices. The Decalogue is the template for discerning concrete acts on behalf of the neighbor in the world.[13]

Stortz perhaps underestimates the extent to which Aristotle was safely and satisfactorily enlisted in the efforts of the Reformation church to shape character (and, it might be noted, the extent to which twenty-first-century heirs of that church might beneficially use Aristotle). Nevertheless, she does help to make clear that at the outset Lutheranism allowed sufficient space for the development of Christian ethics, including the formation of character.

The willingness and even eagerness of church leaders to find a significant place for the work of character formation extended into later generations and locations of the Reformation. Though it was not the intent of his research, and though noteworthy scholars have rightly challenged his conclusions, the work of Gerald Strauss yet provides substantial evidence of the early reformers' tireless commitment to the task of habituation and character formation. Strauss's work, published as *Luther's House of Learning*, is subtitled *Indoctrination of the Young in the German Reformation*. Strauss starts from a well-attested premise about the Lutheran Reformation in Germany:

> It embarked on a conscious and, for its time, remarkably systematic endeavor to develop in the young new and better impulses, to implant inclinations in consonance with the reformer's religious and civic ideals, to fashion dispositions in which Christian ideas of right

11. Ibid., 63.
12. Ibid., 71.
13. Ibid., 70.

thought and action could take root, and to shape personalities capable of turning the young into new men—into the human elements of a Christian society that would live by evangelical principles.[14]

The reformers, Strauss observes, sought to accomplish this goal through widespread efforts of education and catechesis.

Rich with primary source material and references, *Luther's House of Learning* documents the extent of the Reformation's pedagogical effort but ultimately judges the entire undertaking a dismal failure. Strauss bases his negative assessment on his reading of the visitation records still housed in the libraries of various Reformation cities. Here, as Strauss interprets the data, the sorry story of continued and persistent immorality and worldliness, despite the best efforts at Reformation indoctrination and inculcation, belies the efficacy of Reformation efforts at formation.[15]

One could certainly take exception to Strauss's interpretation. Lewis Spitz does, challenging Strauss's underlying assumption that the visitation records truly reflected an accurate picture of the entire society. Further, such a pessimistic interpretation is unwarranted, Spitz contends, since "the visitation reports are almost by virtue of their purpose apt to emphasize abuses and failures" rather than highlight positive outcomes.[16] For the purposes of this study, however, the veracity of Strauss's interpretation is virtually irrelevant. It is sufficient to recognize the remarkable attention and effort that the reformers dedicated to the task of formation. This truth is well documented by Strauss and not subject to dispute. Robert Kolb substantiates this claim, noting the practice of two second-generation reformers. "In any case," writes Kolb, "Spangeberg's and Musculus' calls for the repentance of nobles and burghers demonstrate the deep concern of Luther's and Melanchthon's students that their hearers live the Christian life according to strict moral standards."[17] Spitz goes further, arguing that the efforts may well have been quite effective: "A vast body of other literature—devotional booklets for families, aids for catechetical instruction in

14. Gerald Strauss, *Luther's House of Learning: Indoctrination of the Young in the German Reformation* (Baltimore: Johns Hopkins University Press, 1978), 2.

15. Ibid., 307.

16. Lewis Spitz, review of Gerald Strauss's *Luther's House of Learning*, *American Historical Review* 85 (February 1980): 143.

17. Robert Kolb, "The Devil & the Well-Born: Proclamation of the Law to the Privileged in the Late Reformation," in *Let Christ Be Christ: Theology, Ethics, & World Religions in the Two Kingdoms*, ed. Daniel N. Harmelink (Huntington Beach, CA: Tentatio Press, 1999), 170.

the household (not just by the state), hymnbooks, prayerbooks, well thumbed in extant copies—suggests a vital religious life among the common people."[18]

Whether or not they were successful—and one should be reluctant to follow Strauss in denying any success—the early generations of reformers unquestionably made substantial attempts to promote the formation of Christian character through habituation. As Strauss concludes, "In practice, especially the practice of pedagogy, doubt was not allowed to weaken the proposition that right-thinking and right-living men and women would emerge from a systematic program of religious and ethical indoctrination."[19] The reformers not only proclaimed the gospel; they also sought to shape character through concerted practices of habituation and inculcation.

Considering the evidence from the first wave of reformation, the subsequent generations of reformers, the confessions, and more recent Lutheran thinkers, the conclusion is clear: a reluctance to promote and to practice the cultivation of character and formation in Christian virtue is evidence not of fidelity to Lutheran theology, but of its betrayal.

The Relation between Faith and the Cultivation of Character

Another interesting discussion catalyzed by the material presented in this study is the relationship between faith and virtue. It should be evident from the preceding chapters that the development of character should in no way be considered equivalent to growth in faith. Salvation and the faith that apprehends God's gift of grace are both divine works that transform the individual *coram Deo*. There is nothing that demands development, indeed, nothing that permits development, in the Christian's standing before God. *Coram Deo*, scriptural and confessional integrity demand the maintenance of a strict divine monergism. Justification by grace through faith alone is the precious and enduring legacy of the Reformation. Nothing that has been presented in this book, including even the slightest supporting argument, should be construed as undermining or threatening this legacy.

Still, it must be granted that the shaping of character through the inculcation of right thinking and the exercise of right habits does—in some way—touch also the believer's relationship to God. The truth of this statement is borne out in the ordinary and obvious experience of infants maturing in their Christian faith and learning to trust in their baptisms. This increasing trust (not to be confused with justifying faith), wrought through the unflagging efforts

18. Spitz, review of Strauss, *Luther's House*, 143.

19. Strauss, *Luther's House*, 39.

of parents and parish, is a fruit of formation that certainly has a marked effect on the young believer's relationship with God. While it is supremely true that God accomplishes the gift of salvation and blesses individuals with their new identity—declaring them heirs of divine grace in Christ—it cannot be denied that identity to some extent is also shaped by the practices and habits that result from intentional formation. The ingrained habits of regular church attendance and daily Scripture reading are two common examples of this process at work.

Gilbert Meilaender concurs with these observations and supports the idea that a Christian's actions and habits have an impact on that individual's identity and character—character being, as noted previously, quite simply the manifestation of the person's identity. In his contribution in a collection of Protestant responses to *Veritatis Splendor*, Meilaender concentrates on the importance of the tension inherent in Luther's *simul iustus et peccator*, and concludes:

> No Christian ethic can say everything that needs saying solely through the Reformation language of "faith active in love." If we dare never say for certain that a particular deed makes the simul of faith impossible, we ought not deny that our deeds do shape our character—and that they have the power to make of us people who no longer trust God for our security in life and death.[20]

This is no mere passing thought for Meilaender; neither does he restrict the influence or power of deeds to negative consequences—the loss of trust in God. Extolling the value of C. S. Lewis for developing "a theology for the everyday," Meilaender calls attention to the positive power of deeds:

> In good Aristotelian fashion, therefore, Lewis thinks of all the ordinary decisions of life as forming our character, as turning us into people who either do or do not wish to gaze forever upon the face of God. . . . Every choice counts. Every choice contributes to determining what we ultimately love.

> Protestant readers may, I believe, be especially drawn to this picture because, though they might not articulate the matter this way, it supplies something that is often missing from standard Protestant talk

---

20. Gilbert Meilaender, "Grace, Justification through Faith, and Sin," in Reinhard Hütter and Theodor Dieter, eds., *Ecumenical Ventures in Ethics: Protestants Engage Pope John Paul II's Moral Encyclicals* (Grand Rapids: Eerdmans, 1998), 82.

of forgiveness and faith, pardon and trust. Lewis's picture suggests that our actions are important not only because they hurt or harm the neighbor, but also because—under grace—they form and shape the persons we are.[21]

Meilaender does not, however, need Lewis to escort him into an affirmation of virtuous deeds shaping character. Later in the same volume, he reiterates a similar Aristotelian sort of conviction: "Because structure shapes spirit, moral virtue is simply habit long continued. The inner self—what we are likely to call 'character'—is developed and molded by the structures within which we live daily. Only gradually do we become people whose character is established—who, for better or worse, can be depended upon to act in certain ways."[22] In good Lutheran fashion, though, Meilaender rightly tempers his affirmation of the power of habituation to shape character with an acknowledgment of the believer's continued and complete dependence on God: "Just as God cannot be captured or possessed by our side in any partisan struggle, so true virtue cannot simply become our possession—as if the mysterious working of God's grace on our inner self had no part to play, as if the tree did not have to be made good before its fruit could be good."[23]

A Christian's identity—who one is in Christ—is unquestionably a strong force that drives one's actions and cultivation of habits. This is the well-argued point Robert Kolb makes:

> The art of living the Christian life two-dimensionally is the art of recognizing that my identity—my "self," who I am—is a gift of God the Creator, never a product of my own or other human, creaturely hands, and at the same time—simultaneously—hearing God's voice which calls me to specific acts of obedience in response to specific calls to service. These calls come from him through the neighbor; they are opportunities for playing out our identity in the horizontal realm.[24]

Meilaender is concerned, however, that Kolb's analysis "may not probe the matter deeply enough." While Kolb's view provides a portion of the picture,

---

21. Gilbert Meilaender, *Things That Count: Essays Moral and Theological* (Wilmington, DE: ISI Books, 2000), 131–32.

22. Ibid., 187.

23. Ibid.

24. Robert Kolb, "Niebuhr's 'Christ and Culture in Paradox' Revisited," *Lutheran Quarterly* 10 (1996): 268.

Meilaender contends, as just noted, that "character is formed, in part, from the outside in." He continues, "Thus, true as it is to say that we are the person God declares us to be through the merits of Christ, we are also the person shaped by what—under grace—we do."[25] The Christian's identity is shaped in Christ also in a reciprocal way—by the actions that are done and the habits that have been developed. It is not entirely a unidirectional event. Habits and actions performed by the person certainly do also affect the believer's standing *coram Deo*.[26]

Obviously, standard doctrinal questions about the relationship between divine sovereignty and human agency come into play when an effort is made to determine the source of identity. Rightly appreciating the reality of secondary causes would greatly diminish the perplexity over who or what creates identity. Yet, regardless the doctrinal verities involved, the persistent notion that personal identity is untouched by personal action endures with almost axiomatic authority in most Lutheran circles. It is significant, then, that Meilaender traces this book's central concern—the feeble understanding of character formation within Lutheranism—to an over-simplification of the relationship between a person's identity before God and one's identity before humanity:

So (1) I can be wrong with God even while treating the neighbor rightly, and (2) I can be right with God even while treating the neighbor wrongly. How can these two identities of mine be unified? Or do we end in paradox after all—able to say only that one must trust that one's "true" self is the one who, for Christ's sake, is right with God? If that is all we can say, and if it is rightly said of all who have faith, then holiness of life seems entirely irrelevant to our true identity. And, alas, Lutheranism has no ethic—as its detractors have sometimes suggested.[27]

Meilaender's assessment is altogether accurate. It is important that strong and lively connections between the believer's life *coram Deo* and *coram mundo* be maintained. Yet, a clear delineation of these connections is not only difficult, but dangerous—at least theologically dangerous. Meilaender himself warns

25. Gilbert Meilaender, "Reclaiming the Quest for Holiness," *Lutheran Quarterly* 13 (Winter 1999): 486.

26. For example, the Christian who fails to establish a pious habit of regular worship attendance could well cultivate a detrimental habit of neglect of the means of grace. Such an onerous habit would eventuate in the erosion and extinction of faith.

27. Ibid., 487.

elsewhere against yielding to "the temptation to step across the gap which divides inculcation of the virtues from shaping the soul."[28] The interrelationship between growth in virtue *coram mundo* and individual identity *coram Deo* remains at once tremendously dense and delicate, and wisdom would dictate a marked reticence about offering descriptions of it. While an explication of the relationship remains elusive, it is evident that a relationship does, nevertheless, exist.

One of the strengths of thinking within a creedal framework is the clarification of at least one connection that can be safely traced between the two potentially disparate aspects of faith and character. In the created realm into which the justified person is sent, there is the possibility, indeed the expectation, of continual growth and development. The Christian's character becomes more Christian. The Christian life is marked by the production of abundant good works and the increasing practice of virtue. The development of character does not and cannot win for the believer status before God, yet this status—granted by grace alone—has a decided impact on the believer's growth in character. As Kolb emphasizes, what God declares about the believer unquestionably shapes the person he becomes in his activities *coram mundo*.

Dietrich Bonhoeffer also grasped the importance of this truth. The Christian's life is shaped by the one who redeems and establishes the relationship of faith:

> What matters in the Church is not religion but the form of Christ, and its taking form amidst a band of men. . . . We have now seen that it is only with reference to the form that we can speak of formation in a Christian and ethical sense. Formation is not an independent process or condition which can in some way or other be detached from this form. The only formation is formation by and into the form of Jesus Christ.[29]

Christians strive for virtue not to perfect their nature or to achieve personal fulfillment, still less to win divine favor. They seek to gain a character stamped with virtue because they are acutely aware that this is the standard that Christ himself has established for humanity. And as the creed makes manifest, we were

28. Gilbert Meilaender, *The Theory and Practice of Virtue* (Notre Dame, IN: University of Notre Dame Press, 1984), 126.

29. Dietrich Bonhoeffer, *Ethics*, ed. Eberhard Bethge, trans. Neville Horton Smith (New York: Macmillan, 1955), 21.

created to be fully human. Fully human people are virtuous people seeking the character of the one who shows perfectly what it means to be human.

Meilaender explains the place of Christ as redeemer and exemplar this way:

> Examining our deeds, it may, of course, sometimes seem paradoxical that an identity shaped by such deeds should be one with which God is well pleased. But the unity of our self—and the burden of seeing to it that this unity is one day manifest—lies in God's word of both pardon and power. He is intent upon renewing us after the image of his Son, and we must therefore be just as intent upon seeking that renewal—that holiness—in our being and our doing. Ethics matter—coram deo.[30]

Ethics matters to God because God has a will for creation. God's will for humanity is that each person be fully human—in possession of virtues which make one an able servant to the rest of creation. This is not a pursuit of virtue for the sake of virtue, but for the sake of conformity to Christ who is the perfect standard of what it means to be human, and for the sake of the neighbor who depends on the Christian's service. There is ample room within this framework to reclaim an appropriate understanding of the *imitatio Christi*.[31]

A thoroughgoing pursuit of this potent topic of imitation would lead far from the path that has been determined for this text. It is enough to allow generous space for Köberle to speak with his characteristic eloquence on the place and need for a Lutheran use of the *imitatio Christi*:

> It is necessary to remind ourselves most emphatically what a deep significance the concrete contemplation of the historic picture of the life of Jesus has for our sanctification. For us men who have daily to contend with flesh and blood it is of supreme importance to see how the Holy One of God conducted Himself amid the sinful, wretched, contentious realities of this earth and at the same time preserved His holiness. . . . For that reason only such an example has a liberating effect, which comes from a complete, real human life that was lived

---

30. Meilaender, "Reclaiming the Quest," 491.

31. Roman Catholic moral theology has, not surprisingly, a well-developed concept of the *imitatio Christi*. It is interesting to note that some of their scholars describe "a real participation in the *imitatio Christi*" as "the new 'form' which the infused virtue puts in the believer" (Romanus Cessario, *The Moral Virtues and Theological Ethics* [Notre Dame, IN: University of Notre Dame Press, 1991], 112). This thought bears a remarkable affinity to the present discussion regarding the difference that justification by faith makes in the everyday life of the believer.

in this world and that has known and overcome the needs and trials of humanity. For the formation of the image of God within us, for the renewing of our minds (Rom. 12:2; Eph. 5:17), for the control of our emotions, for the determination of the manner and form of our conduct, the contemplation of the teaching, praying, healing, suffering Savior as He is portrayed in Scripture is indispensable.[32]

Thus the creed, with articles on creation, redemption, and restoration/fulfillment, pulls together the Christian's life *coram Deo* and *coram mundo*. Meilaender provides this succinct summary: "Both identities find their unity in the one Christ, who brings the Father to us and us to the Father. The wholeness and oneness of our identity is God's work. Because he is seriously committed to it, we must also be so committed. Because he is seriously committed to it, we need not doubt that the gap between our two identities will one day be overcome."[33] This rich understanding of the relation between faith and the Christian's life should not be mistaken for a mere motivational connection. Unity in the believer's life is found in Christ. Christ clothes his people with his righteousness. His people strive to become more fully like Christ—more fully human. It is simply what it means to be human. Humans do what humans were created to do. The issue of motivation, or the "why question," is of only secondary importance at best.

The other members of God's creation that stand over against humanity in consistently and correctly serving their Creator do so as they yield to instinct or the "laws of nature." They do what "comes naturally." By being appropriately creaturely, each conforms to God's creative intention for its kind. Thus geese migrate with the seasons, bees gather nectar and inadvertently pollinate flowers, and dogs enthusiastically greet their human caretakers, while cats nonchalantly ignore theirs. Every part of creation moves in conformity with the will of the Creator. So, then, should God's highest creation, humans. For the unbeliever, whether moral or otherwise, this is little more than a matter of conforming, in varying degrees, to the internal and natural knowledge that this is humanity's created purpose—just as Paul has it in Romans 2. For Christians, the desire to be all that they were created to be takes on a deliberate and purposeful nature. Aware of God's grace and God's will, they desire, both by "instinct" and by revelation, to be as God created them to be: fully human—that is, like Christ. Thus the believer's standings *coram Deo* and *coram mundo* are once more tightly bound and interrelated.

32. Köberle, *Quest for Holiness*, 158.
33. Ibid., 491.

FROM THEORY TO PRACTICE

Another objective of this focused study that hopefully, to some extent, has been realized, is the provision of a way to proceed beyond theory to direct application. Stanley Hauerwas once made the pointed observation that "too often theologians spend their time writing prolegomena, that is, essays on theological method meant to show how theology should be done in case anyone ever got around to doing any."[34] Similarly, if a study on theological ethics cannot be translated into tangible application at a personal and parish level, its value and even validity must come under suspicion. Meilaender is cognizant of the frequent disconnect between merely presenting a sublime thought or theory and converting it into action:

> And one thing more: Even if the approach I have taken is sound and is to be recommended, we need finally to acknowledge for ourselves and fellows that the trick is not only to see or say this but to live it. As St. Augustine says at the end of Book VII of the Confessions: It is one thing to see from a mountaintop in the forests the land of peace in the distance . . . and it is another thing to hold to the way that leads there."[35]

Unfortunately, the sought-after application is seldom easily accomplished. While Meilaender is able to contend for the application of theory, he readily admits in another place that this often proves to be an elusive goal. After offering one of his most thoroughgoing attempts at a description of the place of virtue in the Christian life, Meilaender concedes, "We need not deny that it may prove difficult to translate theory into practice and find a way to do justice to both senses of virtue in our lives."[36]

Still, perhaps Meilaender's desire to move from theory into practice is made more difficult needlessly by the tension inherent in his dual understanding of virtue as something that the Christian accomplishes as well as something that God alone can grant. Meilaender does make a move toward the unifying capabilities of narrative that "Christians tell and retell—a story, not yet finished, in which God is graciously at work transforming sinners into saints."[37] He does not, however, specifically fix his duality within a wider horizon that embraces both aspects in a practical way. It would indeed be difficult to apply

34. Stanley Hauerwas, *Sanctify Them in the Truth: Holiness Exemplified* (Nashville: Abingdon, 1998), 34.
35. Gilbert Meilaender, "The Task of Lutheran Ethics," *Lutheran Forum* 34, no. 4 (Winter 2000): 22.
36. Meilaender, *Theory and Practice*, 123.
37. Ibid., 125.

his tension-based understanding in a parish setting. The teaching would be ripe for a harvest of confusion as people inevitably would resolve the tension by affirming one or other of the poles while diminishing the antithesis.[38] As David Yeago convincingly demonstrates in his essay on the misconstrual of the classic Lutheran paradigm, this is precisely the problem that dogs the vital distinction between law and gospel.[39]

What Meilaender hints at with his nod toward a narrative understanding of the Christian life that resolves the practical tensions of the Christian life at the eschaton, the creedal framework makes explicit. The creed is, in fact, essentially a narrative. Dorothy Sayers recognized this fact and offered an eloquent description:

> The Christian faith is the most exciting drama that ever staggered the imagination of man—and the dogma is the drama. That drama is summarized quite clearly in the creeds of the Church, and if we think it dull it is because we either have never really read those amazing documents or have recited them so often and so mechanically as to have lost all sense of their meaning. The plot pivots upon a single character, and the whole action is the answer to a single central problem: *What think ye of Christ?*[40]

The creed in any of its three ecumenical forms—though less simply with the Athanasian—relates the account of God's relationship with this world. The story begins with God's action of creation, unfolds with the account of the redemption of God's rebellious and fallen creation, humans, and culminates in the final restoration and consummation at the resurrection of the dead. This is the narrative that directs and explains not only this world, but the lives of individual Christians. With all the rest of creation, the Christian lives, only by the grace of the Creator, to accomplish the purpose of the Creator by serving the rest of creation, in anticipation of the Creator's promised consummation of all the creation.

---

38. It is possible that this criticism applies also to Köberle's work. Köberle's understanding of the relation between justification and sanctification is grounded in an irresolvable tension that again poses a tremendous challenge in translation to the needs of parish ministry. See Köberle, *Quest for Holiness*, 256–65.

39. David S. Yeago, "Gnosticism, Antinomianism, and Reformation Theology: Reflections on the Costs of a Construal." *Pro Ecclesia* 2, no. 1 (Winter 1993): 37–49.

40. Dorothy L. Sayers, *The Whimsical Christian: 18 Essays by Dorothy L. Sayers* (Boston: G. K. Hall & Co., 1979), 20–21 (emphasis in original).

Gustaf Wingren, of course, did much to restore a dynamic doctrine of creation to theological discussion. In *Creation and Law* he argues for the primary spot of creation and consistently thinks in narrative terms. This allows him to give almost poetic expression to the unifying capabilities that the narrative of the creedal framework lends to Christian faith and the Christian walk:

> While man lives in the world he continues to be affected by the Gospel and his Baptism, but in this he is one with the rest of the world in awaiting an event which will happen not only to him and to the Church, but to all men—the return of Christ, the Last Judgment, and the resurrection of the dead. This last event has already begun with the work of the Spirit in the Church. Everything, therefore, that takes place in the Church takes place with the whole of Creation and for the whole of Creation. What happens in the Church is simply the continuation of what happened when Christ became man. And He became man in order to restore what God had created.[41]

Wingren's grasp of creation as the context for God's narrative of salvation and for human action provides unity to the Christian's life as it relates the two kinds of righteousness together in a meaningful way. Following Sayers and Wingren, the creedal emphasis as presented and expounded in chapter 5 holds tremendous potential as a key for a retrieval of a Lutheran approach to Christian ethics.

Unencumbered by the polarizing tendencies of any of the usual dualities, the creedal framework provides a norming horizon, within which a believer's life *coram Deo* and *coram mundo* can be seen together as a unity. Instead of being concerned to balance some particular tension, the believer is able to see every part of life, before God and before the surrounding creation, as the unfolding of God's creative design. Justification, for example, is not regarded in tension with sanctification. Instead, God's proclamation of justifying grace is recognized as the restoration that enables the believer to return to the created realm with new insight into God's will, and new support for the privileged task of living as God always intended God's creatures to live. There is no polarizing antithesis to be maintained, no dichotomy to be balanced. There is simply God's overarching work for and in God's people.

The work of William Placher is also pertinent and quite helpful to this discussion about the work of God in creating, redeeming, and sustaining creation and our responsibility to live as fully human creatures within God's creation. Placher also reaffirms the relevance of the intriguing doctrinal issues

---

41. Gustaf Wingren, *Creation and Law*, trans. Ross Mackenzie (Philadelphia: Muhlenberg, 1961), 197.

that swirl around questions of divine monergism, human agency, and theodicy. Offering a persuasive account of the historical factors involved, Placher argues that the first generation of reformers, as well as others who had gone before them, understood "human beings . . . as responsible agents in a process that yet owed everything to God."[42] Bringing clarity to an often murky conversation, Placher provides a remarkably apt and illuminating illustration:

> We can debate how many choices Willy Loman had in *Death of a Salesman* and what mix of forces and decisions shaped his tragedy. If someone interrupts our discussions of the relative importance of his family, the company that fires him, and his own character in his tragic fate, to say, "No, you all have it wrong—Arthur Miller was really the force that determined Willy Loman's actions," we do not feel so much that a new point of view has been introduced as that the interruption has changed the subject. *Of course*, the author determined all the characters' actions—but that is irrelevant to our discussion of the characters' motivations.
>
> Similarly, then, given the views of Aquinas, Luther, and Calvin, arguments about the relative weight to be assigned to chance and providence, free will and divine election, make no sense. The author is not one of the characters in the play, and those characters have their own motivations and freedom, independent of the divine author's determination of every outcome.[43]

When approaching a question of theology, then, it is vital to be certain from what perspective, or sphere, the question is being considered—whether from within the play, or from the perspective of the author. Obviously, when it comes to living in the reality of day-to-day life, the more earthbound perspective is typically most practicable.

Moving from the world of literature to the realm of physics, James Voelz makes a similar point with a different image. Considering the question starting from an exegetical outlook, his observation comes in the context of the interpretation of Scripture but arrives at the same place as Placher: "Depending on your vantage point/your perspective, there seem to be two overall systems of theology with their own overall principles or truths. The *first* is characterized

---

42. William C. Placher, *The Domestication of Transcendence: How Modern Thinking about God Went Wrong* (Louisville: Westminster John Knox, 1996), 148.

43. Ibid., 125 (emphasis in original).

by what I shall call *God's initiative*, the *second* by *human concurrence*."[44] With a nod to two patriarchs of the scientific world, Voelz uses the shorthand labels, "Einsteinian" and "Newtonian" respectively, for these two systems. One describes the way that things "truly" are in the infinitely large and infinitely minute realities of the world; the other accounts for the way that things are commonly experienced in routine life. So, what is "true" when it comes to the way that things work at the margins of matter or deep space may not be true with regard to the laws of action and reaction in ordinary life. String theory or the theory of relativity may capture reality in one sphere of inquiry but have little to offer when lining up an eight ball. The application to theology is plain: whether from the vantage of divine monergism or from the perspective of human responsibility, both ways of reading Scripture or doing theology are appropriate and correct—within their fitting sphere or domain.

This two-level way of thinking about what is "real" makes an important point when it comes to a right understanding of theological ethics. Certainly, God accomplishes the entire work of salvation without any contribution from the one God redeems. Yet, it is also true that in another sense—within the created sphere—the ones redeemed are entirely responsible for the lives they live. This is altogether biblical. As Voelz observes, "Much of the Bible is 'Newtonian.' All of Paul's paraenesis is. And we avoid that like the plague."[45] The "Newtonian" category includes, of course, the stuff of human responsibility and the cause-and-effect facts of life in the world. The avoidance of the Newtonian paraenesis, of course, stems from the desire to protect what Voelz would term "Einsteinian" truths about humanity's relation with God, which is founded on absolute passivity and dependence. The insight into the importance of perspective gained from Placher and Voelz reveals the error in denigrating the ethical aspects of Christianity as somehow not quite true when it counts. Within the appropriate sphere, ethics are quite true and matter a great deal—both to the creation, which depends on the service of the redeemed creature, and to the Creator, who places the redeemed into the creation with definite expectations. The encompassing reach of the creedal frame embraces and gives wide latitude of operation to both perspectives. What is true *coram Deo* (the Einsteinian perspective of the playwright) and what is true *coram mundo* (the Newtonian view of the characters within the play) both have free reign as appropriate. Neither view should be privileged; neither should be deprecated.

44. James Voelz, "'Newton and Einstein at the Foot of the Cross': A Post-Modern Approach to Theology," *Concordia Journal* 25, no. 3 (July 1999): 267 (emphasis in original).

45. Ibid., 275.

THEOLOGY AND PRACTICE REUNITED

Among the list of grievances for which Lutheranism is considered culpable, Stanley Hauerwas includes exacerbating the breach between theology and practice that has typified so much of theological thinking and practice in the world of modernity shaped by the Enlightenment: "Once there was no Christian ethics simply because Christians could not distinguish between their beliefs and their behavior. They assumed that their lives exemplified (or at least should exemplify) their doctrines in a manner that made a division between life and doctrine impossible."[46] It should be observed that an expansive creedal frame grounded in the divine narrative of creation and restoration helps to address this concern. By seeing the grand sweep of the story, and their lives before God and within the world as vital aspects of this one story, the gulf between ethics and theology that exists in the minds and lives of many Christians today can be narrowed. In a sense, this observation directly correlates with the discussion of the previous section, but the weight of relevant material warrants separate consideration here.

The effort to rectify the unfortunate divorce between theology and practice Hauerwas identifies is the driving concern in the work of Ellen Charry. Her book, *By the Renewing of Your Minds*, "is concerned with primary Christian doctrines—specifically, their character-forming intentions."[47] The bulk of Charry's work is simply a careful reading of classic and important texts from the church's history that are commonly considered to be doctrinal heavyweights (for example, Augustine's *De Trinitate* and Anselm's *Cur Deus Homo*). Charry's examination reveals a common trait in all of these doctrinally profound theologians: "the irrepressible urge . . . to render theology of genuine use to believers, even as they are clarifying, organizing, and reinterpreting Christian claims about God, the world, the church, and ourselves."[48] In other words, even when doing, or more accurately *by* doing, intensely transcendent and ethereal theology, the church's great thinkers were driven by the needs of ordinary Christian people living ordinary lives in the world. Charry articulates and reinforces the truth that theology is not alien to the routine of mundane Christian life, but intimately intertwined with it.

---

46. Hauerwas, *Sanctify Them*, 20. The entire chapter surrounding this quote is important; see pp. 19–36, esp. 27–28, where Hauerwas tries to make a case for the Reformation's complicity in the division between theology and ethics.

47. Ellen T. Charry, *By the Renewing of Your Minds: The Pastoral Function of Christian Doctrine* (New York: Oxford University Press, 1997), 6.

48. Ibid., ix.

The perceived tension between God's justifying declaration of our identity and our personal achievement of growth in character is also cast in a new light and called into question by Charry's study. "This work," she writes, "assumes that thinking of insight-oriented and practice-oriented options regarding the formation of virtue as a forced choice is a false dichotomy."[49] Elaborating on this fruitful line of thought, Charry argues:

> [Modern] theologians have by and large assumed that knowing God creates the proper conditions for loving God rather than the reverse. But concomitant with dedication to knowing God, the church has stressed participation in Christian community and practices as a way not only of reinforcing the knowledge of God but also of shaping the mind so that knowledge of the love of God fits into a life prepared to interpret it properly.[50]

To put it a bit more succinctly, Christian actions and practices teach the believer about faith and God. Not only does knowledge shape a person and produce right or loving actions, but those right actions or practices reciprocally serve knowledge by opening the way for its proper reception. To create a false choice between what is known and what is practiced is to perpetuate the diminution of the dynamic bond that rightly exists between Christian faith and life.

Also significant in this vein is the study of theological education by Edward Farley. In sympathy with Hauerwas's complaint about the divorce between ethics and theology and in support of Charry's historical assessment, Farley champions the need for fundamental change in the current practice of theological education. Hoping to correct what he considers a wrong turn in modern thinking about theology, he contends that "theology is *practical*, not theoretical."[51] Taking the terminology of Aristotle and his students, Farley describes theology as "a *habitus*, a cognitive disposition and orientation of the soul, a knowledge of God and what God reveals."[52] Theology is more than relevant for Christian living; it is integrally and intimately bound with it.

This desire to affirm and reestablish the union of theology and practice is given resounding support by Luther. The reformer operated with a basic assumption of the absolute relevance of all theology for the life of the believer.

49. Ibid., 4.

50. Ibid., 28.

51. Edward Farley, *Theologia: The Fragmentation and Unity of Theological Education* (Philadelphia: Fortress Press, 1983), 35 (emphasis in original).

52. Ibid.

As one would expect, this attitude is prominently on display in Luther's catechisms. What is most interesting for the purpose at hand, however, is the widespread recognition and approval of this emphasis by contemporary Lutheran theologians. In his study of Luther's catechisms, Arand calls attention to the practical nature of Luther's doctrinal efforts: "Luther provides a seamless integration of doctrine and life. In his day, doctrine had a dynamic and hermeneutical character that shaped and illumined life itself."[53] Certainly, the catechism was particularly intended for sculpting and directing life in the homes of ordinary Christian believers:

> To that end, the Small Catechism provides the household with something of a liturgy, that is to say, the parts of the catechism framed and shaped a Christian ethos for daily living: Upon waking, make the sign of the cross and say the invocation followed by thanks for protection the previous night with prayer to be kept from sin during the coming day. Go to work joyfully. At meals, fold hands and pray. In the evening, call upon the triune Name. Give thanks for the day. Pray for protection during the night. Go to sleep in peace.[54]

Arand makes his point with conviction, and the point is clear that Luther considered theology to be utterly practical, woven into the fabric of everyday life.

Arand indicates that this dynamic understanding of theology should not remain a historical peculiarity of Luther or an interesting bit of trivia about the reformers. Rather, Arand urges that this intentional effort to apply theology to ordinary life find application among the reformers' theological descendants as well.

> Doctrine is not abstract theory to be contrasted with practical skills and how-to steps for daily living. If anything, the Reformers (and the church fathers before them) viewed doctrine as pastoral care. This is what made the study of doctrine so important. This is why they were willing to engage (however reluctantly) in doctrinal debates. Doctrine provides the Christian with a diagnosis of the innermost needs of human beings. It provides a framework for interpreting life and the experiences of life in the light of the triune work of God.[55]

53. Charles P. Arand, *That I May Be His Own: An Overview of Luther's Catechisms* (St. Louis: Concordia Academic, 2000), 20.

54. Ibid., 96.

This emphasis on the practicality of doctrinal work emerges as a consistent theme throughout Arand's study of the catechisms.[56]

Robert Kolb reaches a similar conclusion when considering the confessors at Augsburg. Being "a verbal noun," Kolb explains, *confession* "carries with it a sense of activity."[57] Obviously, that activity at the diet involved the bold stance taken by the Lutheran princes and theologians in the face of imperial power. But the activity of confession extended further. "It also encompasses their activities as they returned to their castles and courts to exercise their God-given responsibilities."[58] The confession of right doctrine was accompanied by the confession of a rightly ordered life. Doctrine and practice came together not only for Luther but for the other reformers and for the laymen as well.

Finally, David Yeago concurs with Arand and Kolb about the close bond that exists between doctrine and practice—a bond that is worthy of reinforcement. "The catechisms," writes Yeago, "not only contain instruction in doctrine, but instruction in prayer and sacramental practice."[59] Christianity, then, is substantially more than a correct exposition of metaphysical or theological truth. "The learning involved in becoming a Christian and persevering as a Christian includes a significant element of 'know-how,' the acquisition of skills related to practices."[60] Yeago is persuaded that this acquisition of "know-how," or training in practices, in conjunction with training in theology must be accomplished as much more than a mere recitation of historical verities or a six-week or even two-year "data dump" of facts about the faith:

> If we do not teach the catechism, if our people do not learn to participate in the liturgy, if our children do not know the Bible stories and cannot sing along in worship, if we do not begin to recover practices of formation, ways of prayer and meditation and fasting and celebration, that bind daily life with the worshiping assembly in a priestly mode of common life, then our churches will simply fade into spiritual inconsequence over the coming decades,

55. Ibid., 114.

56. Ibid.; see esp. 21, 81, 136, and 147.

57. Robert Kolb, "God Calling, 'Take Care of My People': Luther's Concept of Vocation in the *Augsburg Confession* and Its *Apology*," *Concordia Journal* 8, no. 1 (January 1982): 9.

58. Ibid.

59. David S. Yeago, "Sacramental Lutheranism at the End of the Modern Age," *Lutheran Forum* 34, no. 4 (Christmas/Winter 2000): 15.

60. Ibid.

however many new members we have and whatever the outcome of our ecclesiastical politics.[61]

Regardless the eventual amendment or more likely veracity of Yeago's prophecy, he does ably capture the spirit of a number of concerned members of the body of Christ who are eager to reapply today the lessons that Luther and the other reformers seem to have taken for granted in their day. Of course, I am eager to be counted among that number.

There is a marriage between theology and the Christian's life. By emphasizing God's work of creation and our responsibility within that creation, a creedal framework for theology as I've tried to express it will enhance and advance this union. The creed succinctly professes the core doctrines of Christian faith, yet by confessing God's work of redemption and restoration within the wider context of God's creating activity, the profound ontological and theological declarations of the creed are firmly grounded in the ordinary and historical aspects of life within creation. Theology is as much a part of routine life as the recitation of the creed is a routine part of the Divine Service. Those seeking to overcome the divorce between doctrine and ordinary Christian life should find the Christian creed an enormously beneficial norming horizon within which to operate. A creedal view of Christian faith and life that keeps the first article first and affirms the goodness of God's creation, makes space for an active and dynamic practice of ethics, and in the process facilitates the eventual reconciliation of the wrongly divorced pair of doctrine and practice.

APPLICATIONS

Given the overriding thesis of this study, a failure at least to consider and propose possible practical implications would be evident self-contradiction. One more book of theological prolegomena or doctrinal investigation without deliberate application for concrete living is not needed and would betray the purpose of this book. Accordingly, it's necessary to suggest several avenues of concrete practice that seem to spring naturally from what has been argued. As noted at the outset, the initial and precipitating interest of this text has been to consider the possible applicability of virtue ethics within Christian confession. Accordingly, the insights and truths of virtue ethics were situated within the framework of the Christian creed. All that has gone before, however—indeed, all that has been done—has been only for the sake of the actual implementation

---

61. Ibid., 16.

of these ideas at the level of typical and routine parish life. The goal, arguably the only legitimate goal for any theology, is to make a direct and positive impact in the daily lives of ordinary Christian people. It is in the spirit of discharging that responsibility that the following practical applications are offered.

TRAINING IN VIRTUE

Parishes are served by pastors. It should be evident from the case here presented that pastors must take stock not only of their opportunity but of their responsibility to provide the kind of training and teaching that people in their parishes need if they are to grow in the acquisition of virtue. In many ecclesiastical circles, recent decades have witnessed a resurgence of interest in the need for careful and deliberate catechesis, especially for the young. The importance of faithful doctrinal instruction is now widely acknowledged. Hopefully, this study has validated the legitimacy of providing training not only for the sake of spiritual knowledge and doctrinal maturity, but also for the sake of intentional character formation and moral maturity. Masquerading under the guise of confessional faithfulness or historical orthodoxy, a visceral and immediate reaction against any form of "moralism" or "moralizing" continues to haunt many Lutherans. Confronted with this status quo, it is wise—even necessary—to emphasize the theological propriety of intentional and unvarnished training in virtue and cultivation of character.

Gilbert Meilaender is, once more, an articulate spokesman in renouncing this misguided suspicion toward ethics. By reminding us of Scripture's wide scope, he points in the direction that may end in the eradication of this suspicion.

> Protestants, in particular, love to ring the changes on these crucial Pauline themes ["justified by faith apart from works of law," etc.]—almost suggesting, on occasion, that doing so could substitute for moral guidance and direction. . . . Nevertheless, it would be a mistake to suppose that the Scriptures exist only to bear witness to Christ, as if they were the norm for the church's faith but not also for her life.[62]

To insist that the establishment or enforcement of any sort of norm or standard is by definition out of bounds for true Christianity is to extinguish ethics altogether and eventually make it impossible "to distinguish between actions

---

62. Meilaender, *Things That Count*, 60.

that follow Christ and actions that turn against him."[63] Not only is this move misdirected, but so, too, is the ostensibly orthodox thinking behind it.

> The church's moral discipline does not set up conditions for entering the kingdom; rather, it offers a description of what the life of discipleship should be like—a description of what it means to follow Christ. In setting forth such a description of her way of life, in understanding that description as a discipline to be undertaken, the church does not raise any other standard than the Christ who is confessed. . . . We seek, that is, to give content and structure to the meaning of love.[64]

By now, it should be quite obvious that this is not an idea unique to Meilaender. It should be no surprise, of course, to find Hauerwas in outspoken agreement with Meilaender on this score. Hauerwas also identifies an aversion to ethics, or a normed vision of the shape and direction of the Christian life, as a serious problem in the contemporary church.

> In our time, what many call modern times, unbelievers and believers (and even some theologians who actually may be believers!) do not believe that theological claims do any work. I assume that helps explain that no matter how sincerely many believe what it is they believe about God, they in fact live lives of practical atheism. Accordingly, quite profound and sophisticated theological systems can be developed, but the theological discourse seems to "float," making no difference for how we live.[65]

Of course, Hauerwas concurs that intentional training in ethics—cultivating growth in character according to scriptural standards and norms—is a significant step toward overcoming the disorder bred by Christendom's practical atheism. While it is not remarkable to find such ready support from Hauerwas, it is worth remembering that the same approval and endorsement of training in virtue is found also in the Lutheran confessor, Philip Melanchthon: "Since Christians should cherish and support this civil society, this teaching of civic morals and duties has to be known by them. . . . Therefore those who disparage philosophy not only wage war against human nature, but they also

---

63. Ibid., 61.

64. Ibid.

65. Stanley Hauerwas, *A Better Hope: Resources for a Church Confronting Capitalism, Democracy, and Postmodernity* (Grand Rapids: Brazos, 2000), 140.

severely injure the glory of the Gospel, which commands that men be restrained by civic discipline."[66]

It is the repeated refrain and an indisputable conclusion of this study: Christian people need to be trained in virtue. A noble character does not simply happen. For the sake of believers, for the sake of the church, and for the sake of the wider culture, virtues must be cultivated and character shaped. Training in virtuous living should have a place within the church—ideally side by side with catechesis. And training in practical truths of virtuous Christian living that begins in youth should not cease with confirmation but should continue to be an integral component in the church's ministry to adults. Certainly, it would reflect remarkable ignorance—or perhaps hubris—to gainsay a serious study and adoption of the insights into virtue and the shaping of character to be gained from Aristotle and his Christian students in later generations.[67] Christians would not misstep by joining to their study of God's will for humanity revealed in the commandments, a consideration of the cardinal virtues of prudence, justice, fortitude, and temperance.

CULTIVATION OF COMMUNITY

Beyond the what-would-seem-to-be-incontestable conclusion that training in virtue and the cultivation of character deserve to be considered as priorities in the ministry of a congregation, parish pastors would also serve their flocks well by taking to heart the important role of the community in the formation of individual character. This is, of course, a chief principle of virtue ethics.[68] Charry provides a lucid articulation of the role of community in the shaping of virtue:

> Excellent character doesn't just happen—it is formed, crafted among other things by literary or visual examples that companion, expand one's world, stimulate the imagination, engage the emotions, sharpen discernment, and promote practice vicariously. . . . Moral

66. Philipp Melanchthon, *Orations on Philosophy and Education*, ed. Sachiko Kusukawa, trans. Christine F. Salazar (Cambridge: Cambridge University Press, 1999), 81.

67. Naturally, Aquinas and Melanchthon are both to be counted in this number. For an important contemporary example, see Josef Pieper, *The Four Cardinal Virtues: Prudence, Justice, Fortitude, Temperance* (Notre Dame, IN: University of Notre Dame Press, 1967).

68. Hauerwas has devoted at least one entire book to this topic: *In Good Company: The Church as Polis* (Notre Dame, IN: University of Notre Dame Press, 1995). See also Nancey Murphy, Brad J. Kallenberg, and Mark Thiessen Nation, eds., *Virtues & Practices in the Christian Tradition: Christian Ethics after MacIntyre* (Harrisburg, PA: Trinity Press International, 1997), esp. chs. 1, 2, and 4.

formation requires emotional engagement with concrete models for emulation and a social context within which to practice them.[69]

L. Gregory Jones draws the obvious conclusion: "Moral formation occurs through an induction into the friendships and practices of Christian communities."[70] Adolf Köberle also recognizes the role of the church in shaping the morals of its people: "This particularly applies to children," writes Köberle, "who are not to be preached at nor 'converted' but who are decisively formed and fashioned by the visible and tangible influences of the Church in which they grow up."[71] A Christian congregation is indeed the ideal community for the cultivation of character, unparalleled in its ability to supply the fullest possible expression of each of Charry's requirements. In the church, there are concrete examples to be emulated and a social setting within which to hone one's skills. Neither is the character-shaping community of believers bound by the constraints of time or history. As the Apology indicates, included in the community of the church are the saints who have preceded those in the church-yet-militant whose memory and example can also serve the cultivation of character: "Our confession approves giving honor to the saints. . . . The third honor is imitation: first of their faith, then of their other virtues, which people should imitate according to their callings." [72]

While it is unquestionably the case that the majority of faithful Christian congregations already carry out many of these character-shaping functions unintentionally, a concerted and purposeful practice of such shaping is probably nonexistent in most parishes. Congregations and their pastors need to realize the critical role they can play in the right shaping of individual character. Actually, all congregations, by virtue of their intrinsic community influence, are to some degree shaping the character of their members. The question that warrants more careful attention is, What *kind* of character are they shaping? In typically bald and disarming language, Hauerwas bluntly expresses the import of this congregational task with one of his more memorable aphorisms: "I want to be part of a community with the habits and practices that will make me do what I would otherwise not choose to do and then to learn to like what I have been forced to do."[73] Indeed, along with declaring the gospel and delivering the

---

69. Charry, *By the Renewing of Your Minds*, 26.

70. L. Gregory Jones, *Transformed Judgment: Toward a Trinitarian Account of the Moral Life* (Notre Dame, IN: University of Notre Dame Press, 1990), 114.

71. Köberle, *Quest for Holiness*, 201.

72. *Book of Concord*, 238 (Ap 21, 6).

73. Hauerwas, *In Good Company*, 75.

forgiveness of sins, this formation is also part of what a Christian congregation should be doing for its people. It is the reality of what it means to shape character and nurture virtue according to God's will for God's gathered people.

As the congregation cultivates and expands its role in character formation, it will also serve its responsibility to the community that lies beside and beyond the church. This is the intent behind Hauerwas's frequently quoted dictum pair: "the first social ethical task of the church is to be the church," and "the church does not have a social ethic; the church is a social ethic."[74] As the members of the Christian congregation strive to shape character according to God's will, they establish a standard and model for upright living and lend credibility to their first-order task of gospel proclamation. "For the church," Hauerwas asserts, "is finally known by the character of the people who constitute it, and if we lack that character, the world rightly draws the conclusion that the God we worship is in fact a false God."[75] While such deliberate effort at shaping the character of its people does not hold first place in the work of the church, the clear articulation of the gospel and the celebration of the means of grace does not contravene intentional moral formation.

Of course, the pursuit of this vision of character makes the ethic of the Christian community altogether unique and helps to explain its particular and community-oriented nature as well as both its attraction and repulsion to those yet outside. It is different and interesting and champions radical self-giving and love of the other; but it is also demanding, exclusive, and nonconforming to the expectations of the wider culture. The church's understanding of what it means to be a person of character is the church's alone. Hauerwas is consistent in his insistence "that ethics always requires an adjective or qualifier."[76] In other words, there is no universal ethic that encompasses all people of all places and all times, but only the ethics of particular people and communities in particular times and places. Hauerwas explains how this conviction relates to Christian ethics:

> Our ethic is distinctive, not because of the way we go about making decisions, or because it arises out of a tradition or a community. . . . Our ethic is distinctive in its content. Christian ethics is about following this Jew from Nazareth, being a part of his people.

74. Stanley Hauerwas, *The Peaceable Kingdom: A Primer in Christian Ethics* (Notre Dame, IN: University of Notre Dame Press, 1983), 99.

75. Ibid., 109.

76. Ibid., 1.

Therefore, this ethics will probably not make much sense unless one knows that story, sees that vision, is part of that people.[77]

So it is that as the church community makes a priority of shaping character according to its unique norm—that of faithfulness to the way of Christ, it is authentically accomplishing its divine duty to be salt and light in a sin-ridden world.

ETHICS FOR ORDINARY LIFE

An emphasis on the cultivation of character and growth in the virtues finds a fertile field of application in the everyday aspects of routine individual and family life. In this arena, the most daunting challenge is typically the mundane ordinariness of daily existence. Focusing on the character of the person and the attendant virtues which incarnate that character is an exercise that is relevant even on the most usual days doing the most regular things. Careful and conscious attention to the application of virtuous character in the normalcy of life stands in sharp contrast to the purview of typical ethical consideration. In popular understanding, it is generally and justifiably assumed that ethics is preoccupied with extraordinarily complicated, borderline situations of life that most people rarely face. These artificial situations that bear so little resemblance to the circumstances of real life have become a standard feature of many efforts at "doing ethics," and are now almost standardized. Two recognizable favorites remain: "Should a person lie to protect the life of an innocent person from murderous pursuers?" and some form of the "overloaded lifeboat" in which students with minimal résumés of each "survivor" are asked to determine who should and should not retain a position in the boat. The tremendous practical benefit of learning from thinkers in virtue ethics is their aversion to this sort of theoretical speculation and their interest instead in the ethical needs and questions encountered in the daily lives of regular people. It is interesting and not surprising that Melanchthon, too, had little use for theoretical speculation about hypothetical borderline ethical dilemmas. In his 1521 *Loci Communes,* he wrote: "Cicero discusses the duty of the man who, after being shipwrecked, chances upon the same plank that a certain wise man is holding. Away with such stupid questions which hardly ever arise in actual human affairs!"[78] When incorporating the insights of virtue ethics as practiced in the context of the

---

77. Stanley Hauerwas and William H. Willimon, *Resident Aliens: A Provocative Christian Assessment of Culture and Ministry for People Who Know That Something Is Wrong* (Nashville: Abingdon, 1989), 102.

78. Philipp Melanchthon, *Loci Communes Theologici,* in *Melanchthon and Bucer,* trans. and ed. Wilhelm Pauck, The Library of Christian Classics 19 (Philadelphia: Westminster, 1969), 148.

Christian creed and community, ethics is moved from irrelevant speculation into the ebb and flow of utterly practical routine living.

Emphasizing the need for continual growth in virtue and the cultivation of character leads people to understand life more comprehensively. In the context of the wide narrative horizon provided by the creedal framework, the continuous expression of God's salvific activity on humanity's behalf is detected in all of life. Believers thus taught to recognize the activity of God throughout the whole of creation will learn to reflect a corresponding interest in living all of their lives as godly people of virtue—increasingly conforming themselves to God's norm for God's highest creation. In time, this perspective will overshadow and displace the fragmented view of life and ethics that results from attempts to discern the "right" decision to be made in a particular circumstance. Hauerwas captures this thought when he writes, "For the Christian life is more a recognition and training of our senses and passions than a matter of choices and decisions."[79] One does not live as one chooses and then resort to ethical considerations only when faced with a perplexing dilemma or choice. Seen in the context of character formation and the practice of virtue, all of life becomes a matter of ethics.

For the Christian believer, making ethics a way of life means seeking to conform to the standards of Christ-like virtue—for no other reason than that this is God's will for human creatures. The Christian recognizes that every human being is—in the most comprehensive sense—created for such virtue. We are to be fully human, and it is Christ who perfectly exemplifies what it means to be fully human; it is Christ who perfectly makes the Christian fully human. Ethics is not about choices and weighing options. It is a matter of being what God created the person to be. Josef Pieper captures well the difference that it makes when one thinks about ethics in terms of virtue:

> With a doctrine of commandments or duties, however, there is always the danger of arbitrarily drawing up a list of requirements and losing sight of the human person who "ought" to do this or that. The doctrine of virtue, on the other hand, has things to say about this human person; it speaks both of the kind of being which is his when he enters the world, as a consequence of his createdness, and the kind of being he ought to strive toward and attain to—by being prudent, just, brave, and temperate.[80]

79. Hauerwas, *Peaceable Kingdom*, 149.
80. Pieper, *Four Cardinal Virtues*, xii.

Understood in this way, ethics becomes an integral aspect of all life—and coheres seamlessly with Christian confession. Indeed, were this understanding of ethics to be welcomed and embraced in Lutheran congregations, the tired criticisms of Lutheranism's ethical irrelevance and ultimate failure could not long be sustained.

At the risk of stating the obvious, and broaching a topic beyond the limited consideration of this book, spiritual habits such as daily prayer (yes, even the use of rote, memorized prayers), regular use of the liturgy, making the sign of the cross, and a prominently emphasized church year should all be recognized not only as pious practices of some Christians, but as significant tools to be used in the formation of character. Spiritual habits such as these become a part of the believer's everyday life and directly influence both spiritual and moral development, if indeed the two may be so easily distinguished. An acknowledgment of the rightful place of character development and cultivation of virtue within the Christian congregation may even create the space necessary for a reevaluation of what constitutes a "good, biblical (and/or confessional), sermon." Perhaps virtue ethics exercised within a creedal framework may so broaden ethical thinking and understanding in Lutheran circles that homilies in the spirit of Luther's great catechetical sermons may once again be heard even from twenty-first-century pulpits.

SIGNS OF LIFE

Lutheranism has long and legitimately enjoyed a reputation for theological precision and profundity. It is not surprising, therefore, to find within the theology of the Lutheran reformers and their heirs an able response to those who would charge the Lutheran confession with an inability to articulate a coherent and meaningful ethics. Perhaps more significantly, the rich heritage of Lutheran doctrine also reveals the serious error of those adhering to the Lutheran tradition who would dismiss or even castigate efforts at Christian ethics as a threat to the "pure gospel." Lutheranism is quite able to attend to the concerns of real people in real situations without in any way diminishing an accurate and effective proclamation of the gospel. The reformers understood and taught the full breadth and richness of Christian doctrine. So should we. Thus, even as faithful Lutheran pastors, theologians, and parishioners should proclaim and hear the gospel, so also should they attend to the concerns and situations of everyday routine life.

The Lutheran church of recent decades has struggled half-heartedly and finally futilely to find its ethical voice. Meanwhile, Lutheran theology itself is and always has been fully equipped to present an ethic for daily life that is altogether adequate and eminently practical. Most importantly, though, Lutheranism is quite able to expound a Christian ethic that is meaningfully connected to the central doctrine of justification by grace through faith alone. Within the framework provided by the creed, the doctrine of justification can be proclaimed in all of its glory and comfort, and the insights of virtue ethics can be brought to bear on individual lives with all of their concrete relevance. Wingren is quite right: "What happens in the Church is simply the continuation of what happened when Christ became man. And He became man in order to restore what God had created."[81] At the cross the restoration was accomplished, a fact wholly realized even now in the lives of believers, *coram Deo*. And, a fact increasingly revealed, *coram mundo*, as believers grow into God's will, becoming, incrementally, more of what God created them to be: fully human. This is the rich and unified reality available when Christian theology and Christian living are considered together within the context of the creedal frame—a framework that points to creation's ultimate telos—the consummation of God's will at the parousia when reality *coram Deo* and reality *coram mundo* are made fully and finally one.

There is no reason for Lutheranism to be afflicted with an ethical paralysis prompted by a nervous fear of legalism. Such a fear is misguided and empty. It is, however, most probably a result of this fear reinforced with an array of other factors, that the charge of Lutheranism's ethical irrelevance is too often vindicated by contemporary Lutheran theologians, pastors, and parishes. A faithful appropriation of their theological heritage, however, is categorically *not* one of those reinforcing factors! Perhaps rightly directed Lutheran doctrine may yet vanquish this errant fear; and on a not-so-distant day, a discussion of Lutheran ethics will not be greeted with indifference, hostility, or even amusement. On that day Lutheranism's ill-suited, yet sadly deserved, reputation for ethical irrelevance finally will be overcome and the church will be poised to fulfill its holy calling. If this short book serves that end, it will have succeeded in at least one of its purposes.

Perhaps it is not unreasonable to suggest that another result of this investigation might be to temper somewhat Hunter's declaration of character's demise. This is not to say that Hunter's observation about the state of character formation in American society is incorrect. Quite the opposite, his premise is altogether accurate: in the culture of America, character is quite dead and memorials and requiems for the departed are altogether appropriate. But this is not the case in the church. Within the church the funeral should be postponed

---

81. Wingren, *Creation and Law*, 197.

if not canceled, assuming that what is called church is being faithful with what it has been given. Of course, that often may be assuming too much. Whether character and its conscientious cultivation endure in the life of the church is too often an open question. By some accounts, the bell tolls for character even within America's churches. Churches that capitulate to the culture and accede to the demands of religious relativism and doctrinal inclusivity in which all well-intentioned and good people eventually arrive at the same place have forfeited all power to shape character.[82] This may seem an extreme claim, and many will argue against it, or at least hope that it isn't true. But character cannot grow in a culture without a foundation that supplies the necessary definitions of fundamental concepts like the telos of human life, the meaning of good, and the virtues that attend right human being. Character, as Hunter fully understands, depends on a community that is founded on "a creedal order that constrains, limits, binds, obligates, and compels."[83] But that is precisely the sort of foundation rejected by the culture—and even by many who would claim a place within the church.

All is not lost, however. The church in America and in the rest of the Western world is in grave danger of losing its creed and confession to the siren song of the wider culture with all of its threats and enticements both crass and subtle. There are, though, those that remain faithful. There are places where the creed is confessed in the spirit of Nicea and Chalcedon. There are places where the scriptural text is preached in unity with Paul, and Chrysostom, and Luther. There are churches that believe that there is a truth that sustains and directs all of creation and all creatures, a truth that proceeds from the Creator. There are churches that hold to "a creedal order that constrains, limits, binds, obligates, and compels." These are the churches that can cultivate character. These are the churches that have what the world urgently needs: yes, the gospel of God's forgiveness and free grace, but also the truth of God's will, the law that provides a concept of "the good," defines justice, and makes possible the cultivation of character.

---

82. The remarkable extent to which the churches in America have already succumbed to the culture is well attested. See especially Christian Smith, *Soul Searching: The Religious and Spiritual Lives of American Teenagers* (New York: Oxford University Press, 2005), and C. Edwards, *Plain Sense of Things*. Smith has contributed the term "moralistic therapeutic deism" to the contemporary discussion of the church's fidelity and vitality. Edwards gives us the label "normal nihilism." Neither offers any substantial hope that the church may hold fast to her creed; thus, I would add, neither gives us much reason to believe that the church may succeed in forming genuine Christian character.

83. Hunter, *Death of Character*, xv.

Character is not dead everywhere. The faithful church can still mold and form its people into God's fully human people. The church can shape character. Alasdair MacIntyre concludes *After Virtue* with a now legendary passage that is more wistful than hopeful: "What matters at this stage is the construction of local forms of community within which civility and the intellectual and moral life can be sustained through the new dark ages which are already upon us."[84] Such communities, it is quite certain, are already in existence. It is the faithful church, the lowly congregation of gathered believers that is this community. Overlooked, derided, and dismissed by the culture, the faithful church is nevertheless precisely the place most needed by the culture. Faithful churches proclaim the gospel. Faithful churches cultivate character.

---

84. Alasdair MacIntyre, *After Virtue: A Study in Moral Theory* (Notre Dame, IN: University of Notre Dame Press, 1981), 263.

Index of Subjects and Names